Frogs in a Well

Frogs in a Well

Indian Women
in Purdah

Patricia Jeffery

Zed Books Ltd
London and New Jersey

Frogs in a Well was first published by Zed Press (Zed Books Ltd), 57 Caledonian Road, London N1 9BU, UK, and 165 First Avenue, Atlantic Highlands, New Jersey 07716, USA, in 1979.

Cover designed by Andrew Corbett.
Cover photo by John and Penny Hubley.
Illustrations by Les Brown from photographs by
John and Penny Hubley and Patricia Jeffery.
Printed and bound in the United Kingdom
at Dotesios Ltd, Trowbridge.

Seventh impression, 1991.

ISBN 0 905762 20 7
ISBN 0 905762 32 0 Pbk

Contents

Illustrations

Preface

Since the Partition of India in 1947 and the creation of Pakistan as a homeland for South Asia's Muslims, the position of Muslims in India has been
somewhat anomalous. This is perhaps particularly so of the subjects of this
book, who are the hereditary custodians or *pirzade* at a Sufi shrine in Delhi,
once at the heart of Muslim culture in the subcontinent but now a busy
cosmopolitan city which has almost overwhelmed the shrine. The *pirzade*
are reminders of the old days, with their Persianized Urdu speech, their
refined manners, and their secluded womenfolk.

This book about them has arisen from work which began in 1975: the
Social Science Research Council (U.K.) funded my research and have been
most patient about the unexpected turn which it took. My special thanks, of
course, go the *pirzade* themselves, because their hospitality and tolerant
co-operation have made my work possible. My research has also been greatly
aided by the kindness of friends, among them Hayat Bouman (who introduced me to the *pirzade*), Muhammad Nasimuddin (who translated some
Persian and Urdu documents for me), and Les Brown (who has produced the
line drawings). There are also many who have generously given me their time
and helped me to clarify my thoughts. Among them, special thanks must go
to Imtiaz Ahmad, Michael Anderson, Hermione Harris, Penelope Hubley,
Rosemary Johnson, T.N. Madan, Adrian Mayer, Regula Qureshi, Ursula
Sharma, Peggy Duncan Shearer and Hilary Standing. My greatest debt is to
Roger Jeffery, who, more than anyone else, has encouraged me throughout
and made the research and the writing of this book a challenging and valuable
experience.

Note on Transliteration
For the ease of the reader who is unfamiliar with India, I have restricted my
use of Urdu words in the text. But the transliteration from Persian script has
posed several problems. Roman consonants generally have the same value as
in English, though *q* represents a gutteral 'k' and *gh* a gutteral 'g'. The vowels
are more problematic: *y* is short, *i* long, *e* is as 'ay' in day, *u* is as 'oo' in cool
and *o* as in long. Problems over typesetting have meant that the long and
short *a* have not been distinguished. In the following words, the *a*'s are short:
aurat, duppatta, haj, Hazrat, izzat, Moharram, and *sharm.* Other words

repeated in the text should be pronounced as follows (long *a* is signified by 'aa'): *khandan* (Khaandaan), Nizamuddin (Nizaamuddin), *pirzada* (pirzaada), Ramzan (Ramzaan), *taziya* (taaziya), *Quran Sharif* (Quraan Sharif). I have retained the familiar spelling *purdah* (parda).

Patricia Jeffery
Edinburgh
January 1979.

'Ladies not allowed' – women kneeling at the shrine

Introduction

The images which *purdah* conjures up in the Western world often bear only a superficial relationship to the rather dull everyday reality experienced by the Indian Muslim women — the wives and daughters of the custodians of a shrine near Delhi — who are the subject of this book.

Foreign travellers to British India were often struck by the phenomenon of seclusion. Along with *purdah*, matters such as female infanticide, the plight of the child widow who could never re-marry, and the immolation of widows on the funeral pyres of their husbands caught the imagination and often crowded the diaries and memoirs which were destined for the Western reader. Such material generally seems to assume that the opinions of the women themselves are self-evident, uncomplicated, unproblematic; that the women themselves feel oppressed and would eagerly welcome the removal of the yoke of *purdah*. But social life is rarely so simple. These practices have their niche in a complex social system, and abolishing female infanticide or the immolation of widows is merely attacking the symptoms of something much more pervasive. That these practices — along with *purdah* — have almost exclusively been the prerogatives of the most wealthy and privileged sectors of a highly stratified society tends to be submerged under the condemnations which they attract.

On the other hand, recent years have seen the accumulation of sociological material about India, often village studies which contain detailed accounts of the division of labour between the sexes, the arrangement of marriages by the elders of the bride and groom, the restricted movements of women, the many and subtle ways in which the worlds of men and women are kept separate. The dispassionate documentation, the attempts to understand Indian life from the inside, have their attractions over the sensationalism and condemnations of other sources. The one approach has been unashamedly critical; the other has eschewed evaluation and judgement, and has been steeped in a tradition of cultural relativism.

And yet both types of material are unsatisfactory. In neither is sufficient attention paid to the relationships of *purdah* to the wider social system of which it is an integral part. The general perspective has been too narrow, for seclusion is embedded in an intricate social setting. Moreover, even in the sociological material, women are given little opportunity to express their

1

views of *purdah*. Until recently, most sociological studies have been conducted by men, for whom the very existence of *purdah* has presented obstacles to their talking freely to Indian women. My intention in this book is to try to rectify these gaps.

I was confronted with *purdah* the first time, not in India, but in Pakistan where I was doing fieldwork in 1970. Exposure to it in no way attracted me to a life in seclusion, but my training enabled me — perhaps compelled me — to try to suspend judgement while I looked into the workings of a society dominated by the rigid separation between men and women, with the men's world outside the home where they work to support their families, and the domestic realm of the women who only leave their homes when fully shrouded by their long garments. At that time, my own distaste for *purdah* was neutralized by the views of the women among whom I was working. They seemed to accept the Islamic ideals of 'different yet equal' and the strikingly different lives which such notions entail for men and women in practice. For the moment, I was lulled into complacency about *purdah*.

Consequently, when planning my next period of fieldwork — which I did in Delhi in 1975-76 — the interests which had grown out of my stay in Pakistan were but marginally related to the question of *purdah*. My research proposal centred on how parents arrange the marriages of their children and the liking of some North Indian and Pakistani Muslims for marriages between close relatives.[1] Clearly, a system of arranged marriages can be controlled more easily if young men and women have little opportunity to meet, and marriages between close kin could reasonably be expected to have some relationship to the status of women in their families. But wrongly, as it happened, I imagined that *purdah* would be marginal to my other interests.

As a woman, I could gain an entree which would have been denied to any unrelated man, and the Urdu which I had learnt in Pakistan enabled me to converse with the women I met in *purdah* directly and intimately. Within days, my attention began to be drawn repeatedly to the women's comments about *purdah*, and their often contradictory responses to their positions. Not only were the women speaking up loudly, but I was becoming more aware of the complexities and ambivalences which surround the institution of *purdah*. No longer could a dispassionate pretence be justifiable, for the women were often pungent in their complaints; but no more could *purdah* be dismissed with mere condemnation, for it is far too subtle and complex.

Behind the Curtain

The experiences of the women whom I knew in Delhi fall within a broad range of styles of behaviour which is loosely included in the term *purdah*. *Purdah* is a Persian word widely used in India, not just among Muslims, meaning 'curtain'. The curtains over windows and across doorways are all called *purdah*. But the word *purdah* is also used in phrases such as *purdah rakhna* (to keep *purdah* or to place a curtain), *purdah ke pichhe rehna* (to live behind the *purdah*) and *purdah nashin* (a person who sits behind the *purdah*). In this latter type of usage, reference is being made to the concealment of women and the separation of the worlds of men and women which is a major aspect of *purdah*. But this separation may be created in numerous ways. Something of the problems which can arise when trying to define *purdah* succinctly can be seen from such apparently discrepant comments as 'one can generalize without fear of inaccuracy in saying that at least 95% of Moslem women, perhaps even more, observe *purdah* consistently and logically' and 'though a close estimate is impossible, it is doubtful if even at the height of the *purdah* period more than 15% of adult women were ever in seclusion.'[2] Much of the difference in these assessments can be attributed to the complexity which the term *purdah* contains.

For one thing, *purdah* is not just an Islamic institution in the Indian subcontinent. While this book is primarily about some Muslim women, it is important to note that many Hindu women observe *purdah* too. But it would be incorrect to suggest that the *purdah* of Hindus is the same phenomenon as that of Muslims.[3] For Muslim women, *purdah* in the sense of complete veiling seems to operate after *puberty* in relation to all men, except very close kin. In northern India, for Hindus, *purdah* in this sense is largely a question of veiling only after *marriage* and in relation to the husband's older male kin. Hindu women do not veil themselves in the place where they were born and where their own kin live, unless their husband or one of his male relatives is present. There are also differences in the way Hindu and Muslim women veil themselves: the *burqa* is a garment almost restricted in its use to Muslim women, but Hindu women can conceal themselves satisfactorily using a shawl or draping the end of their *sari* over their head and face. On the other hand, other elements which are generally included in the term *purdah* seem to be parallel in Hindu and Muslim practices. Young Hindu women are often given no more freedom to move around outside their homes after puberty than are Muslims; and the general stress on bodily concealment and the separation between the sexes — while differing in detail — can be found in Hindu and Muslim *purdah* alike.

Even among the Muslims, there are variations in *purdah* practices. The general feature of separation between the sexes remains, but differences in wealth as well as differences in context affect the precise character of that separation.

In some homes a curtain is indeed used to separate the *zenana* (women's area) from the *merdana* (men's area), while in others the separation is effected by more solid structures. This is possible only for the wealthy; poor people who wish to maintain this separation of physical space can often only do so by limiting entry to their homes to men from whom the women do not have to keep *purdah*. If the women have to leave their homes, the more wealthy may be able to transport them in curtained cars or, in days gone by, in shrouded sedan charis called *palki* or *doli*. Buses and trains also provide separate areas where women may be concealed from the public gaze.

But *purdah* entails much more than the physical separation of men and women. There are multitudes of complex social arrangements which maintain *social* and not just physical distance between the sexes. Of these, the symbolism of clothing is perhaps the most striking. Concealment of women is an important dimension of *purdah,* and a wide range of degrees of concealment can be effected by the styles and adjustments which the women can make to the clothes they wear.

Most conspicuous to the outsider is the way in which some of the women are veiled when they leave their homes. The older women I knew talked of how they used to leave their homes wrapped up in a *chaddar* (an enormous shawl) with their bodily features and faces concealed, though if they were going outside the village they would be transported in a curtained sedan chair. Nowadays, most of the women I knew wear a *burqa,* a garment whose use in India is practically restricted to Muslims. The old style *burqa* is perhaps the most effective means of concealing a woman, for it consists of a circular piece of material, with its centre intricately embroidered to create a skull cap, which drops right down to the ground around the woman, giving a rather ghostly impression. In fact, most of the women I knew wear the new style *burqa,* which consists of a long coat with sleeves, and a separate shoulder-length cape tied over the head with chiffon veils which fold down over the face.

The effect of all these garments is the same, though, for the woman is rendered anonymous, a non-person, unapproachable, just a silent being skulking along, looking neither to right nor left. To those who do not know her personally, she is nameless and faceless. Within a few months, however, I came to recognize the women whom I had seen unveiled in their homes, by the colour of their *burqa* or by their gait, by their sandals or by the shape of their feet. I never did overcome the unease of talking to such women who, I could only presume, were smiling at me through their veil. But women in the street would not normally engage in conversation with any one: the *burqa* cuts them off from the social world around them.

The *burqa,* though, is one of the more crude mechanisms for maintaining social distance between men and women. The different styles of *burqa,* the various qualities of cloth, and the cleanliness of the garment can indicate to the tutored eye the wealth or poverty of the wearer and possibly her age, but little more information than this is conveyed.

There are, however, many Muslim women who cannot afford to acquire a *burqa,* and they have to resort to other tactics of concealment. By dint of refusing to don a *burqa* myself, I had to learn some of the more subtle ways in which a woman can cut herself off from social contact with strange men and can be acceptably modest without hiding herself completely. I learnt about *purdah* through action and experience, not just observation. There is the importance of wearing some form of trousers to hide the legs, and a dress on top which is loose over the body, and has a high neck and sleeves; there is the *duppatta,* a chiffon scarf which is wrapped over the head and shoulders to cover the hair and bosom; there is the slightly bowed head and the eyes lowered to avoid eye-contact with men, and the unwavering gaze at the ground a couple of paces ahead. Only when I went out at dusk or wore

sunglasses could I feel free to look around. I had to avoid incurring any suspicion that I chatted with shopkeepers or encouraged the attentions of men in
the *bazar.* Men who received me warmly in the privacy of their homes, or
chatted to me in the shrine — as they did to women pilgrims — would
doggedly ignore me in the street, lest their greeting reflected badly on my
modesty and their respectability. ~~I was treated — and expected to behave —
as if I was the invisible creature I would have been in a *burqa*.~~

The *burqa* is only relevant when a woman goes outside her home. But
even within the home, relationships between men and women who may meet
— particularly between young women and older men — are generally characterized by restraint, by distance, by a certain aloofness. Where I worked, the
women often do their housework with their *duppatta* round their shoulders,
and indeed it is often tucked out of the way: but the arrival of an older man
makes a woman drop her work and re-adjust her *duppatta*, so that her head
and bosom are properly covered. A woman is also expected to cover her
head out of respect when she hears the call to prayer from a nearby mosque,
and when she prays she will wrap her *duppatta* closely round her so that even
her hair is hidden. When an elderly man — say a father or father-in-law —
comes into the room, there is an instant lull in the young women's chatter,
and they only speak audibly in response to a question or instruction from
him. It is also expected that young women, especially new brides, should
avoid direct eye-contact with the older men of the household. Even today, a
bride must conceal her face from her husband's older male relatives, though
maybe only for a few days: women in her mother's generation would
probably have hidden their faces until their first child was born. Unmarried
girls are also expected to remain aloof from their elder sisters' husbands, and
to adopt a pose of *ankhon ka purdah* (*eye purdah*), as one woman termed it.

In brief, the social distance between the sexes does not simply depend on
the *burqa*, let alone on physical separation, for there is a complex of little
signs being given off by the women about the different degrees of social
distance between themselves and men, whether they be older kinsmen, distant
relatives or total strangers. Indeed the variations are such that Cora Vreede-
de Stuers, for instance, in her study of Muslim women in and near Delhi,
talks of strict, partial, intermittent and absent *purdah*.[4] Some women always
wear their *burqa* with the veil down, while others never wear a *burqa* at all;
but between these two extremes are variations. Individual women may shift
between these different types of *purdah* at different stages of their lives, even
within one day. In some parts of Delhi, women prefer to wear their *burqa*
with the veil down over their face, in others they like to wear the *burqa* like
a coat and expose their face, in some parts the *burqa* even makes a woman
conspicuous rather than invisible.

Vreede-de Stuers' categories of *purdah* primarily refer to the styles of
wearing the *burqa*, or to its absence. But, as I have indicated, women who do
not wear the *burqa* may nevertheless be able to distance themselves from
strange men. Even those people who consider themselves 'modern', who
condemn the *burqa* and the rigid seclusion of women, even those who

practise no veiling and permit their women to attend school and college, are greatly influenced by notions of womanly modesty and the practice of 'eye-*purdah'*. Mixed social gatherings are more often characterized by stiff formality than by ease and comfortable interaction. Men and women are likely to polarize to different parts of the room, or the women may creep into their symbolic shells, lowering their eyes and taking little part in the conversation. In this most minimal sense, *purdah* is almost universal in northern India.

The social segregation of the sexes has one very important implication for the role in society of women living in some degree of *purdah*. Outside the home the economic role of women is sharply curtailed: in most families, it is the task of the men to obtain employment to support the women and children who are their dependants. The tasks of the women are generally restricted to the domestic sphere: cooking, cleaning, sewing, and childcare, but almost certainly not shopping for the family's daily food requirements, let alone going out of their homes to work. In fact, many poor families depend heavily on the earnings of their women, and it would be incorrect to presume that work outside the home is completely incompatible with maintaining some semblance of *purdah*. Few families appear to like their women to work outside the home, and there is even evidence that women may be required to live in more strict *purdah* once their families can dispense with their earnings: concealment of women and the ability to withdraw them from the public realm are costly but widely valued achievements.[5]

There are, however, those families at the upper end of the scale who can afford to educate their daughters for work which can be performed while maintaining *purdah*. It is still rare for women to perform office work in India. but work in the spheres of health and education often permits gainful employment without compromise to family honour since few women patients are prepared to be treated by male doctors and there are few co-educational schools particularly at secondary level. Provision of schooling and health care for girls and women is a virtual monopoly of women teachers and doctors, and in this way the employed women and their clients alike can leave their homes without necessarily having contact with strange men. Nevertheless the strictest forms of *purdah*, which follow through the logic of segregating men and women and separating the tasks which they perform in society, generally also entail the economic inactivity of women outside the confines of their homes. This is the case for the women who figure in this book.

Pirzada Women: The Frogs in a Well

The site which I had selected for my fieldwork in 1975 was the shrine of the Sufi — that is, Muslim mystic — Saint Hazrat Nizamuddin Auliya, which is situated about four miles south of Old Delhi. Adjacent to the shrine is the village named after the Saint, where the custodians and their families live: they are the *pirzade* (sing. *pirzada*) and they claim descent from the Saint's relatives and disciples. The village was the preserve of the *pirzade* until 1947 when the British administration partitioned India: ~~Pakistan was created to be~~ ~~a homeland for the Muslims of the Indian sub~~-continent. During the upheavals about half of the *pirzade* – like millions of other Muslims living in areas which were to become part of independent India – went to live in Pakistan. The migration of Hindus and Sikhs in the opposite direction resulted in a massive growth in Delhi's population, and in many parts of the city land was allocated for new residential colonies in which refugees were settled. The village of Hazrat Nizamuddin is now flanked to the south and east by just such a colony, and some non-*pirzade* even live within its confines now.

It is difficult to imagine a more impressive location for fieldwork: my first images remain, of the magnificent architecture spanning Islamic styles from the time of Hazrat Nizamuddin's death in 1325 A.D. until the nineteenth century. Delhi is a noisy place: throughout the day, from dawn until late at night, the ears are assaulted by sounds of bus and car horns, by the blaring of favourite songs from the latest hit films, by the cries of numerous street vendors. During the monsoon – the time when I arrived – it is also a muddy, steamy and bedraggled place.

To be taken for the first time to the shrine, stopping briefly by the flower stalls by the gate to remove footwear before going inside, has a stunning impact. During festivals, the shrine bustles with the throngs of pilgrims, but just now the impression is one of quiet purposeful activity – of barefoot pilgrims shuffling silently to and fro making their devotions, of *pirzade* sitting in the shade checking and rechecking their notes in the registers of pilgrims. Immediately, the visitor is taken right back into history: pilgrims and *pirzade* have been giving life to the shrine in just this fashion for centuries.

The main court of the shrine, paved in black and white marble, is bounded on its west side by the arched facade of the red sandstone mosque, which is said to be the oldest mosque still in regular use in India. In the centre of the court, directly opposite the main arch, is the tomb of Hazrat Nizamuddin Auliya. The grave of delicately carved white marble is in the middle of a small chamber whose walls are finely carved marble tracery screens, and whose ceiling is covered in mother of pearl. At all times, the grave is discreetly covered with velvet drapes and a canopy. The tomb chamber is surrounded by a small colonnade raised above the level of the rest of the court, and there in the shade some of the *pirzade* men sit, reading the *Quran Sharif,* checking their registers or chatting to guests in gracious Urdu. All the while, there is a steady trickle of pilgrims coming to honour Hazrat Nizamuddin. The men bring small wicker baskets heaped with rose petals and other flowers which they buy from the shops at the entrance to the shrine. They cover their heads and go inside the tomb chamber to pray and scatter their flowers. A notice above the lintel sternly warns 'Ladies are not allowed', so the women walk around outside, clutching at the marble screens and peering through the holes into the gloom. Myriads of ill, barren or simply worried women seek the Saint's help, and the hundreds of tiny ragged pieces of cloth which they tie onto the marble tracery are testimony to their vow of gratitude should their wish be granted. The atmosphere is thick with the heavy scents of joss sticks which

the men light before they leave, and, as they make to go, the *pirzade* on duty
encourage them to place their donations in the trunk outside the tomb
chamber.

Around the walls of the courts are the cells of the *pirzade,* where members
of the public bring their problems for resolution, and wait patiently, watching
and overhearing the people who arrived before them: the worried parents of a
child with pains no doctor has been able to diagnose; the boy concerned
about his imminent examinations; the woman plagued with miscarriages and
another whose husband blames her for only giving birth to daughters. For
each person's problem, the *pirzada* tries to produce a diagnosis and a remedy,
whether it be some powder to swallow or an amulet to hang around the neck.
Dotted about the courts are many graves, for it is an honour to be buried near
to the Saint. Some are of members of the Mughal royal family, set apart from
those of commoners by marble tracery enclosures, and some of the women
sit and relax in the privacy which the screens provide. When there are singing
sessions at the shrine, women pilgrims take over these enclosures, hazy dark
shadows, themselves hardly able to see out.

The pilgrims are all manner of humanity. Some of the women are well
dressed and veiled, some ragged and poor and hobbling painfully on calloused
feet. But none is a *pirzada* woman. This calm and beautiful retreat from the
outside world is far too public for them. Some of the older *pirzada* women
have not been inside the shrine since childhood, and it is rare for any *pirzada*
women to go except for some special occasion, late at night or at dawn,
huddling themselves up inside their *burqa* to make themselves as inconspicuous
as possible.

On my first visit to the shrine, I meet some of the elderly *pirzada* men and
explain my wish to meet their womenfolk and learn about their way of life.
The next day, I am escorted from the shrine to one of the homes by a dimin-
utive middle-aged manservant who scuttles hurriedly ahead of me along a maze
of narrow alleys, past the *bazar*, which buzzes with the conversation of men
and boys making their purchases from one-roomed stores perched a few feet
above the ground.

The part of the village called the *kot* is slightly higher than its surroundings,
and some parts of its medieval ramparts are still in evidence. Elderly *pirzade*
can even remember the hunting parties which sometimes took place outside
their village, but now the protective rough-hewn wall is tumbledown in many
places. The *Kota Derwaza* — the village gate — is about 500 yards south of the
shrine and is still virtually intact. It used to be the main point of entry to the
pirzada territory until the Partition of India in 1947. Before then, any
outsiders who tried to go through the gate would be challenged by shopkeepers in the *bazar*. But now, many outsiders live in the village, and two
pirzada households live outside the confines of the *kot*. The old wall has been
breached in many places, sometimes as a result of monsoon rains, sometimes
because *pirzade* living on the periphery have found it convenient to provide an
alternative entrance to their homes. This unkempt little village is no longer a
bastion against the dangers of the outside world.

But it does seem a haven of peace after the noise of the *bazar*. There are no shops inside the walls, though travelling vendors sometimes visit the village. There is a cloth merchant, who sits in the alleys outside his customers' homes and sends in cloth lengths for them to inspect; there is the woman who fits the *pirzada* women with glass bangles, and, besides her wares, brings all the latest news from Old Delhi; and there is the vegetable seller, who calls each day with his bicycle piled high with goods and who drops samples for inspection into baskets which hidden women hand out through the door. By and large, though, the village is the preserve of those who live there, and the alleys are the haunts of a few children and the lumbering myopic water buffaloes on their way to be milked.

The seclusion of the women in their homes is dramatically signalled in the construction of the houses. All were originally of one storey, but, as the roofs are flat, several households have extended their living-space by building new rooms on top. The plastered or bare brick walls present a blank facade to the outside, for they are windowless, except for small lights set high into the wall, which are only opened when there is need of a cooling through draught At intervals there is a doorway a couple of steps up from the alley.

Finally we arrive at one such studded wooden door, and the servant grasps the heavy iron chain which secures the door from the outside when no one is at home. He raps loudly, several times. A muffled voice asks who is there, and he explains. He tells me to step inside, and the next thing I know, he has vanished, closing the door behind him. For a few seconds I stand nervously, with all the symptoms of stage fright, wondering how my un-practised Urdu will withstand the barrage of questions, fiddling with my chiffon *duppatta* to make sure that my head and shoulders are decently con-cealed. I draw aside the curtain hanging inside the door, and at last I am in the world of the women: a physically enclosed world, a world of chatter and laughter, a world of domestic activity, of sewing, of cooking, of lulling babies to sleep on the floor with their head supported by tiny bolsters, a world of helping children to read the *Quran Sharif,* or of resting in the cool under the electric ceiling-fan listening to the radio.

Several of the rooms which open on to the central courtyard have an entire wall made of pillars separated by doors which fold back like shutters. In the height of summer, the doors are closed and the women maybe even retreat into the pleasantly cavernous inner rooms without direct access to the outside. In the cool months, the doors are thrown open, and the women often sit in the sun to chat while they do their work. There is little furniture: clothes and other goods are stored in tin trunks in small side-rooms. During the day, the beds are stacked against the walls or pushed to the sides of rooms, and the life of the women is mostly conducted at ground level. Floors are covered with mats, and here the women sit to prepare vegetables for cooking, or to sew the clothing and bedding for the household. At mealtimes, a cloth is spread over the mats and those present sit around it cross-legged to consume their meal.

I discard my sandals at the door of the main room and add them to the

pile of shoes already cluttering up the threshold, and the women come to
greet me, each placing her right hand first on her forehead and then over her
heart. They are all simply dressed: a cotton dress or *qemiz*, with long sleeves,
over baggy *shalwar* trousers, some with *duppatta* covering their head, others
with them draped carelessly over their bosoms, all with their hair parted in the
middle and tied back into a single plait, and the only jewellery small earrings
and nose studs and some glass bangles.

Like all guests, I am directed to sit 'above' on the special rug placed along
the back wall and recline upon the round bolster placed on top. They were
expecting me, and all work in hand is put aside. One young woman is deputed
to prepare some tea. Her mother-in-law reaches her *pan* box and prepares a
pan for me. She places a moist *pan* leaf on her palm, and with a spatula spreads
it with a red herbal paste and lime, sprinkles it with chopped areca nut and
cardamons, folds it neatly into a cone which she pegs with a clove, and presents
it to me on a tiny tray. The other women of the household cluster round us,
and begin to bombard me with questions.

What is life like in Britain? How do marriages come about when parents do
not arrange them for their children? Does not the mixing of the sexes result
in high rates of divorce and illegitimacy? Is it not better that boys and girls
alike should trust their parents' good judgement in selecting their marriage
partners? What do men in Britain think about having many children? What is
my husband's view? Do most married couples practise family planning? How
did I learn to speak Urdu? What was Pakistan like? And why have I now come
to India? What interest could it hold for someone from Britain? What makes
me think that I will possibly find them worthwhile companions? Am I not
embarrassed to talk to such ignorant people, who have hardly ever left the
confines of their homes?

Such questions were on the lips of all the women I met, and during the rest
of the year among the *pirzade* problems related to the status of the women
kept being brought to the fore. Talking about arranged marriages unearthed
the apprehensions of the unmarried about the in-laws their marriage would
bring. The Government sterilization programme gave impetus to discussions
about family size. Even when I was asking about genealogies, it was impossible
to escape the implications for the women involved. Since old women are very
important in the arrangement of their juniors' marriages, I had hoped they
would be mines of information. But they would often plead that their knowledge was sharply curtailed by being kept in strict *purdah* from the age of
nine or ten. By the end of the year, *I* was telling the women about their own
ancestors, much to their wry amusement. Moreover, my insistence that I
wanted to know about female as well as male forebears was as much a puzzle
to the women as to the men: for 'blood' comes through the male line, so it
does not matter exactly who a man's wife is, as long as she comes from a
good family. People who were often perplexed when asked how many sisters
their grandfather had, perceived no irony in being able to trace their connection through the male line right back to the Prophet Muhammad's daughter
Fatima. Women are continually lost from genealogical memory, they are

structurally irrelevant. No line continues unless there are sons, and yet the production of sons relies on the presence of wives.

Not surprisingly, then, my interests began to broaden. I found that the men did not puzzle over the question of *purdah:* it was not something which they thought to query. But for the *pirzada* women, seclusion was very problematic. The women had their own perspectives on *purdah,* which they continually wished to voice. A young woman told me a joke which went as follows: a bored Mughal emperor demanded that his courtiers recount something new, and one told him about seeing two women seated on a balcony above the street. 'What's new about that?' scoffed the king. 'Ah, Sire', responded the courtier, 'they weren't saying anything!' 'That', I was told scornfully, 'is what men think about women'. But like many jokes, there is an element of truth in the calumny. In the absence of men, the *pirzada* women were assertive and lively conversationalists. They often reverted to complaints about the restriction on their movements outside their homes; about the sheer physical discomfort of having to cover their clothes with a *burqa* when they go out, especially in hot weather; about the shame they feel when strange men taunt them in the streets and about the shame which they would feel if they discarded their *burqa;* about their embarrassment at being unable to tell me what they considered the simplest things about the way the shrine is organized; and about their self-designation as *kue ka meyndak* – a frog in a well – as people with intellectual and physical horizons limited to the tiny patch of sky directly above their heads.

Compared with the women I had known in Pakistan, the lives of the *pirzada* women are much more restricted: they themselves talk of their *purdah* being *sakht,* harsh or strict, in comparison with that of others. They are not involved in work outside their homes: indeed, they rarely leave their village. For the most part, they are invisible, virtually non-existent, to the outsider. Generally they are kept busy with their domestic work. All but the youngest wear a *burqa* when they leave their homes. They mostly have little contact with the men of their own households, let alone other men, for the *pirzada* men spend much of their time at the shrine or engrossed in their business elsewhere, and do not always come home even to eat or sleep.

If the *pirzada* women complain so much about *purdah* (while the men scarcely talk about it) it is no longer possible to pretend that the perpetuation of *purdah* rests on the accord of the women. But, then, if they are so often resentful, why are the women's lives still based in their homes, why do young women often fail in their bids to escape wearing a *burqa* when they go out, and why, indeed, do some elderly women play active parts in preventing adolescent girls from continuing at school? Why are the lives of these women still dominated by separation from the outside world and from unrelated men?

My experiences in Hazrat Nizamuddin challenged me to unravel the roots of sexual segregation in the village, and almost compelled me to follow up new lines of questioning. But in addition to this, I had to confront the possibility of being a detached observer. I had to contend with my own

confused and ambivalent response to the seclusion of the women who
became my friends. I tried to put myself in their position. Just what would
it really be like? I could make tentative efforts to 'live *purdah*' – but I had
the luxury of knowing that my experiment would only last for a year. What
must it feel like to face a lifetime of *purdah?* Do they feel as I would about
the numerous ways in which their control over their own destinies is so
limited? I could not enjoy watching the trauma which even crossing the road
on their own caused some of them. I could scarcely smile at their laughter
over getting lost or even misdirected through their ignorance of their own
city. How could I approve of a system which creates women who are so
'ashamed' that they rarely leave their homes during daylight (even though their
double veil completely conceals their facial features), or who always peep
cautiously outside to check that there are no men in the alley before they set
foot outside their homes? At the same time, how could I fail to be cheered by
the various ploys which the women made use of to evade the system or cover
up for one another?

I also found myself brought up against the responses of the *pirzade* to
myself and my husband. In some respects, Papanek's view – based on her
own fieldwork in Pakistan – is correct, that the foreign woman has advantages
in a society dominated by *purdah*.[6] On the one hand, she has access to local
women which no man, foreign or local, could attain. On the other, her very
foreignness, her being outside the local marriage market, mean that the demand
of modesty can be relaxed somewhat and it is possible to be acceptable to
local women while also conducting 'neuterized' relationships with local men.

Even so, I did sometimes find that it took several months to persuade the
pirzada men that I was capable of fathoming the intricacies of the shrine's
organization. To many of my questions came the answer that it was a very
complicated matter, and it was only through my persistent questioning that I
was able to convince some of the men that I was both interested and
intelligent enough to understand the full import of what they might tell me.
This was not a response which came from all the men, but it contrasts with
the way in which the women received me. I had no need to persuade the
pirzada women of my seriousness: that they presumed. Several were clearly
influenced by my having bothered to learn their language, by having come so
far from my home, that my interest and sympathy were not felt to be in
doubt. Some early suspicions that I might somehow be connected with
Mrs. Gandhi's Emergency were briefly reactivated at the start of the compulsory sterilization programme in April 1976, but for the most part I was
warmly received. My questions were taken in good spirit – and more often
than not reciprocated by the *pirzada* women – and my explanation that I
intended to write a book about them and their customs was welcomed by
these persons unused to the flattery of prolonged attention.

My husband's fate was different. He had his own work to do, but during
his occasional visits to the shrine the *pirzada* men warmly welcomed him.
Some of the older women even talked about him as their 'son-in-law' – but
this did not mean that they were prepared to meet him. I have images of one

woman in her fifties recounting how he had delivered my camera to her when she was alone at home during a festival. She told of how she had been too frightened to say a word to him, and almost too frightened even to go to the door — and all the while, she was breaking off to laugh at herself and cover her mouth with her hands in embarrassment. Several women caught glimpses of him from behind the veils of their *burqa,* but were unwilling to appear unveiled before him. During a picnic after a religious procession, for instance, several *pirzada* women were present, and he had to be relegated to the edge of the party, where he sat with his back to the group and his head bent. When the women visited me — which only a few would agree to do — normally lively and vocal women would be struck dumb, hang their covered heads and cast their eyes down in his presence. I had either to arrange for his absence or else put *him* in *purdah.* And then I had to listen solemnly to their praises that he is so 'noble' that he always avoids mixed company!

There is much more to it than this, though, for despite my reservations about the system of *purdah* which permeates the lives of these women, there are also respects in which they are privileged in relation to other Indian women. *Purdah* may restrict and seclude, but it also shelters, and means that secluded women do not seriously have to concern themselves with the harsh economic realities of life in India.[7] That is a matter for their menfolk, while the women only bother themselves with preparing meals, cleaning the house and caring for the children. How is it possible to compare the comparatively calm (if dull) lives of the *pirzada* women with those of the poorest women of India, who perforce do menial and ill-paid jobs out of sheer economic compulsion, and who do indeed really have to worry about how the next meal will ever materialize?

I had anticipated little of this confusion, nor the preoccupation of the *pirzada* women with their own position, but in the end such concerns became a central part of my work in Hazrat Nizamuddin. At the time I merely recorded what I saw and heard, but felt that my training had ill-equipped me to analyse the position of these women. In effect, this has been a book forced on me by the women themselves.

I hope to portray the lives of the *pirzada* women in such a fashion that this book can be both approachable to the general reader and of interest to the specialist. There will possibly be some — Islamic scholars, historians and sociologists of the Indian sub-continent — who would wish for a less perfunctory treatment of the doctrines of Islam, or the historical position of women in India, or who would want the text to be larded with more references to the sociological and anthropological material. There are many sub-themes which I have excluded so that the reader is not distracted from the main purpose of the book: that is, a detailed analysis of the position of these particular women living in *purdah,* a specific case of a phenomenon with widespread analogues. I hope that new light can be shed on the question of the position of women in India, and, in part, I have tried to achieve this through extensive quotation from my conversations with the *pirzada* women themselves, thereby giving a public voice to a normally silent and invisible sector of humanity. I always talked to them in Urdu without an interpreter or tape-recorder. Generally, I made few notes at the time, since this slowed down conversation, but I made full notes, mostly in English, immediately afterwards. I have tried to be true to the spirit and tone of the women's often pithy comments in order to present their taken-for-granted world most directly to the reader.

But there has to be more than this. The chapter which follows this Introduction puts the *pirzada* women into the general context of seclusion practice: a context of stratified, but not necessarily Islamic, societies.

References

1. The fieldwork on which this book is based was funded by the Social Science Research Council of the U.K.
2. The first quotation is from V.R. and L. Bevan Jones, *Woman in Islam: a Manual with Special Reference to Conditions in India*, (Lucknow, 1941 p.226, while the second comes from F. Hauswirth Das, *Purdah: The Status of Indian Women*, (London, 1932), p.85.
3. H. Papanek, 'Purdah: Separate Worlds and Symbolic Shelter', *Comparative Studies in Society and History*, 15 (1973), pp.289-325; D. Jacobson, 'The Wives of North and Central India: Goddesses and Wives', in C.J. Matthiasson (ed.), *Many Sisters: Women in Cross-Cultural Perspective*, (New York, 1974), pp.99-175; both contain material on different *purdah* practices in the Indian sub-continent. See also D. Jacobson, 'The Veil of Virtue: *Purdah* and the Muslim Family in the Bhopal Region of Central India', in I. Ahmad (ed.), *Family, Kinship and Marriage among Muslims in India*, (Delhi, 1976), pp.169-215, and her thesis *Hidden Faces: Hindu and Muslim Purdah in a Central Indian Village*, (Ph.D. thesis, Columbia University, 1970).
4. C. Vreede-de Stuers, *Parda: A Study of Muslim Women's Life in Northern India*, (Assen, 1969), pp.84-97.
5. The employment of women in India is considered below in Chapter 1. There are numerous references to women becoming more strictly secluded when the financial position of their family improves. See, for instance, M.N. Srinivas, 'The Changing Position of Indian Women', *Man (New Series)*, 12 (1977), pp.221-38; Z. Bhatty, 'Status of Muslim Women and Social Change', in B.R. Nanda (ed.), *Indian Women From Purdah to Modernity*, (Delhi, 1976), pp.99-112; V. Saifullah Khan, 'Asian Women in Britain: Strategies of Adjustment of Indian and Pakistani Migrants', in A. de Souza (ed.), *Women in Contemporary India*, (Delhi, 1975); Z. Bhatty, 'Muslim Women in Uttar Pradesh: Social Mobility and Directions of Change', in de Souza (ed.), *ibid*.
6. H. Papanek, 'The Woman Fieldworker in a Purdah Society', *Human Organization*, 23 (1964), pp.160-3.
7. Papanek, 'Purdah', pp.315-25, deals with the sheltering aspects of seclusion.

Woman reading the Quran

1. Sexual Apartheid

The substance of this book focuses on the seclusion of the women who form part of the 250 or so population of *pirzade* who depend on the shrine of Hazrat Nizamuddin Auliya, but, first of all, it is important to place this small population of Muslim women in a wider context.

Their lives are not freak aberrations. No doubt many particulars of their case could only be found among the *pirzade*, yet there are general features in the seclusion of the *pirzada* women which find their echoes far beyond the tumbledown walls of Hazrat Nizamuddin village: the almost total removal of the *pirzada* women from the public world of the men outside their homes; their rare forays outside, generally completely veiled and chaperoned; their complete exclusion from economic roles outside their homes; and the elaborate forms of modesty behaviour when they are confronted with men. There are probably few populations where all these features are as rigidly and strictly followed as among the *pirzade*. But they all have their parallels over a very widespread area, including the Middle East and Mediterranean as well as the Indian sub-continent. The lives of the *pirzada* women must be comprehended within these wider patterns. In this chapter, I want to suggest some tentative explanations to account for the widespread existence of the seclusion of women, and to provide an orientation for the main body of the book.

Islam and the Seclusion of Women

In the West, the seclusion of women is commonly thought to be a characteristically Islamic institution. Indeed, as far as the *pirzade* themselves are concerned, their women are secluded in their homes and veiled on the rare occasions when they leave them, because of the demands and requirements of Islam. They consider the tenets of Islam to be crucial.

One of the purposes of this chapter is to establish the weakness of this stance, and to suggest that Islamic doctrines can, at best, provide only a partial explanation for the seclusion of women. However, since the *pirzade* themselves put so much stress on the requirements of Islam, a brief presentation of Islamic doctrines as they relate to the position of women is called for.

17

Islam is a monotheistic religion which developed out of the Judaeo-Christian tradition. Jesus of Nazareth and the prophets of Judaism are all accepted by Muslims as prophets or messengers of God, though the greatest and final prophet was Muhammad. He lived in Arabia during the eight century (of the Christian era), and within a couple of centuries of his death, Islam dominated the Middle East.[1] The word 'Islam' means submission to the will of Allah (God), and a 'Muslim' is a person who so submits. The major book of Islam is the *Quran Sharif* (Holy Quran), which was revealed to Muhammad on behalf of Allah by the angel Gabriel. Muslims also turn for guidance to *Hadiths,* the sayings of Muhammad, and the *Sunna,* the reports of the Prophet's acts, which are considered worthy of imitation.

In the realm of worship, the obligations of Muslim men and women are identical. There are five 'pillars' of Islam, the first three of which are considered feasible and therefore obligatory for all Muslims, rich and poor, male and female. They are the confession of faith, the five compulsory prayers which are performed daily, and fasting from before dawn until sunset each day during the month of Ramzan. The two other pillars are only incumbent on those who are wealthy enough to bear the expense: the pilgrimage to Mecca (the Haj), and the payment of alms (levied at various rates on different types of property). A woman may not go to Mecca alone, but if she has the means, she should arrange to be accompanied by a male relative. Similarly, since women may own property and receive income in their own right, they are expected to pay alms on their own behalf. The rewards of piety are the same for both sexes: 'But the believers who do good works, whether men or women, shall enter the gardens of Paradise. They shall not suffer the least injustice.'[2]

That, however, indicates but the barest bones of Islam, and anyone wishing to present a concise version of the Islamic position on any topic is immediately confronted with immense problems. Islam is far from monolithic, for there are rival schools of interpretation, and although the text of the *Quran Sharif* is not disputed, the meanings attributed to particular verses often are. Moreover, the different schools have collections of the sayings and acts of the Prophet which are not in complete agreement with one another. There are disputes about what 'Islam' decrees in particular instances and there are discrepancies between the Traditions which rival schools adduce to support their stands.

The question of women is no exception to this. Do the texts in the *Quran Sharif* which refer to the veiling of women relate only to the female relatives of the Prophet Muhammad, or is veiling an absolute requirement for all pious Muslim women? Debate on this sort of question has been energetic, particularly in the past century or so, when Islamic reform movements have challenged many of the orthodox positions. In India, for instance, the demise of the Mughal empire under the onslaught of the British made many Muslims question deeply the reasons behind their downfall. The deliberations of opposing schools of thought have generally included the question of *purdah* and the status of women. Aziz Ahmad — a historian with a special interest in Islamic history in India — has outlined two major strands of interpretation which began to develop in the nineteenth century.[3] On the one hand was the position of the reformists who generally considered that the Mughal empire had failed to withstand the invasion of the British because of its traditionalism and obscurantism. Islam must move with the times, new scientific discoveries must be accommodated and accepted. Some parts of the *Quran Sharif* are eternally relevant, but others refer to issues relevant only in the time of Muhammad. It is the obligation of Muslims to excise from their practices all those which are no longer relevant, and in accord with the spirit of Islam. From this point of view, the seclusion of women was seen as problematic, if not downright un-Islamic. Ameer Ali — one of several proponents of this line of thinking — comments that Muhammad

> recommended to the women-folk the observance of privacy. But to suppose that he ever intended his recommendation should assume its present inelastic form, or that he ever allowed or enjoined the *seclusion* of women, is wholly opposed to the spirit of his reforms. The Koran itself affords no warrant for holding that the seclusion of women is a part of the new gospel.[4]

On the other hand is the line of thinking which attributes the fall of the Muslims to divine punishment, meted out because of their failure to follow to the letter the demands of their religion. Only a return to the original pure religion of Islam can save Muslims from a further decline. When the *Quran Sharif* talks of seclusion and veiling — so this argument goes — it refers to all women and to all times. Many Muslims in India today — including many of the *pirzade* — would take this line of argument. It is impossible to summarize adequately the numerous and diverse strands of thinking within the Islamic world, so the account which follows is (I hope) a fairly uncontentious portrayal of how orthodox Indian Muslims see the position of women.[5]

Equality in the 'religious' sphere does not preclude differences between the sexes. Indeed, it is the assertion of differences which is used to justify the seclusion of women. Khurshid Ahmad, a Pakistani academic lawyer, says that men and women are considered equal as human beings, but nevertheless they have different functions in society. The woman is primarily concerned with the family and with the upbringing of children, while the man is responsible for earning a living: 'This is a functional distribution of roles and activities and is regarded as essential for the proper functioning of different institutions of society and for its moral and social health and well-being.'[6] What is the basis for this differentiation? Of the orthodox school, Maulana Abul A'la Maududi — an Indian Muslim theologian who moved to Pakistan after India was partitioned — has written an influential commentary about the position of women, which comprehensively vindicates the Islamic view, as he sees it.[7] Originally written in Urdu before the Second World War, this book has been translated into Arabic as well as English and — like much of the material which addresses itself to this topic — is continually looking over its shoulder to life in the West. One of the purposes of the book was to combat what he saw as the danger of the corrupting sexual standards of the West infiltrating into Muslim circles in India through the Islamic reform movements there. The arguments presented are perhaps the most lucid systematization of the ortho-dox Indian Muslim view of *purdah*.

Maududi is concerned with the 'laws of nature' and the social system of Islam, at whose base is the social separation of men and women, a God-given social order in tune with nature. As he sees it, 'the most important problem of social life is . . . how to regulate the sexual urge into a system and prevent it from running wild.'[8] The human sexual urge is relatively unlimited and also uncontrollable. It is not intended just for the propagation of the species, or for pleasure, but for the creation of enduring bonds of affection which provide an atmosphere suitable for the rearing of children. Islam does not require the curbing of the sexual urge: there is a valued place for it, in marriage. All Muslims should marry and give outlet to their sexual desires in the proper context. An ordered social system can only be maintained if there are safe-guards preventing the arousal of sexual urges, except between a married couple Muslims should be so imbued with Islamic ideals of modesty and decency that they would not behave in ways which they should have learnt to consider unnatural; and if education fails, there should be severe punishments for offenders against morality. Finally, in the event of faulty moral education, social order is protected by preventive measures, which Maududi supports by quoting Quranic sources and the sayings of the Prophet.[9]

Several of the preventive measures relate to dress. The *Quran Sharif* tells Muslims: 'O Children of Adam! We have revealed unto you raiment to conceal your shame . . .'[10] There are parts of the body – the *satr* – which men and women must always hide. For men, this area is between the pit of the stomach and the knee. For women it is the whole body except the face and hands, even in the company of other women. Only spouses may see one another's *satr*, but even between them complete nudity is abhorrent.

Bodily concealment is only one aspect, for men and women alike are instructed to lower their gaze and be modest. Women are also told not to be alluring in their speech[11] and 'to display of their adornment only that which is apparent, and to draw their veils over their bosoms . . . And let them not stamp their feet so as to reveal what they hide of their adornment.'[12]

Generally, argues Maududi, unrelated women and men should have little cause to meet. Men should not enter other people's homes without permission and even men of the household should refrain from rushing inside, lest the women are inadequately covered.[13] Conversely, 'Islam has not approved that a woman should move out of her home without a genuine need.'[14] When a woman does leave her home, she should be accompanied by a male relative, and she should conceal herself from public view: although the veil or *naqab* is not mentioned in the *Quran Sharif*, Maududi considers that it is Quranic in spirit.[15] Even among orthodox Muslims this point remains a matter of debate, however. Siddiqi, who agrees in most essentials with Maududi, is one of those who consider that a woman need only cover everything but her face, hands and feet, and that complete veiling is not required by Islam.[16] Further women are exempted from participation in public religious activities. A man's most meritorious prayers are said in congregation in a mosque, especially on Friday and during festivals, but a woman should normally pray alone at home. Women should not attend mosques during daytime, and they may not lead public prayers, but should pray silently behind the rows of men. Women are also under no compulsion to participate in funeral processions, and during the pilgrimage to Mecca, men and women are kept as separate as possible.[17]

In several ways, then, society should be organized so that men and women are kept apart, for human sexuality is dangerous and the *purdah* system must at all costs be preserved, for it is the 'bulwark against the sex anarchy'.[18]

But there is another reason for *purdah:* nature has endowed men and women with different physical structures and capacities, and any equitable and fair social system must take these differences into account. 'The female physical system is evolved in order to bear and bring up children',[19] asserts Maududi, who argues that menstruation, pregnancy, post-partum weakness and two years of suckling each child all put women at a physical disadvantage. Moreover, 'the mother's lap is the best place where a child can be most naturally nourished and brought up.'[20] He goes on: 'Will it be just and fair to require [a woman] to undergo all sorts of hardships set for her sex by nature and also to earn her living in the economic field?'[21] But justice is only one part of it, for requiring women to do 'manly jobs is utterly against the will and design of nature', since women have been psychologically endowed to suit their 'natural duties' of motherhood and domesticity.[22]

These supposedly physiological and psychological 'natural differences' between the sexes might appear inescapable. However, to ensure that things do not go awry, the full force of education must make women fitted for their 'natural' roles. We are told that Islam has not distinguished between men and women as far as religious and mundane knowledge and cultural training are concerned, and yet Islam

> recognizes a difference in the type of education meant for the man and the woman respectively . . [A woman's] sphere of activity is the home. Therefore, she should be trained primarily in those branches of knowledge which make her more useful in that sphere.[23]

Thus, sexual apartheid entails 'separate development' as well as segregation. The apologists for the seclusion of women say that this is merely bowing to nature and in no way implies a lack of respect for women. Maududi considers that Islam permits men and women alike to attain success, honour and progress — in their own natural spheres.[24] For a woman, those spheres are motherhood and creating a stable home life. Similarly, Khurshid Ahmad asserts that there is equality of rights alongside a demarcation of responsibilities, with the roles of men and women complementary rather than competitive. Different roles 'do not mean difference in basic status as human beings. Rose and jasmine, daffodil and tulip are different, but to say that they are unequal is simply confusing the issue'.[25]

Even within the framework of Islam, however, the question of equality between the sexes is rather problematic. The *Quran Sharif* contains a verse which says: 'Men are in charge of women because Allah hath made the one of them excel the other, and because they spend of their property (for the support of women).'[26] Khurshid Ahmad tosses this off as 'in the interests of proper organization and management within the family', but I think it is impossible to dismiss it as lightly as that.[27] In the next two chapters I shall delineate the rights which Muslim women may have in property and in marriage, and — to pre-empt slightly — their rights are not always the same as those of men, and indeed do not compare favourably with those granted to men. Despite protestations by the advocates of *purdah,* there is little evidence that separate ever is equal (whether in the field of sex or race) even when it is dressed up as functional interdependence, and I certainly think that the question of equality between the sexes is at the heart of the matter. For the orthodox Indian Muslim, however, the volatility of human sexuality and the different capacities of men and women necessitate — and justify — a separation of the spheres of existence and the tasks of men and women. The *purdah* system is in tune with nature and ordained by Allah.

Seclusion and Social Stratification

There is, however, another dimension of inequality which is also relevant to the question of seclusion: social stratification. This raises the question of the relationship of seclusion to ranking in society, and its relationship with wealth and poverty. Explanation only in terms of Islamic ideals can give but a partial view of the institution of *purdah.*

Firstly, there is the problem to which I have already alluded: the problem of delineating just what are 'Islamic ideals' about the position of women in society. As Reuben Levy comments, Quranic provisions are often vague, and interpreters sometimes went beyond what was unequivocally enjoined, even inventing 'Traditions' to buttress their own stance.[28] In similar vein, Papanek writes: 'Purdah among Muslims is obviously related to the broad lines of the status of women in Islam, but it is an illusion to believe that this status can be fully explained in terms of the Quran and the commentaries'.[29] In other words, the tenets of Islam are themselves open to debate among Muslims — and it seems impossible for them to provide a completely satisfactory explanation for the existence of *purdah.*

A more critical objection to trying to explain *purdah* in terms of Islamic requirements is that the seclusion of women is not just an Islamic institution in India, or elsewhere. In South Asia for instance, many Hindus, as well as members of other religious communities, keep their women in seclusion. Indeed, right across Eurasia, from India, through the Middle East, the Balkans and even some parts of northwestern Europe, to the Iberian peninsula, there are reports of women secluded in their homes, of a sharp separation and differentiation between the spheres of the men and the women, of systems of arranged marriage and the use of chaperons when women leave their homes, and of notions that a woman should have no close contact with men, other than her husband and close kin whom she may not marry. The seclusion of women is a very general phenomenon — and not found just among Muslims — and Islamic ideals alone (whatever they might be) can give only a very limited insight into it.

Much of the sociological material which deals with this topic tries to account for the seclusion of women by reference to the twin notions of 'honour and shame', notions which are more widely applicable than Islamic ideals. Women are the locus of family 'honour', and their vulnerability to assault by outside men necessitates constant vigilance over their virtue. Many women rarely emerge from their homes, and there is an emphasis on bodily concealment (even if not on full veiling) and 'modest' behaviour, which includes averting the eyes and not talking to strangers. Chaperons are used and marriages are often arranged by guardians rather than by the parties to the marriage. While there are, of course, many differences discernible in the literature, a broadly similar picture emerges of the position of women in Eurasia, whether Muslims or not.[30] The *purdah* of the *pirzada* women has much in common with that observed elsewhere, especially in the Indian sub-continent, and more particularly in northern India and Pakistan, and the *pirzade*, too, use the words *izzat* or honour, and *sharm* or shame.[31]

Most of the regions under discussion have at some stage been dominated by Muslim influences, and it might be that the general notions of honour and shame represent the transplanting of Islamic notions into non-Islamic contexts. However, according to Levy, the early interpreters of the *Quran Sharif* were 'men who originated in Persia, a land in which women had long been secluded', and the *purdah* system was probably fully established in the Muslim world about one and a half centuries after the death of Muhammad.[32] Further, as I shall indicate in more detail below, there is also evidence from the Indian sub-continent that some women were secluded before the Muslim invasions which took place from the tenth century onwards. Thus, the source of any cultural diffusion which might explain the seclusion of women is by no means unambiguously Islamic.

More seriously, explanations in terms of cultural diffusion rarely focus on the perpetuation of institutions. A history of the diffusion of *purdah* would by itself provide an inadequate answer to why such similar patterns are still found today, and what is more, still found in different religious contexts. This implies the need to search for other widespread and more fundamental patterns which might relate to the seclusion of women.

In this quest, the notions of honour and shame are at best partial answers. Values — which no doubt legitimate the seclusion of women — must be related to other elements of social organization and not considered in isolation. It is not that 'Islamic ideals' or 'honour and shame' are unimportant, but that they are related in complex ways to other features in societies where women are secluded.

The major factor which undermines the strength of employing values as an explanation for the seclusion of women is that not all women in Eurasia — not even all Muslim women — are actually secluded in their homes, or excluded from work outside the home, or expected to have their marriages arranged by their parents. These may be widespread ideals in this geographical area, but in practice they are most particularly associated with people who are not poor. Keeping women in seclusion may be something which most people desire, but it can entail expenses which the very poor cannot meet. The income which a woman could bring if she were economically active outside the home must be forfeited; more extensive domestic quarters may be required; the assistance of servants may be called for; even a special garment to conceal the women when they leave their homes may be beyond the purses of the poorest. On several counts, the seclusion of women has to be seen as a 'luxury', a status symbol, in which only the relatively wealthy can afford to indulge themselves. Different patterns of behaviour sometimes relate to different systems of values: certainly there are 'modernists' throughout this area who deny that women should be restricted to the domestic sphere and be excluded from involvement in economic matters outside the home. Nevertheless, it is also clear that many women who work outside the home do so out of economic necessity rather than because they disdain the life-styles of their wealthy neighbours.

Two recent publications make analyses which are of particular relevance here: Jack Goody's work on *Production and Reproduction,* which was clearly much influenced by Ester Boserup's discussion in her *Women's Role in Economic Development.*[33] The perspectives in both these books are very broad: both are concerned with vast areas and there are probably plenty of specific instances which fit into their extensive sweep uneasily. Nonetheless, their efforts to uncover general patterns do suggest some interesting leads about the seclusion of women.

Goody argues that a broad distinction can be made between Eurasia and Africa, at the root of which are differences in agricultural production. While Africa is characterized by hoe agriculture, Eurasia has plough agriculture which permits the production of agricultural surplus, and a complex division of labour, as a result of which some sectors of the population are not directly involved in subsistence production. Plough agriculture allows greater population densities than are normally found in Africa, and land may thus become scarce and valuable. In much of Eurasia, land is still the major productive resource, and its unequal distribution is the major dimension in the system of stratification in the area.

Unequal access to land is something which landowners wish to perpetuate in their own favour, and Goody relates this to the patterns of inheritance, seclusion of women, arranged marriages and the prevalence of dowry systems. In Eurasia, in contrast to Africa, women generally have rights in the parental estate along with their brothers. Often these rights, it is true, may be hedged around with various types of restrictions. For instance, women may inherit land only as 'residual heirs', when they have no brothers; and generally they receive their share as a dowry (often made up of cash or household goods) which they get at the time of their marriage and which establishes a new conjugal estate. Among those who have property, Goody suggests, the position of women will be of particular concern, and there will be a preoccupation with the 'propriety' of matches, with preventing misalliances through the seclusion and concealment of women, the use of chaperons and the arrangement of marriages on behalf of the parties involved. Such are not likely to be the concerns of the poor. They have no property to pass on, they have little to fear from the misalliance which so frightens the wealthy, and their women may have to work outside the home, in any case, where they can be protected only with difficulty. Societies in Eurasia are characteristically stratified into groupings which internally are relatively homogeneous economically and within which most marriages take place.

Boserup approaches the matter from a slightly different but not inconsistent perspective. She differentiates between male and female systems of farming, the latter being characteristic of Africa, tribal India and Latin America. Where women work in the fields, Boserup suggests that polygamy and bridewealth are generally found, along with relative freedom of movement and even some economic independence for women. Male systems of agriculture, by contrast, are marked by settled plough agriculture in which women have, at most, a marginal role. Where women do not work in the fields, the pattern is of monogamy (except for the very wealthy), veiling and dowry, and the economic dependence of women. In male systems of agriculture, women tend to be evaluated not in terms of their productive capacities but in terms of their reproductive capacities, that is, their fecundity and especially their ability to provide a man with male heirs.[34]

The exclusion of women from agricultural production in male systems of farming applies most consistently to women from wealthy families. Often even the men from rich families actually do no manual work, but perform supervisory roles. Those who work the land come from landless families — or families with insufficient land for subsistence needs — who either hire their labour out, or are tenants of the landowners. The men do much of the work, especially the ploughing, but, among the poorest families, women may also do agricultural work such as weeding or transplanting rice seedlings.

Seclusion prevents affairs of the heart, before and after marriage. In wealthy families, parents can prevent misalliances — indeed, they can try to dispose of their children in economically or politically advantageous matches. Further, the seclusion of the women of relatively wealthy families — whose major task is the bearing and rearing of heirs for their husbands — ensures the correct paternity of a woman's children, and thus safeguards the transfer of property to a man's real heirs. The notions of honour and shame are important ideological buttresses in this state of affairs.

In other words, the ability to keep women in seclusion and uninvolved in economic activity outside the home is an important index of relative wealth, and it is closely tied up with the possession and transfer of property. The seclusion of women is a function of a family's worth, in an economic sense, but it also becomes indicative of their social worth, or their honour.

Women in India

What I want to do now is relate the perspectives of Goody and Boserup to the question of women in India, in order to provide a more detailed backdrop to the *pirzada* women in Hazrat Nizamuddin.

There is such a paucity of historical material that it is very difficult to determine when *purdah* originated in India.[35] Such few references as there are to women in India are generally restricted to women from the most wealthy — often royal — families. What is clear from this, though, is that the seclusion and veiling of women was not unknown before the Muslim invasions, which took place from about the tenth century onwards. Nevertheless, most writers consider that the Muslim invasions were a watershed and that *purdah* became more widespread during and after that period. Imitation of the invaders as well as protection of women in troubled times are the most common reasons given.[36] The case, in fact, is unproven, for the statistical material which could establish any change in the extent of *purdah* is simply not available. In any case, any increase in *purdah* might have been less to do with the fact that the invaders were Muslims than with the establishment of dominion, which was maintained over most of north and central India through a vast administrative bureaucracy whose personnel often lived lives of great splendour and wealth. But whatever was the case, some *purdah* at any rate pre-dated the Muslim invasions, and the general picture is of wealthy women being strictly secluded, while poor women often had to work outside their homes.

The present-day situation is considerably clearer. Land is still the basic productive resource of India: over three-quarters of India's population lives in villages and most of them are directly involved in agricultural production. In some areas at least, British rule resulted in the entrenchment of the position of big landlords, and land reform legislation since Independence in 1947 has not brought about any marked shift in the inequitable patterns of land ownership. There are quite wide variations among the states of India, but the general picture is of the concentration of land in the hands of a very small percentage of the population, with most people in the villages owning very little or no land.[37] The extent to which relationships of production in the agricultural sphere are becoming capitalist is a matter under lively debate at present. In addition, any description of the Indian economy must be further complicated by the merchant and industrial sectors, which in absolute terms are sizeable — when compared with other Asian or African countries — though small in relation to the Indian agricultural sector. Large-scale industry is split amongst state enterprises, a few large indigenous capitalist organizations, and subsidiaries of multinational corporations. In spite of the often close diplomatic connections with the U.S.S.R., then, India can be seen as a peripheral capitalist country.[38]

While the complexities of the Indian economy are hard to summarize, one thing is clear: India is a country of contrasts. At one end of the scale, is the wealthy businessman or landlord, living in a domestic splendour which is maintained not just with the use of labour-saving devices, air conditioners and the like, but with the employment of a staff of servants to wait on members of the family. At the other extreme are the families of the unemployed or under-employed, the day labourers on farms who may only find work seasonally, the poorly paid workers in service jobs in urban centres. Such people may live in squalid wattle and daub huts, often in sites liable to flooding, with no sewage disposal or adequate water supply. These are the people whose skeletal frames contrast with the obesity of the wealthy, whose children have the matted chestnut-coloured hair of malnutrition. Between these two poles comes an enormous range of existences: the poorly paid school teacher living in tiny quarters, struggling to make ends meet; the well-fed and hard-working independent peasant farmer, who can even produce some surplus for sale in the local market; the nightwatchman for a wealthy family, paid a pittance in cash and totally dependent on his employers for food, clothing and shelter; the civil servant, with his government housing, pension rights and security of employment.

Within this framework of contrasts, the position of women varies enormously: I cannot of course portray here the full range of regional, religious, caste and socio-economic differences, but I shall highlight themes which will recur in later chapters.[39] Indian society is highly stratified, and plough agriculture is characteristic of most areas. Thus it can be expected that the perspectives of Goody and Boserup will be applicable to the Indian situation. Firstly, then, I shall examine the position of women in India in the work-force and then go on to consider marriage and motherhood. Both Goody and Boserup, though, are primarily concerned to view society as a whole, and there is another dimension which I want to consider here too: that is, the question of women's status within their families.

Employment of women

There are considerable difficulties in using aggregate data to summarize the position of 'working' women in India. Different censuses have employed different definitions of 'work', and the delineation of employment trends is made even more problematic because of changes in the economic situation of India and different age structures of the population at different times.[40] In the Indian censuses (which must presumably be run mainly by men!), domestic work is considered 'unproductive' and women involved in it are registered as 'inactive'. However, the extent and type of work outside the home which a woman (or any person, indeed) has had to do before being added to the 'working' population has varied from census to census, and this is particularly problematic with agricultural work, for many women are predominantly engaged in domestic work but participate sporadically in work outside the home, such as during harvest periods.[41]

Nevertheless, several patterns may be delineated. While the level of male work participation remains more or less constant over the whole country, that for women varies quite considerably from region to region. Different parts of a single state may display marked differences, but an overall difference between the northern and southern regions of the country can be discerned.

Generally, women living in northern India are much less likely to be 'economically active' than women in the south. Boserup attributes this to the larger tribal population in the south, amongst whom women generally play a very important subsistence role, as well as to the greater influence of Islamic cultur in the north.[42] In addition, as Veena Das suggests, wet rice agriculture predominates in the south, and the vast amount of weeding and transplanting wo that has to be done quickly must therefore be generally done by women as well as men.[43]

This points to another general feature of the employment of women in India. Just as agriculture is the major source of employment for men, so it is for women. Women in urban areas are much less likely to be involved in work outside the home than women in rural areas. While 7% of urban women (that is about three million) are registered as workers, about 13% of rural women (some 28 million) are regularly involved in work outside their homes.[44] Of these rural workers 87% are involved in agricultural work, where they are generally paid less for their work than men.[45] Several writers point to a decline in the absolute numbers of women involved in industrial work, reported in the employment censuses between 1952 and 1962. Among these, Chitnis suggests that labour legislation protecting women has made them less attractive as employees than they used to be.[46]

Economic 'inactivity' of women, then, is characteristic of northern urban India in particular. The Muslims of India — a bit over 10% of the whole country's population — are concentrated in the northern and eastern areas, where they are a somewhat more urban population than the Hindus, and *purdah* is often considered to be a predominantly Muslim phenomenon. However, even allowing that 'Islamic ideals' might result in the seclusion of a greater proportion of Muslim women, it is clear that this alone cannot accoun for the more than 90% economic 'inactivity' of urban women in north India.[4]

Further, poor women are more likely to be employed than women from wealthy families: several writers comment on the greater prevalence of wage labour for women at the bottom of the hierarchy, which, from Goody's perspective, is what might be expected.[48] Again, in line with this is Baig's assertion that economic differences are more important than religious differences: a poor Muslim woman is more likely to work outside her home than the wife of a Hindu landowner.[49]

It is important, though, to note here that some women from wealthy backgrounds are working outside their homes in India. Most are women from 'westernized' urban families, generally women with high levels of education; but in terms of the overall picture such women form a very tiny part of the population of working women. Educated women may find openin in the medical and educational sectors, for instance, where they need have little contact with men, and there are smaller numbers of educated women in other types of work.[50]

For women involved in well paid work — and also for women in wealthy families who do not work outside their homes — there is a vast pool of workers available for domestic service. As Barbara Ward comments, the 'liberation' of a tiny elite of highly educated women carries implications in India which have no relevance in the West, for domestic chores may simply be taken over by servants, male and female.[51] On the other hand, many working women have to cope with the double role of housework and paid employment, because their incomes do not give sufficient surplus to enable them to employ servants. Given the dearth of domestic equipment and convenience foods to lighten the work of the Indian housewife, this double role is far more burdensome than it is in the West.

The employment of women in India, then, is not just a consequence of the necessities of subsistence, but it is largely that. For the most part, as several writers note, work outside the home is avoided by women: most women who do work, do so out of economic necessity and there is a great deal of prejudice against women working. The Indian women who are least likely to work come from the middle ranks and wealthy traditional families.[52] Overall, domestic labour in their own homes is the main work of women in India. This is especially so in urban areas — where only 7% of women are registered as working — in part because there are fewer employment opportunities for uneducated women in urban areas than there are in villages.[53] Typically, Indian women of whatever religion are dependent on the men of their families — and work outside the home is rarely seen as a privilege.[54] Perhaps, given the back-breaking nature of the work which most women would be expected to do, this is hardly surprising. As Das comments, it is not possible to draw the simple conclusion that a woman's status improves if she goes out of her house to work.[55] Indeed, the way in which work is perceived has to be related to the general notions of the *indignity* of manual labour, for men and women alike, in India.

Marriage and Motherhood

The roles for which most Indian women are destined are those of wife and mother. Marriage is nearly universal, and much of a woman's life is spent in bearing and rearing children.[56]

Indicative of the importance of marriage is the age at which women marry in India. The mean marriage age of females has risen from about 13 (in the early years of this century) to about 17 currently. Further, in 1971, only around 20% of females over the age of ten were recorded as unmarried. Less than 2% of rural women remain unmarried by the age of 30. As Boserup predicts, polygamy is very rare. In 1971 there were 1024 married women for every 1000 married men. Polygamous marriages are generally only found amongst the most wealthy.[57]

Most Indians trace descent through the male line (patrilineally), and for women who are not involved in work outside the home, their major importance is not reckoned by their earning capacity but by their fecundity, by their ability to bear sons to perpetuate their husband's line.[58] The wealthy often place great importance on their lengthy genealogies and the continuity of their lines, and the wife who fails to provide her husband with male heirs faces cruel stigmatization. The poor rarely have long genealogical memories, but nonetheless motherhood is not irrelevant for them: poor women may simply have to combine their work outside the home with having children, and for rich and poor alike, sons are considered insurances against destitution in old age.

Recent material suggests that women in the age group 40-44 have had an average number of 6.4 live children born to them. Because of problems of recording stillbirths, perinatal mortality and natural abortions – all of which are likely to be prevalent in India, given the nutritional status of many women – this figure of 6.4 children probably does not relate closely to the average number of conceptions per woman, but it can give some impression of the extent to which the lives of women in India are dominated by motherhood. Despite national campaigns to persuade couples to limit their families, only about 13% of married couples in the reproductive age group are employing some mechanical means of family limitation, though the figure for Delhi is estimated at 30%.

The importance of motherhood is reflected in statistics which indicate that males and females have differential chances of living until old age.[59] Apart from two states, the pattern over India is for there to be more males than females, and this is a reflection of differential mortality rates. Females are particularly vulnerable in infancy and again during the prime child-bearing years. It is generally argued that sons are more valued than daughters (since daughters cannot be expected to support elderly parents, as sons are) and that this is reflected in the infant mortality rates and age-specific death rates which – while appallingly high for boys – indicate that girls have even less chance of surviving to puberty. Also, from 15 to about 40 years of age women are more likely to die than are men, and this is largely attributable to the dangers of pregnancy and childbirth in a context in which pregnant women are often undernourished and have little or no access to hygienic medical facilities. It is only after 40 that the life chances of women begin to surpass those of men. Over the last 50 years, life expectancy at birth has dramatically improved, but the small differential between the sexes in 1921 had widened by 1971 (47.1 years for men and 45.6 years for women), suggesting that males have benefited more than females from improvements in the field of public health and nutrition.

A further indication of the importance of marriage and motherhood in India comes from literacy statistics and material about the educational levels of boys and girls.[60] Women are much less likely than men to have been enrolled at school, or to have learnt to read at home. At all levels of formal education, girls are outnumbered by boys, and higher up the educational scale the differential widens, though the enrolment of girls has increased in relation to boys at all levels since 1950. Generally it is said that parents consider the education of boys to be much more important than that of girls, and when families must choose how to allocate resources, the schooling of girls tends to lose out in relation to boys. Moreover, there is still widespread opposition to 'wasting' money on schooling girls whose future is likely to be home-based, performing tasks which they can more easily, cheaply and usefully learn from their mothers. Not surprisingly, then, there are sharp differentials between men and women in relation to literacy as well as educational attainments at different levels: overall, the literacy rates for men are more than twice those for women, with an even more marked difference in the age groups over 35. The national rate of literacy for women is only about 19 per cent, though this conceals massive variations between the different states as well as between rural and urban areas: the urban literacy rate for women is just over 40 per cent. Female literates are slightly more likely than males never to have been to school at all and about 90 per cent of female literates either had left school by the age of 10, or had never attended school at all.

These overall differences between men and women in terms of mortality and education — important indicators though they are — should not be allowed to conceal other dimensions of differentiation. People in urban areas have greater access to medical and educational facilities than do those in rural areas, for instance. There are also differences between the regions, with women's life chances and educational attainments being lower in the north — in general — than in the south, which parallels the lower involvement of women in the work force in northern India. Another major factor of differentiation in the Indian sub-continent is that by wealth: wealthy women have better life chances than poor men, let alone poor women; they are less likely to suffer for want of an adequate diet or medical treatment than are poor people; and they are more likely to receive some formal education.[61]

I would suggest that the perspectives of Goody and Boserup fit well into the general picture of the position of women in India. Indian society is a highly stratified and predominantly agricultural one, with the plough forming the backbone to its male farming system. Few women work outside the home. Those who do, mainly do so out of necessity; those who do not, spend their lives based in their homes, emerging veiled or at least well-concealed, and their adult lives revolve around housework and the bearing and rearing of children. One point which needs to be stressed, though, is that the seclusion of women is not just a rural phenomenon. It has also been long associated with the urban elites, with the royal courts and the households of their followers, and with wealthy traders and businessmen. In stratified social systems, a common feature is the emulation of the rich by the less wealthy; and to this day, in India, *purdah* is widely — though not universally, it must be stressed — associated with respectability and family honour. *Purdah* is part and parcel of stratification in India.

Factors Affecting the Status of Women within the Family

But stratification at the level of the whole society — while crucially significant — is not the whole story. The work of Goody and Boserup will indeed form an important backdrop to the rest of this book, but much of the material which is presented below is more concerned with the *pirzada* women *within* their families, and with the interplay between stratification at the wider societal level and stratification within the family. Several features are often said to have a bearing on the status of women within the family, and it is to these that I briefly want to turn now.

A major factor is that of working outside the home. I have already indicated that very few women in India work outside their homes: most are dependants of the men of their families, and those women who do work generally do so because of poverty. Where possible, Indian women have typically avoided work outside their homes. Recent anthropological material, however, has given attention to this question, and it is often suggested that control over economic resources is crucial for the attainment of domestic power. Since the products of labour outside the home may be appropriated or de-valued, work outside the home does not guarantee power within it, but where women do not work outside their homes at all, where they are not involved in the production or distribution of vital goods, they generally appear to have little autonomy or control over others.[62]

The Indian situation, then, presents a paradox. It is mainly — but not exclusively — women from the poorest sectors who work outside their homes, and have greatest equality with their menfolk at home. By contrast, the cloistered women who do not work are women whose menfolk wield the greatest influence in the world outside the home, and who, as several writers have commented, experience marked inequalities between spouses in these richer families, often signalled by the women when they cover their heads, lower their eyes, or employ polite and circumlocutory forms of address.[63]

Another factor which affects the status of women in their families is household structure in different sectors of society. As with the question of women working outside their homes, household structure largely parallels differences in wealth. Extended households are associated with wealthy urban or landowning rural families, while poor people tend to live in small, often nuclear households.[64] Whereas the poor bride may only have her own husband to contend with, the bride in wealthy families may be as much under the thumb of older women as of the men of her husband's family, though she can hope to move up the female hierarchy as the years pass.[65] In relation to the wider system of stratification, then, women in wealthy families have high status *through their menfolk,* but their power in the home is likely to be circumscribed within a hierarchical structure, and their power outside the home is virtually non-existent.

The way in which marriages are arranged also appears to affect a woman's status within the home. Arranged marriages are particularly associated with families which can afford to keep their women more or less cloistered. Generally in India, marriage involves transfers of property. Major among these is the dowry — the gifts which the bride's parents send with her to her conjugal home — which is characteristic of the relatively wealthy, rather than the poor.[66] It is often said that parents dread the burden of many daughters because of the financial demands their marriages involve, and, indeed, the size and contents of the dowry are often matters which are disputed by the parties involved in a marriage. The pressure is always on the bride's family to give as much as they can — and the fear is always that, if they fail, the bride will be ill-received in her husband's home. The non-working daughter is a drain on the family's resources. A son, by contrast can be expected to support his aged parents, as well as provide their line with continuity.

Another dimension of the arrangement of marriages in India concerns the way in which eligible matches are chosen. A broad distinction can be drawn between the north and south of the country.[67] In the south, it is common for marriages to be arranged between people who are already related, and Das suggests that brides who are already known to their in-laws will be treated with greater love and consideration than others. In the north, the marriage regulations generally exclude a much wider range of relatives from the pool of potential marriage partners. In addition, the groom's family is always treated as if they are the superiors of the bride's, even if there is no great disparity in wealth between the families: the very act of giving a bride makes one an inferior.

Typically, then, women living in urban areas of northern India do not work outside their homes, especially among the relatively wealthy sectors. That much fits well with the accounts of Boserup and Goody. But focusing on the level of the family provides a rather different picture. Seclusion and the economic 'inactivity' of women are characteristic of relatively wealthy, high status families, but seclusion and economic inactivity are also likely to have a deleterious impact on some aspects of the position of women within their families. Moreover, in relatively wealthy north Indian circles, a bride is likely to be not just a stranger, but an inferior one, entering at the bottom of the ladder in an extended household, subordinate to older women as well as to her husband. The dowry — depending on its scale — which her parents have managed to provide may simply make her vulnerable, or, alternatively, it may help her to rise in the estimation of her in-laws. But it is her own ability to bear sons for her husband that is her best hope for bettering her status in her conjugal home. The rather unenviable domestic position of such women in relatively wealthy families goes hand-in-hand with high status in the overall stratification system of Indian society.

Pirzada Women and Seclusion

In this chapter I have been suggesting that *purdah* cannot simply be regarded as an Islamic institution, although 'Islamic ideals' or notions of 'honour' and 'shame' are important in providing religious and moral justification for the seclusion of women. Concentrating on values diverts attention from the crucial economic dimension to the seclusion of women, to which Goody and Boserup both point. The types of relationship which they outline, linking seclusion with relative wealth, and contrasting the position of women under different modes of production are very important. The seclusion of women is not just for Muslims, but neither is it for the poor (no matter what their religion), nor for those who live in the more egalitarian systems based on hoe agriculture. The seclusion of *some* women is but one integral part of a particular type of social system.

The *pirzade,* though, are Muslims and for them — and for the men in particular — Islamic tradition provides a great deal of backing for their assertions that Islam decrees purdah. And yet the *pirzade* fit most of the expectations outlined above: the women are economically 'inactive', marriage and motherhood are the destinies to which girls are directed, they spend most of their time at home, and nearly all the *pirzada* households are extended. Only on the question of dowry and the arrangement of marriages do the *pirzade* depart from the north Indian pattern. While they give dowries, they claim that they place little importance on the content — unlike outsiders — and they say that no bride suffers if her dowry is small. Further, they often, though not always, marry among themselves: this contrasts with the general pattern of marriages in northern India, where brides usually move some distance at marriage into a household of strangers. This is only sometimes the case among the *pirzade,* and indeed among some other north Indian Muslims.[68] Both these factors could be expected to moderate the adverse effects of women's economic inactivity on their status, and the usual position of brides in extended households.

The maintenance of *purdah* is very important for the *pirzada* men. Their position as custodians of a shrine, their dependence on the incomes which pilgrims bring, provide very compelling economic reasons why the men should wish to appear 'orthodox' with respect to *purdah. Purdah* makes the *pirzada* women conspicuous by their absence in the world outside their homes, but, as the next chapter indicates, the seclusion of the *pirzada* women has implications for their status within their families as well as for the ability of their menfolk to cut a convincing and respectable pose to the pilgrims at the shrine.

References

1. There are too many works on Islam to list here, but the following provide good introductions: H.A.R. Gibb, *Islam,* 2nd. ed., (London, 1975); R. Levy, *An Introduction to the Sociology of Islam,* 2 vols., (London,1931-3); M. Rodinson, *Mohammed,* (London, 1971).
2. There are many translations of the *Quran Sharif,* none of them entirely satisfactory. The two most easily available are N.J. Dawood (translator), *The Koran,* (Harmondsworth, 1968), and M.M. Pickthall (translator), *The Meaning of the Glorious Koran,* (New York, n.d.), and I have quoted as appropriate from both of these. This quote is chapter 4 verse 124.
3. Aziz Ahmad, *Islamic Modernism in India and Pakistan 1857-1964,* (London, 1967), pp.35, 63-4, 72-5, 94-5.
4. S. Ameer Ali, *The Spirit of Islam,* Rev. ed. (London, 1922), p.249. See also Cora Vreede-de Stuers, *Parda: A Study of Muslim Women's Life in Northern India,* (Assen, 1968), pp.52-8.

5. V.R. & L. Bevan Jones, *Woman in Islam*, (Lucknow, 1941), gives a more detailed summary, and is a mine of useful information despite its age.

6. Khurshid Ahmad, *Family Life in Islam*, (Leicester, 1974), p.16.

7. S. Abul A'la Maududi, *Purdah and the Status of Women in Islam*, (Lahore, 1962). See also M.M. Siddiqi, *Women in Islam*, (Lahore, 1952).

8. Maududi,*op. cit.*, p.145.

9. *Ibid.*, pp.164-82.

10. *Quran Sharif*, 7:26.

11. *Ibid.*, 33:32.

12. *Ibid.*, 24:31.

13. *Ibid.*, 24:27-8 and 24:59.

14. Maududi, *op. cit.*, p.150, and *Quran Sharif*, 33:32.

15. *Ibid.*, p.198, and *Quran Sharif*, 33:59 and 24:60.

16. Siddiqi, *op. cit.*, p.128.

17. Maududi, *op. cit.*, pp.205-15.

18. *Ibid.*,p.224.

19. *Ibid.*,p.115.

20. *Ibid.*,p.119.

21. *Ibid.*,p.119.

22. *Ibid.*,pp.121-2.

23. *Ibid.*,p.156.

24. *Ibid.*,pp.161-2.

25. Ahmad, *op. cit.*, pp.29, 31 and 16 (note 28).

26. *Quran Sharif*, 4:34 and 2:228.

27. Ahmad, *op. cit.*, *p.29.*

28. Levy, *op. cit.*, vol. 1, pp.179-90.

29. Hanna Papanek, 'Purdah: Separate Worlds and Symbolic Shelter', *Comparative Studies in Society and History*, 15 (1973), p.303.

30. Again, there are too many works to list fully here. The following are a selection drawn from a range of ethnographic areas. R.T. Antoun, 'On the Modesty of Women in Arab Muslim Villages', *American Anthropologist*, 70 (1968), pp.671-97; N.M. Abu-Zahra 'A Reply', *American Anthropologist*, 72 (1970), pp.1079-88; R.T. Antoun 'Antoun's reply to Abu-Zahra', *American Anthropologist*, 72 (1970), pp.1088-92; Abner Cohen, *Arab Border Villages in Israel*, (Manchester, 1965); B.S. Denich, 'Sex and Power in the Balkans', in M.Z. Rosaldo and L. Lamphere (eds.), *Woman, Culture and Society*, (Stanford, 1974); E. Friedl, *Vasilika: A Village in Modern Greece*, (New York, 1962); S. Harding, 'Women and Words in a Spanish Village', in R.R. Reiter (ed.), *Toward an Anthropology of Women*, (New York, 1975); J.G. Peristiany (ed.), *Honour and Shame: The Values of Mediterranean Society*, (Chicago, 1965); J.G. Peristiany (ed.), *Mediterranean Family Structures*, (Cambridge, 1976); J. Pitt-Rivers (ed.), *Mediterranean Countrymen*, (The Hague, 1963); J. Pitt-Rivers, *The Fate of Shechem or The Politics of Sex*, (Cambridge, 1977); R. Reiter, 'Men and Women in the South of France', in Reiter (ed), *op. cit.*; J. Schneider, 'Of Vigilance and Virgins', *Ethnology*, 10 (1971), pp.1-24.

31. For translations of Urdu words I have relied on J. Platts, *A Dictionary of Urdu, Classical Hindi and English*, (London, 1911). For general

material on North Indian parallels see Papanek, 'Purdah', *op. cit.,* T.N. Madan, *Family and Kinship,* (Bombay, 1965); A.C. Mayer, *Caste and Kinship in Central India,* (London, 1960); D. Pocock, *Kanbi and Patidar,* (Oxford, 1972); S. Vatuk, *Kinship and Urbanisation,* (Berkeley, 1972); W. and C. Wiser, *Behind Mud Walls 1930-1960,* Rev. ed., (Berkeley, 1971). For material on North Indian Muslims see I. Ahmad (ed.), *Caste and Social Stratification Among the Muslims,* (Delhi, 1973); I. Ahmad (ed.), *Family, Kinship and Marriage Among Muslims in India,* (Delhi, 1976); F. Barth, *Political Leadership Among Swat Pathans,* (London, 1965); Z. Eglar, *A Punjabi Village in Pakistan,* (New York, 1960); S.C. Misra, *Muslim Communities in Gujarat,* (London, 1964); C. Pastner, *Sexual Dichotomisation in Society and Culture,* (Ph.D. thesis, Brandeis University, 1971); R.N. Pehrson, *The Social Organisation of the Marri Baluch,* (New York, 1966); C. Vreede-de Stuers, *Parda: A Study of Muslim Women's Life in Northern India,* (Assen, 1968).

32. Levy, *op. cit.,* vol. 1, p.180.

33. J. Goody, *Production and Reproduction,* (Cambridge, 1976), especially chapters 1-4, of which the following is a precis. See also E. Boserup, *Women's Role in Economic Development,* (London, 1970).

34. *Ibid.,* pp.50-1.

35. The following account is based on these sources: A.S. Altekar, *The Position of Women in Hindu Civilization,* 3rd. ed., (Delhi, 1962); A. Appadorai (ed.), *Status of Women in South Asia,* (Bombay, 1954); S.C. Dube, 'Men's and Women's Roles in India: A Sociological Review', in B. Ward (ed.), *Women in the New Asia,* (Paris, 1963); F. Hauswirth Das, *Purdah: The Status of Indian Women,* (London, 1932); R. Misra, *Women in Mughal India (1526-1748 A.D.),* (Delhi, 1967); M. Mujeeb, *The Indian Muslims,* (London, 1967); K.M. Panikkar, 'The Middle Period', in T.A. Baig (ed.), *Women of India,* (Delhi, 1958); R. Thapar, 'The History of Female Emancipation in Southern Asia', in Ward (ed.), *op. cit.;* P. Thomas, *Indian Women Through the Ages,* (London, 1964); M. Yasin, *A Social History of Islamic India,* 2nd. ed., (New Delhi, 1974).

36. Some writers say that *purdah* was introduced into India by the Muslims. See, for example, Mrs. Meer Hassan Ali, *Observations on the Mussulmauns of India,* (2 vols., London, 1832), vol. 1 p.317, and K. Mayo, *Mother India,* (London, 1927), p.108. But this seems to be incorrect.

37. P.C. Joshi, 'Land Reform and Agrarian Change in India and Pakistan since 1947', in R. Dutta and P.C. Joshi (eds.), *Studies in Asian Social Development No.1,* (Bombay, 1971); H. Laxminarayan and S.S. Tyagi, 'Some Aspects of Size-distribution of Agricultural Holdings', *Economic and Political Weekly,* XI (1976), pp.1637-40.

38. For a survey of the debates on this issue see D. McEachern, 'The Mode of Production in India', *Journal of Contemporary Asia,* 6 (1976).

39. Indian Council for Social Science Research, *Status of Women in India,* (New Delhi, 1975); D. Jain (ed.), *Indian Women,* (New Delhi, 1975); A. de Souza (ed.), *Women in Contemporary India,* (Delhi, 1975); B.R. Nanda (ed.), *Indian Women from Purdah to Modernity,* (New Delhi, 1976). Some relevant statistical material has been collected in an appendix.

40. D.R. Gadgil, *Women in the Working Force in India,* (Delhi, 1965). See also Table 1, in the Appendix.
41. B.E. Ward, 'Men, Women and Change', in Ward (ed.), *op. cit.*
42. Boserup, *op. cit.,* pp.89-90.
43. V. Das, 'Indian Women: Work, Power and Status', in Nanda (ed.), *op. cit.* See also A. Beteille, 'The Position of Women In Indian Society', in Jain (ed.), *op. cit.;* V.S. D'Souza, 'Family Status and Female Work Participation', in de Souza (ed.), *op. cit.*
44. A. Bose, 'A Demographic Profile of Indian Women', in Jain (ed.), *op. cit.* See also Table 1, in the Appendix.
45. *Ibid;* see also S. Chitnis, 'International Women's Year: Its Significance for Women in India', in de Souza (ed.), *op. cit.,* and Tables 1 and 2, in the Appendix.
46. Chitnis, *op.cit.;* S.R. Deshpande, 'The Position of Women in Different Social Stratifications and Occupations In India', in Appadorai (ed.), *op. cit.;* Gadgil, *op. cit.;* P. Sengupta, 'In Trades and Professions', in Baig (ed.), *op. cit.*
47. See India, Census Commissioner, Series 1 — India, Paper 2 of 1972. *Religion,* (Delhi, 1972).
48. Sengupta, *op. cit.*; M.N. Srinivas, 'The Changing Position of Indian Women', *Man (New Series),* 12 (1977), pp.221-38.
49. T.A. Baig, 'The Family and the Home', in Baig (ed.), *op. cit.*
50. See Table 29, in Jain (ed.), *op. cit.,* p.172.
51. Ward, 'Men, Women and Change', in Ward (ed.), *op. cit.*
52. D'Souza, *op. cit.*
53. Boserup, *op. cit.,* pp.157-93; Papanek, 'Purdah', *op. cit.,* p.292, talks of *purdah* as a typically lower middle class urban phenomenon.
54. Beteille, 'The Position of Women', in Jain (ed.), *op. cit .;* Bose, 'A Demographic Profile', in *ibid.*
55. V. Das, 'Marriage Among the Hindus', in *ibid.*
56. See Tables 3 and 4, in the Appendix.
57. Bose, 'A Demographic Profile', in Jain (ed.), *op. cit.,* pp.131-2 and 179-80.
58. Boserup, *op. cit.,* pp.50-51; E. Friedl, *Women and Men,* (New York, 1975), pp.66-70; Ward, 'Men, Women and Change', in Ward (ed.), *op. cit.,* pp.76-87.
59. Bose, 'A Demographic Profile', in Jain (ed.), *op. cit.,* pp.146-8.
60. *Ibid.,* pp.162-7.
61. G. Myrdal, *Asian Drama,* (London, 1968), pp.1533-1829; A. Rauf, *West Pakistan: Rural Education and Development,* (Honolulu, 1970).
62. Friedl, *Women and Men, op. cit.,* pp. 7-11; M.Z. Rosaldo, 'Woman, Culture and Society: A Theoretical Overview', in Rosaldo and Lamphere (eds.), *op. cit.;* P.R. Sanday, 'Female Status in the Public Domain', in *ibid;* V. Das, 'Indian Women: Work, Power, and Status', in Nanda (ed.), *op. cit.;* K. Young and O. Harris, 'The Subordination of Women in Cross Cultural Perspective', in Women's Publishing Collective (eds.), *Papers on Patriarchy Conference,* (Lewes, 1976).
63. Thapar, in Jain (ed.), *op. cit.;* Srinivas, *op. cit.;* Das, 'Marriage Among the Hindus', in Jain (ed.); 'Men, Women and Change', in Ward (ed.) *op. cit.*

64. Dube, 'Men's and Women's Roles', in Ward (ed.), *op. cit.;* Ward, 'Men, Women and Change', in *ibid.*
65. Srinivas, *op. cit.;* Das, 'Indian Women', in Nanda (ed.), *op. cit.*
66. J.R. Goody and S.J. Tambiah, *Bridewealth and Dowry,* (Cambridge, 1973); Goody, *Production and Reproduction, op. cit.;* Boserup, *op. cit.*
67. Das, 'Marriage Among the Hindus', in Jain (ed.), *op. cit.;* L. Dumont, 'Marriage in India: The Present State of the Question III: North India in relation to South India', *Contributions to Indian Sociology,* 9 (1966), pp.90-114.
68. Vreede-de Stuers, *Parda, op. cit.,* pp.28-38; W. Crooke (ed.), *Islam in India,* (London, 1921), pp.56-88; S.A. Husain, *Marriage Customs Among Muslims in India,* (New Delhi, 1976), pp.56-89; Eglar, *op. cit.,* pp.207-9; V. Das, 'The Structure of Marriage Preferences: An Account from Pakistani Fiction', *Man,* New Series, 8 (1973), pp.30-45.

Woman pilgrim consulting a pirzada man

2. Priestly Power

The purpose of this chapter is twofold. On the one hand, it is important to locate the *pirzade* in the Indian social system. My discussion of the work of the *pirzada* men in the shrine and the incomes which they receive from devoted pilgrims indicates their position of relative privilege in terms of the overall picture which the Indian situation presents. That their womenfolk, therefore, are economically inactive and secluded in their homes should come as no surprise.

However, to link relative wealth within a stratified social system to *purdah* in Hazrat Nizamuddin does not explain how the women are persuaded to accept restraints on their movements. Goody, whose writings have already been referred to, is concerned with the connections between property transfer, agricultural production and social stratification at the level of the social system as a whole. He blandly talks of 'the seclusion of women' — a fate which, I hazard, he would find unpalatable — and does not make the shift in focus which would be required to examine adequately the question of stratification *within* the domestic unit.[1] My book is concerned with exploring the factors behind the perpetuation of *purdah* among the *pirzade*, and for that it is impossible to view the *pirzada* women in isolation. The *pirzada* women hardly figure in this chapter, for the very good reason that the control over economic resources which the men possess is a crucial element in the perpetuation of *purdah*. Thus, this and the next chapter are concerned with the different spheres of the men and the women, with the separation between them, and the vital importance of the exclusion of the *pirzada* women from the world of the shrine, which is the source of livelihood for the *pirzade* as a whole. I want to demonstrate not just relative privilege in terms of the wider Indian system, but also the utter dependence of the *pirzada* women.

The Public and the Private

Purdah may be seen as an extreme example of a common phenomenon: the dichotomy between the private domestic sphere and the public sphere.[2] In Hazrat Nizamuddin, for instance, there is a marked spatial separation between the shrine — the world of the *pirzada* men — and the bounded area of the village where the women spend most of their lives. During the daytime, indeed, the older *pirzada* women in particular do not leave their homes much: if they have to, they put on their *burqa,* and lower both veils over their faces, even to scuttle a few yards along a lane from one domestic haven to another. The village is the world where the men are marginal, for they spend most of their waking lives at the shrine, or conducting their business elsewhere, visiting guests, buying in stock for their stalls. They rarely enter the homes of other *pirzade,* unless occasionally to visit their married sisters, and, for many men, home is merely the place to take a quick bite or to snatch some sleep before more work in the shrine. Sometimes their work is so pressing that they scarcely come home at all — maybe there is no one to take their place in the service rota (see below) and a child or servant is sent with their meal, or maybe some festival programme runs through the night and they must sleep in the shrine. Religious and economic roles outside the home are the preserve of the *pirzada* men; the women are presented with a limited range of roles to play — motherhood and domestic labour. In other words, the different work which men and women perform parallels the division between the public and private spheres. As I shall indicate in the next chapter, though, women living in *purdah* perform work within their homes which is crucially important to the world of the shrine outside.

Although separation between the spheres of men and women *may* provide room for an autonomous female sphere over which men have little control, it seems that women's status generally tends to be lower the more they are excluded from extra-domestic roles. As Rosaldo argues, women tend to be

> oppressed or lacking in value and status to the extent that they are con-
> fined to domestic activities, cut off from other women and from the
> world of men. Women gain power and a sense of value when they are able
> to transcend domestic limits, either by entering the men's world or by
> creating a society unto themselves.[3]

The public/private dichotomy may thus be taken as an indicator of likely subordination of women, of differential power being allocated to men and to women, of differential access to activities and goods which are valued. Two particularly important areas over which men and women may have differential control are income and the reproductive powers of women. It seems that it is not so much women's role in production which is an important determinant of their status within the home and the public sphere, but their control over what is produced. There are plenty of examples, from around the world, of women spending more hours in productive work than men, and yet having very little power in their society. What is more important is who has the right to make decisions about 'the domestic and extra-domestic distribution of strategic resources'.[4] Working outside the home does not guarantee that women can make such decisions, but the woman who does not work outside the domestic sphere is even less likely to have much say in how resources are used. It is also important to consider who has rights over the sexuality and reproductive powers of women. Does each woman have the right to dispose of her own sexuality? Does she have the right to choose her own marriage partner, or even the right to choose not to marry? Who decides how many children a woman should have? And who has greatest say when a marriage becomes unhappy? Hints in Goody's material suggest that the seclusion of women is closely tied up with systems of arranged marriage and the importance of a woman's fertility, since she is expected to produce heirs for her husband's line.

We can perhaps expect that women living in *purdah,* where there is a sharp demarcation between public and private spheres, have little legitimate power outside their homes and are subordinate to men inside. For the moment this rather stark picture will suffice to orient the material to be presented here, but it should be borne in mind that women may exercise various types of power and that women themselves — like men — are not all equally powerful or powerless. However, if women in such a situation typically have less power than men of the same age, it is important to explore how the women's subordination is maintained.

In a recent paper, Kate Young and Olivia Harris have suggested that there are three main dimensions to the subordination of women — the political, the ideological and the economic — which may co-exist in different balances with one another.[5] Political subordination may involve the exclusion of women from important decision-making processes and a blunt ignoring of their opinions, but it can also extend to physical violence (or the threat of it), which may include sexual violence and the danger to women who leave their homes unaccompanied. The *pirzada* women are certainly excluded from much that goes on in the shrine, but I never witnessed or heard of any physical violence employed by the men to control their women. On the other hand, though, taunting by non-*pirzada* men in the streets clearly restrains the women's movements.[6]

Ideological subordination persuades women of their own inferiority and unimportance and may thus reduce the necessity for physical violence. To a very large extent the *pirzada* women accept that the proper place for them is in the home, that women should marry and have children, that they should not strive for economic independence but rely on their menfolk, and that men and women should not mix freely. Ideological subordination may also include menstrual taboos, alienation from the process of reproduction and the exclusion of women from ritual, all of which are important among the *pirzade.*[7]

Economic subordination, according to Langton and Halpern in their critique of Young and Harris, is 'often contained in the restriction of [women's] control over economic resources to those resources which are directly for household consumption.'[8] Although ideological subordination is present and important among the *pirzade,* it is economic subordination which is the mainstay of the perpetuation of *purdah.* The *pirzada* women are excluded from the shrine, and the men control the income from it. The women are dependent for their subsistence needs on the men, and they also have little control over their own marriage, sexuality and fertility. But, it remains true that, to the extent that women concur with this situation, to the extent that they co-operate in rearing girls who fit into this setting, ideological factors clearly buttress and legitimize the economic subordination of the *pirzada* women. If the women themselves believe in the *status quo,* their subordination can be fairly smoothly maintained.

However, there are limits to the ideological subordination of the *pirzada* women. No doubt these limits make the perpetuation of *purdah* more complex than it might otherwise be, but they are apparently not such — at any rate not yet — to disturb the *purdah* system fundamentally. For this reason, I shall leave a consideration of the ideological subordination of the *pirzada* women until later: for it is not the most important means of maintaining their subordination. In this and the next chapter, then, I shall be concentrating on economic subordination. This chapter is concerned with the public sphere, the shrine in which the *pirzada* men obtain the income on which they and the *pirzada* women and children subsist. The next chapter deals with the women's world in the village, looking at the connections between the public sphere and the childbearing and household tasks of the women.

The Men's World of the Shrine

The main resource of the *pirzade* is the shrine, the *Dargah Sharif* of Hazrat Nizamuddin Auliya: their incomes are almost solely derived from the cash which pilgrims present at various points during their devotions to the Saint.

Muslims believe that Muhammad was the final prophet sent by Allah. However, there are also many in the Islamic world who believe that men who came after Muhammad may have had exceptional spiritual qualities. The reverence with which the memories of such men are invested is often condemned by theologians, but, nevertheless, such saints have a very important place in popular Islam. During their lifetimes, such men attracted followers whom they advised or inducted into discipleship and trained in the skills of mysticism (known as Sufism in the Islamic context). The most prominent of these saints founded schools or *silsila,* the leadership of which was passed down a line of spiritual heirs. Many renowned Sufi saints are remembered to this day, and their burial sites have become important places of pilgrimage.[9]

While Sufism was apparently known in the Middle East within a couple of centuries of Muhammad's death, it was only after the Mongol invasions of central Asia during the twelfth and thirteenth centuries and the resulting flood of refugees to India, that Sufism had any impact there, mainly in the north. The Sufi saints of India, who are particularly revered today, nearly all lived within a couple of centuries of this time. One of the more important of the Sufi *silsila* in India is the *Chishti silsila:* this was founded by Khwaja Adu Ishaq in Chisht (in eastern Iran) during the tenth century and the *silsila* traces a 'spiritual genealogy' back to the Prophet Muhammad. Khwaja Muinuddin Chishti (who was born in Iran and claimed both spiritual and biological descent from the Prophet) introduced the *silsila* into India in the early years of the thirteenth century. His shrine at Ajmer in Rajasthan is a major place of pilgrimage. The four saints who followed immediately in his line are among the most important Sufi saints of India. Of these, Hazrat Nizamuddin Auliya was the penultimate, living from about 1240 A.D. until 1325. His successor, Khwaja Nasiruddin Chiragh Delhi (the 'Light of Delhi'), was unable to find a disciple of suitable spiritual calibre to succeed him. His death in 1356 marks the end of an epoch. The short-lived excellence of the Sufi saints of India — a classic case of the routinization of charisma — can be attributed to several causes : to the dispersal of disciples under government orders, which weakened the central organization of the *silsila*, to the break in the tradition of poverty and aloofness from politicians and statesmen, and especially to the growing importance of positions in the *silsila* based on inheritance rather than spiritual qualities.[10]

Hazrat Nizamuddin, like the rest of the great Chishti saints, was given to a life of contemplation and abstinence, sleeping little and often praying through the night, regularly keeping fasts and engaging in exercises of self-discipline. His special qualities are marked by the titles by which he is affectionately known in India: Mehboob-e-Elahi (Beloved of God) and Sultan-ul-Mashaikh (supreme among the Shaikhs). He eschewed contacts with the rulers, and established his monastery near the banks of the river Jumna, a few miles north of the contemporary capital Kilokhri. The ruins of the monastery still remain, beside the walls of the tomb of the first Mughal emperor, Humayun, and the site of the present shrine is about half a mile to the west.

Hazrat Nizamuddin and his disciples lived off gifts presented to them; Hazrat Nizamuddin would only accept gifts of food or other items which could be given away immediately. Hundreds of beggars are reputed to have been fed every day and Hazrat Nizamuddin ensured that everything received each day would be given away by nightfall. Sultan Jalaluddin Khilji once offered a *jagir* (grant of land and villages), the rents from which would provide a sure income for the monastery, but Hazrat Nizamuddin refused to accept it.[11] On another occasion, Khusro Khan usurped the throne and tried to win popularity by sending gifts to important people. Hazrat Nizamuddin was among those included, but he promptly gave all the money away to the poor. When Khusro Khan himself was assassinated, his successor tried to retrieve all the cash so liberally dispersed, but Hazrat Nizamuddin responded that the money had come from the people's treasury in the first place and he had simply returned it to the people.[12]

Among the most spiritually endowed of his disciples, Hazrat Nizamuddin nominated several to be his *khalifa* or spiritual successors, of whom Nasiruddin was the most important. Most of the *khalifa* moved to other parts of India and began to induct their own disciples. Their spiritual descendants perpetuate a branch of the *silsila*, which is now sometimes called the Chishtia-Nizamia *silsila*. Other disciples remained by the Saint's side, even after his death. The *pirzade* of today recount how Hazrat Nizamuddin's disciples were concerned about what would happen to them when he died. He said that none would be under any compulsion to remain at the graveside, but he undertook to entreat with God that those who remained would never go hungry or naked. That prayer, they say, has been answered right to this day: the world *'pirzada'* itself literally means the son of a *pir* or holy man and the *pirzade* of Hazrat Nizamuddin belong to three *khandan* or Families (there were four until about 100 years ago) which claim to be descended in the male line from three of Hazrat Nizamuddin's kinsmen and disciples.

I shall go into the question of descent among the *pirzade* in the next chapter, while discussing reproduction; for the moment it is important to note that the *pirzade* claim to be Syed — descended in the male line from Muhammad's daughter Fatima — as well as to have close spiritual and genealogical connections with Hazrat Nizamuddin. In this context, such claims to 'purity of blood' and 'holiness' are — like the seclusion of women — important elements in their claims to be entitled to act as custodians of a famous Saint's tomb and to receive gifts from pilgrims in recognition of the services which they perform. Although some young *pirzada* men object to 'just sitting' in the shrine, on the whole the assessment made by a British woman some 150 years ago remains fair:

> There are men in charge of Shah Nizaam ood deen's mausoleum who lead devout lives, and subsist on the casual bounties gleaned from the charitable visitors to his shrine. Their time is passed in religious duties, reading the Khoraun over the ashes of the saint, and keeping the place clean and free from unholy intrusions. They do not deem this mode of existence derogatory; for to hold the situation of darogahs, or keepers of the tombs of the saints, who are held in universal veneration amongst Mussulmauns, is esteemed an honourable privilege.[13]

This 'unproductive' life of the *pirzade* is not unusual in India. While the Indian economy is predominantly agricultural, there is a great deal of manufacturing and other industry — both large and small-scale — and people in all these sectors have access to various types of 'service personnel'. It is into this category that the *pirzade* would place themselves.

The *pirzade* used to own sizeable tracts of land, mostly around the village of Hazrat Nizamuddin, which were worked by hired labourers. In the early years of this century, land to the west of the village was bought up for the construction of the Delhi-Agra railway line. Then in 1911, the British administration moved the capital from Calcutta to Delhi and further encroachments began to be made during the building of New Delhi. But the village and shrine were left untouched: during discussions about the siting of government buildings and new housing developments, it was explicitly pointed out that the shrine and its attached village were of such architectural and religious significance that they should not be disturbed.[14] However, elderly *pirzade* can remember numerous small villages in the vicinity of their own which were swept away in the tide of new building. The final closing-in has occurred in the last thirty years, with the establishment of residential colonies for refugees from the Partition troubles. Nowadays few *pirzade* own any agricultural land at all, though most own small plots and house-sites which they rent out. For several of them, incomes from rents are an important part of their livelihood.

However the prime orientation of the *pirzade,* even if not always their major source of income, is to the shrine. In their work there, the *pirzade* consider that they are serving both the public and the Saint himself, through services which they can render because of their close links with Hazrat Nizamuddin through the centuries. It is they who are responsible for the up-keep of the buildings around his tomb and they who arrange for any repairs which wealthy pilgrims sponsor. They organize the major public festivals at the shrine to honour the Saint, festivals which draw huge crowds of pilgrims and provide a large part of the incomes of the *pirzade.* Among these the most important are the death anniversaries of Hazrat Nizamuddin and his poet disciple Amir Khusro who is also buried there; the birth anniversary of Hazrat Nizamuddin when the Saint's 'naked' tomb is given a 'first bath'; the Prophet Muhammad's festival, when several relics of the Prophet, believed to have been left at the shrine by Bahadur Shah Zafar during the 1857 uprising, are shown to pilgrims; and Basant, a Hindu Spring festival, which is the only major festival at the shrine which is timed according to the solar rather than lunar calendar. The *pirzade* also guide pilgrims around the shrine, pointing out notable monuments, and they instruct pilgrims in their devotions.

Since Hazrat Nizamuddin refused to accept grants of land which could provide the shrine with a permanent and stable income from rents the *pirzade* depend on the fluctuating contributions which pilgrims make.[15] There are four main sources of income for the *pirzade* at the shrine, over which they collectively have a virtual monopoly, but in all but one of these the *pirzade* are in competition with one another for the donations of the pilgrims.

The Flower Shops
Immediately on arrival, the pilgrim is confronted with the flower shops at the main gates of the shrine. Particularly if the pilgrim arrives by car or taxi and looks moderately wealthy, a chorus of cries and shouts builds up: 'Brother, come here – buy your flowers here!' 'No, Brother, come this way if you please – my flowers are fresher and I have more fragrant joss sticks!' For the uninitiated the experience is bewildering: all the stalls stock a virtually identical range of items which the pilgrims need for their devotions. The main body of the stall is taken up with neatly arranged patterns of red rose petals, chrome yellow and white daisies and tiny white 'pearls', which are piled on to wicker baskets for the purchaser, and behind the vendor are stacked the boxes of joss sticks to be lit beside the tombs of the Saints, the tiny bottles of *'itr* (essence of rose petals), and tiny white sweets which the *pirzade* will bless.

The Pleaders and their Guests
During his travels in India in the middle of the nineteenth century, von Orlich

visited the shrine and reported that 'several fakirs and idlers have taken up their abode near these tombs: some did not suffer themselves to be disturbed in their devotions, while others came forward and offered themselves as guides . . .'[16] Today's visitors, too, once inside the threshold of the shrine complex, are likely to be crowded by *pirzade* eager to attract their attention, to monopolize them, to guide them around the shrine, help them with their devotions, and finally produce with a flourish their 'book' — a register which pilgrims sign after presenting a cash gift. Once a pilgrim has become the *mehman* or 'guest' of a particular *pirzada* in this fashion, the *pirzada* considers himself the pilgrim's *wakil*, his agent or pleader, who henceforth has a pre-emptive right over that pilgrim's gifts.

Some pilgrims come with 'referral notes' from *pirzade* at other shrines, and can sidestep the wheedling and flattery by going straight to the *pirzada* they want to meet. But many new pilgrims come unprepared. Over them occurs permissible competition: for they become the eagerly sought prey of the vigilant *pirzade*. There are some accusations of 'poaching' of 'guests', but the *pirzade* keep a close watch to ensure that 'guests' do not wrongfully escape into the clutches of other *pirzade*, and generally the system runs fairly smoothly.

The major point here is that this system of *wakil* and their *mehman* is the lynchpin of the incomes of most of the *pirzade*, with takings much larger than can be expected from a flower shop. It is also a system which rests not just on the physical presence of the pilgrim, for many 'guests' send money through the post, and during quiet periods at the shrine many of the *pirzade* go on tour around the country (and even abroad), staying with their 'guests' and hoping for more gifts and new 'guests'.

Advice and Remedies

Many of the pilgrims at the shrine are less concerned to make devotions to the memory of Hazrat Nizamuddin than they are to seek remedies for problems, and not always 'spiritual' ones. Some of the *pirzade* practise *piri-muridi*, which, in its original meaning, entailed the attachment of an aspirant or *murid* to a preceptor or *pir* in order to attain spiritual advancement through the study of religious texts and learning the Sufi 'Way' or *Tariqa*. This is but one rather minor element in *piri-muridi* in Hazrat Nizamuddin.

In the cells around the courts of the shrine some of the *pirzade* give advice on social (often marital) and medical (often gynaecological) problems. While most 'guests' seem to be men, many of the people who report to *piri-muridi* 'surgeries' are women. The *pirzada* women themselves never attend the shrine for this purpose, for if there is an illness in the family, their menfolk can prescribe remedies without the women needing to leave their home. Most of the women who do come to the shrine apparently come from Old Delhi, and problems which affect women particularly, such as infertility or persistent miscarriages or the lack of sons, come fairly high in the list of issues which they raise with the *pirzada* men. The *pirzade* prescribe remedies — often amulets of various kinds — and are paid small sums for these services. Most *pirzade,* in fact, concentrate on cultivating their 'guests', because *piri-muridi* is regarded as a very difficult task with heavy responsibilities. But the man who is able to inspire confidence in his counsel and his remedies can hope to build up a large following of *murid* through the recommendations of satisfied customers: success in this field, with the financial rewards which go with it, is very important in the bids for supremacy at the shrine.

The Rota System

Alone among the sources of income at the shrine, that from the *Bari Dari Nizam,* or rota system, almost excludes competition among the *pirzade.* Pilgrims are encouraged — even cajoled — into placing donations into the trunks which sit outside the tomb chambers of Hazrat Nizamuddin and his disciple Amir Khusro. Each week, the takings are divided up according to a rota which the *pirzade* believe to be of great antiquity. Those on duty during the week are expected to sit in the shrine, help pilgrims with their prayers — for instance, going inside the tomb chambers to strew flowers on the graves for the women, or blessing sweets and distributing them among the people round about — and when there are major festivals, it is they who are responsible for all the decorations and organization.

The rota system is extremely complicated: it now takes 96 weeks to complete a full cycle and each week's rota itself is greatly fragmented, with specified owners of shares at each point. Basically, though, there are two types of share, the personal and the ancestral. A personal share, the *zati* or *hayati hyssa* is collected for each man, woman and child of the *pirzada* Family on duty. Many years ago, however, some lines died out, and their shares were frozen and taken over by other *pirzade* as *maurossi hyssa* or ancestral shares which are transmitted by the normal rules of inheritance. Generally, but not always, there is agreement about who should be on duty and the size of their share from each turn of duty in the shrine.

These, then, are the major sources of income for the *pirzade* at the shrine. Individual households may have members involved in several spheres: one son might be deputed to sit on duty in the rota, while one runs a flower shop, another sets himself up in *piri-muridi,* and the father is left free to concentrate on developing his links with his 'guests'. Aside from this, one man runs a small tea shop, and another has a couple of bookstalls where he sells plaques with quotations from the *Quran Sharif,* rosaries, amulets and prayer caps, as well as books and tracts about Islam, Sufism and Hazrat Nizamuddin. Several *pirzade* are enthusiastic pamphleteers, and have printed and marketed their own products.

There were several factors, however, which hampered any assessment by me of the size of the income at the shrine. The numerous sources of income — in the shrine, through the post, as well as during visits to 'guests' — the round the clock service, and the seasonal fluctuations, with festivals followed by slack periods, all made for practical difficulties. Further, Mrs Gandhi's Emergency — during which there were many tales of income tax enquiries — made people suspicious of questions about money, and anyway the *pirzade* themselves wish to minimize their incomes because of their desire to portray themselves as mendicants without a care for the morrow, just relying on the bounty of Hazrat Nizamuddin for their simple wants. It was also impossible to assess the balance between the tiny contributions of the many very poor people who came to the shrine, against the often massive contributions made by prominent politicians and military personnel, as well as some famous film stars. Much of the renovation work around the shrine, and other expenditures, such as feeding hundreds of beggars each day at dusk during Ramzan — the month of fasting — were funded by extremely wealthy people.

Inasmuch as the *pirzade* extract payment from pilgrims at various points in their devotions, they can, however, be considered to be in a common class position in the shrine. Ultimately, the *pirzade* subsist on the surpluses generated by the poor, whether directly from the pilgrims at the shrine, or indirectly through the dispersal of wealth from film stars, businessmen or politicians, who themselves siphon off wealth from beneath. But the *pirzade* would not see things in this light. They consider their incomes to be just rewards for the services which they perform. I am no special advocate of the *pirzada* cause, but their efforts to alleviate human suffering should not be lightly dismissed as cynical attempts to make an easy living off the backs of the poor and credulous. In the absence of widespread welfare facilities in an inequitable social structure which shows little sign of change, their pastoral and medical care is part of a not insignificant matrix of safety valve mechanisms, locating the rectification of misfortune in the pilgrim's faith and in the Saint's powers to heal or to intercede with God.

In their work in the shrine, some of the *pirzada* men have succeeded in tapping more fertile sources of income than others, through their counselling abilities, their interactive skills, their spiritual qualities or their perspicacity. 'Money follows money', as one young woman commented, and men who develop links with pilgrims who become prominent public figures can anticipate more such links and hefty contributions to their private finances as well as to the shrine. Several *pirzada* households have television sets, a couple own motor vehicles, and the bulk of the *pirzade* are able to finance school and college education for their children (especially their sons) and can meet medical bills and so on. The undoubted variations in income, though, do not always show up in the food and clothes which households consume: for most of the time, the *pirzade* dress and eat in very similar and fairly simple fashion. In large measure, this is because much of the cash flows through the hands of the men and never reaches the domestic sphere. Further, the *pirzada* men are living in an 'expense account' economy, and much of their income is in the form of payments to do specific, rather privileged things, which cannot easily be translated into cash — for instance opportunities to travel, maybe even to go on the Haj pilgrimage to Mecca.

It is the life-styles and life-chances that their work makes possible which are important. Not only is the work which the *pirzada* men perform sedentary and non-manual, but it affords them a comfortable standard of living at home as well as attractive opportunities outside it. The *pirzade* cannot compete with the opulence and extravagance of the wealthy businessman or the successful film star, but their position within the Indian economy is still an enviable one.

Controlling the Purse Strings

The incomes of the *pirzade* are earned through the activities of the *pirzada* men: it is they who receive the donations of the pilgrims at the shrine, whether through selling them flowers, becoming their *wakil* or practising *piri-muridi*. It is also the men who control most of the purse strings at home. The women even do very little shopping for household needs: the men purchase most of the everyday requirements of food from the local *bazar*, though generally at the behest of the women of their household. But before the household needs are met, before the women receive any benefits from the earning power of the men, the men themselves cream off money for various purposes, primarily business.

The *pirzada* men constantly need to maintain and cultivate links with their patrons, for otherwise they would have no income. Just to keep the shrine functioning, to keep pilgrims coming to honour the Saint and to keep the sick or worried coming to have their problems solved, there are several expenditures. A rich harvest of pilgrims depends on a great deal of preparatory investment of time and money.

Those who run flower stalls have to keep replenishing their stocks of joss sticks and scents, and every day they have to buy in fresh flowers for the pilgrims to purchase. Those who are concerned with maintaining their relationship with their guests send out printed invitations to all those registered with them when any festival approaches, and after the festival they send small pieces of blessed sweets to all those who sent money to help with the festival expenses; they also extend their hospitality to their 'guests', and several of the *pirzade* have built or hope to build special guest-houses so that they can house as well as feed their 'guests' in proper comfort, without causing domestic disruption to themselves. Further, the *pirzade* like to tour during slack periods, and the travel expenses, though not board and lodging, have to be met from their incomes at the shrine. Those who practise *piri-muridi* have to buy some expensive items such as musk, which is used to write out amulets; one man even had a black velvet robe embroidered with gold thread made up in order to impress the public, though most of the other *pirzade* considered this outrageously showy.

Out of the takings from the rota system, the shrine expenses have to be met, for instance the lighting, the payment of the cleaners and the watermen who carry water in leather sacks to replenish the supplies of water for the pilgrims to drink. The singers also have to be paid retainers, and during the major festivals several of the more wealthy *pirzada* men also organize large public singing and poetry recitals in which they compete with one another to attract audiences.

Some of the *pirzada* men are also involved in legal disputes, mainly with one another. Most of the *pirzade* heartily disapprove of the squabbles among their number. However, a great deal of the economic competition among the *pirzade* in the shrine has become deflected into lawsuits. Some concern property, but many others revolve around the question of precedence at the shrine, and the disputed genealogical connections of the different *pirzade* with Hazrat Nizamuddin.

What all this amounts to is that the *pirzada* women are excluded from the shrine, for they are neither directly involved in the economic enterprises the men conduct there, nor do they have much say over the distribution of the incomes derived from the pilgrims. In line with the image of decency and respectability which the *pirzade* try to project, the *pirzada* women rarely go to the shrine at all. Even young women who have succeeded in persuading their elders that they need not wear a *burqa,* all have a *burqa* specially set aside for wearing in the shrine. Comments such as these indicate the general position of the women in relation to the shrine.

(A woman in her late fifties):
Yes, certainly some women go to the shrine during the daytime — but they aren't *pirzade.* I hardly ever go, but one thing I like to do is go around dawn during Ramzan [the month of fasting] when there are special prayers and readings. There aren't any strange men around that early.

(A teenage girl explaining her presence one day with her mother and several other women):
You know how we've been having such trouble with our tenants? Well, they moved out today, at long last. My mother made a *mannat* [vow] that she would give a mantle of flowers for Amir Khusro's tomb and one of flowers and cloth for Hazrat Nizamuddin's, if the tenants left.

(During the Prophet Muhammad's festival, when I located some of the *pirzada* women inside one of the royal tomb enclosures):
Peace be with you! Tell us, what's happening out there? We can't see anything through this marble screen. Have they shown any of the relics yet? [When I said that they had not, and why did they not come with me to stand by the main tomb where they could see the relics properly] Oh no! We couldn't do that — someone would be bound to recognize us. Then there'd be trouble. [But they came eagerly enough when I said that I would take all the blame.]

(At about midnight, after the completion of a programme only attended by *pirzade,* commemorating Hazrat Ali, the Prophet's son-in-law):
Listen, do you know what *I'm* going to do now? It's such a long time since I've been in here, that I've almost forgotten what the place looks like. Come round with me. Let's do a private pilgrimage, while there isn't anyone here to watch!

The *pirzada* women do not go to the shrine regularly. Some elderly women have scarcely been there since childhood. If the women do go, it is for some special reason, preferably during the night or at dusk, and only rarely when there are many pilgrims at the shrine who could catch a glimpse of them. In addition, the belief in menstrual and post-partum pollutions means that women cannot go to the shrine at all at such times.[17] And no woman — *pirzada* or outsider — may ever enter the actual tomb chambers of Hazrat Nizamuddin or Amir Khusro.

Indicative of this separation of the women from the shrine is their ignorance about many matters concerning it. The shrine is the men's world *par excellence:* it is the site of their work and of their specialist knowledge. What they see fit to tell the women about the shrine organization, the women may learn. Otherwise, the women remain in ignorance, for they have no chance of learning about it directly. Few women felt they could initiate enquiries; so what they learnt, they learnt by the grace of the men. As one middle-aged man commented: 'Naturally my wife does not understand these matters. Why should she? She's far too busy with housework for me to bother her about how the festivals are organized.'

Few women had any idea of the complexity of the rota system, for instance, and those who knew of the intricacies could not furnish any details. One woman was less cautious and during several conversations she provided various accounts. But they contradicted one another and disagreed with the very detailed account which older men could provide. In general, the women said that the rota system is a matter for men and I would obtain a more accurate answer by asking them.

Comments of the same kind emerged when I asked about imminent festivals at the shrine: the standard response was that women never attended them or, if they did, were put in such sheltered places that they could not see. 'You'll have to ask the men — it's their job to organize these things, not ours.' Similarly, one woman of about 30 was surprised when I told her that her first cousin was practising *piri-muridi* in the shrine. In contrast, many of the *pirzada* men could rattle off the names of the *pirzada* Families or *khandan,* the present membership of them, and the different versions of their connections with Hazrat Nizamuddin — indeed several of them have written books and tracts on this very subject. This, too, was very much a male preserve: several of the women could not tell me all the names of the Families (one could not even tell me which Family her husband belongs to), let alone their present-day membership. This, like the rest, is a *bahar ki bat,* an outside matter, and 'the men don't tell us about shrine business'.

The women are not so untutored about the shrine, however, that they are unaware of the rights which they have in financial shares from the rota system, rights albeit which they are generally denied in practice. Women rarely inherit ancestral shares from their parents, for a set of brothers will normally divide such shares among themselves without including their sisters. Several women said that the shares would become impossibly fragmented if sisters took their portion along with their brothers. One elderly woman put it this way:

These shares are undoubtedly our *haq* [right] but a woman can 'forgive' her brother so that he no longer has any obligation to share the inheritance with her. That's what I did with my brother — after all, he's a poor man and I'm well settled here. So why should I bother to press my claims?

Not only this, but women rarely receive their personal shares. These shares are collected, normally, by the male head of the household or his deputy on behalf of his sons and their children, as well as his sisters and daughters. Generally, though, these shares are used for household expenses, and the married daughters and sisters of the household head often do not actually receive their shares. Many women receive their shares only on two types of occasion. If their Family chances to be on duty during a major festival and the income from the rota increases dramatically, their brothers or father may ensure that they receive their entitlement. A woman in her fifties commented:

Of course, I *should* receive my share regularly — that's my right. But my brothers don't send me anything normally. They say that they have enough children of their own to feed and they can't afford to give me my share. But if they happen to be on duty during an *'urs* [death anniversary festival] then they may send me my share. With all the pilgrims, there's more money to share out.   So maybe I'll get five or ten rupees each day during a festival.

The other occasion when women generally receive their share is when a child is born into their Family, when the *hyssa charhana* — literally, the stepping up of the share — is performed and the baby's name is added to the Family. During the ceremony, the child's father or paternal grandfather puts some money into the trunk outside Hazrat Nizamuddin's tomb chamber, and this is divided equally among all the members of that Family. This is known as the 'fortune money'. One young woman told me that people had received two paise when she was born, and that the money for two children born into her Family during my period of fieldwork had been five and ten paise — hardly the stuff of economic independence.

While the *pirzada* women have been granted — in theory — one tiny foothold in the shrine economy, through their shares in the rota system, they have no direct access to any of the other sources of income at the shrine. And even their rights in the rota system are often denied in practice. Men 'sit' on duty in the rota, not the women, and they have prior control over all the income which they receive in the shrine. If they choose not to hand over the share to which their womenfolk are entitled, there is little that the women can do. A few of the men are scrupulous in ensuring that their sisters and daughters do receive the ancestral and personal shares which are their right, but most do not. In any case, the rota system is generally less remunerative than the income from the 'guests' and from counselling, and even when women are given their rights in the rota, it is not clear that they are being conceded anything more than pin money.

In all ways, then, the women are marginal to the shrine: they hardly ever go there, they remain in almost total ignorance of what takes place there and how the shrine is organized, and they rarely receive those economic rights in it to which they have been entitled. But to say that they are marginal does not imply that the shrine is unimportant to them. On the contrary, they are as dependent on it as the men, for they have no separate productive resources of their own.

The Economic Dependence of the Pirzada Women

The adult *pirzada* women spend their lives in housework and the bearing and rearing of children, and this work is the subject of the next chapter. Apart from a few very minor exceptions — which I shall discuss later — the *pirzada* women do not earn cash for themselves by any work outside their home, or by work which they perform at home for outsiders. They are excluded from the shrine, and they have no other sources of substantial income. For their every subsistence need, they depend on their menfolk throughout their lives, firstly on their fathers and brothers and later on their husbands.

Muslim apologists always insist that women have not been deprived of economic rights, for the *Quran Sharif* is meticulous in laying down women's entitlements to maintenance, to inheritance, and to a settlement at the time of marriage.[18]

A Muslim woman is, it is true, entitled to maintenance throughout her life.[19] Until her marriage, she is supported by her father. If he is dead, then her brother or some other close male relative is appointed her guardian, and it is his duty to feed, clothe and house her as well as to arrange her marriage in due time. Once she is married, it is her husband who is obliged to maintain her, though with the very important proviso that she remains obedient to him. While women may contribute to their husband's household expenses from income or property of their own, there is no expectation that they should do so. When a woman is widowed, her sons — if adult — take over their father's responsibilities, but otherwise her own father or brothers may have to maintain her. In all this, the *pirzade* follow the requirements of Islam. When it comes to the question of inheritance and marriage settlements, though, their claims to 'orthodoxy' appear rather shallow, for the *pirzada* women rarely receive their dues.

Women's Inheritance Rights
Muslim women are entitled to inherit property — which they can hold in their own right — from relatives. The detailed rules by which a deceased person's property is divided are very complex, for there are several classes of heirs.[20] The claims of some heirs have priority and they can exclude other more peripheral heirs altogether. It is only in their positions as wife, mother or

daughter of a deceased man or woman that women can never, in theory, be excluded. In essence, a woman generally receives a share half the size of that which goes to a man in an analogous position. For instance, when the deceased has sons and daughters, the part of the estate reserved for them is so divided that each son receives a share twice that of each daughter. This distribution is not considered inequitable by Muslim writers, for they argue that women have the right to be maintained throughout their lives, while men always have the obligation to support their dependants.

What is more important here, though, is that Muslim women often do not receive even their entitlement, unless there are no close male relatives. This seems to be common in the Indian sub-continent, and is generally the case among the *pirzade,* unless their parents are wealthy or a woman has no brothers.[21] A few men have insisted that their sisters take their due, but many women receive nothing.

Several of the *pirzada* women pointed out that a woman may waive her rights, or 'forgive' her brother, provided that she does so 'out of happiness' and not 'under pressure'. If a man dies without giving his sister her due, he will suffer in the after-life, unless she has forgiven him. But it is considered honourable for a woman to forgo her rights. Further, there may be practical problems in dividing up the property equitably, when most of it is in the form of buildings or household items rather than cash; moreover, a woman well settled in her husband's home should think of her brothers' obligations to their own wives and children; and particularly if she might still expect a brother to house her in the event of her widowhood or divorce, she should not greedily press her claim. But there is more to it than that. Here is a typical statement:

> Certainly it is the case that a woman receives a share half the size of her brothers. But in my case, I took nothing when my father died. My brother was poor and he needed the rents from the houses more than I did. That was my personal wish, but I've heard that several of the men have refused to let their sisters forgive them. You mustn't think that women do badly out of this, though, for, at the end of the day, a man has to give a lot to his sister. He must take her in if she is widowed or divorced — and people will lift their fingers at him if he does not — and on top of all that, he has to send presents to her, right up to her dying day.

Until her marriage, a girl is maintained by her father or brothers. Then, at the time of her marriage, she receives the major set of gifts from them, her dowry, the *jahiz.* Among the *pirzade,* this should at least contain a bed, with its embroidered sheets, quilts and a pair of pillows, an areca-nut box, a metal jug and drinking bowl, and one piece of gold jewellery. The desire to endow daughters equally sets limits on how much a bride is given, but most parents try to give more than the basic, including several sets of clothes, cooking utensils, tableware and furniture. 'Out of happiness', the bride's uncles, aunts and married cousins may add their contributions.

But the giving does not stop once she is married. For the first year after her marriage, during festivals and when she visits her parents, her own kin are expected to send her various types of foodstuffs, mostly sweetmeats, and, of these, the gifts which are sent at the major Muslim festivals, the two Eids, continue to be sent throughout her life. When she bears children, her parents send gifts for the baby and for other members of her conjugal household, and the beginning and completion of each child's first reading of the *Quran Sharif* are marked by more presents. So, too, are the marriages of her children.

A daughter is often called a 'guest', for she will soon be taken away to her real home with her husband. But even after this, her parents and brothers have obligations to her. It is said by the *pirzade* that 'a daughter takes for ever', or 'a daughter takes throughout her life'. However, while sons generally receive such immovable property as their parents owned, a daughter receives only a sporadic trickle of movable goods — mostly non-durable items, such as food and clothing, and only rarely cash — until she dies. In death her brothers or father have their obligations to her, for it is then that they send the 'final gift' of the white shroud in which she is wrapped before burial.

The Marriage Settlement

When a woman marries, her husband is obliged to contract to pay her the *mahr* or marriage settlement, which is supposed to provide for her in difficult times.[22] Also, since the party initiating divorce forfeits the *mahr,* it is supposed to prevent thoughtless and capricious divorce. Often, as among the *pirzade,* the sum is specified in the marriage contract, but its payment may be 'prompt' or 'deferred'. While astronomical sums are sometimes named by the very wealthy or pretentious, most commentators agree that small sums which a man can realistically be expected to pay are in line with the spirit of *mahr,* for the Prophet Muhammad suggested only a small sum as the *mahr* for his daughter Fatima. The sum may be increased or decreased by agreement after the marriage, and if the husband dies without paying the sum, his wife's claim takes precedence over his other heirs.[23]

In practice, though, the wife often receives only limited benefit from the *mahr.* The verse in the *Quran Sharif* which is considered the primary instruction to give the marriage settlement, also contains a crucial escape clause: 'And give unto the woman, (whom ye marry) free gift of their marriage portions; but if they of their own accord remit unto you a part thereof, then ye are welcome to absorb it (in your wealth).'[24]

In India, at any rate, it seems that even the 'prompt' *mahr* is often left unpaid, and the question of payment rarely comes up unless the couple are divorced. Even large sums are not necessarily any deterrent to divorce, according to Jones and Jones, for a man may maltreat his wife until she feels impelled to initiate divorce proceedings, or he may simply omit to summon her back from a visit to her parents, without formally divorcing her.[25] As with inheritance, Muslim women apparently often — though how often is uncertain — do not receive their entitlement.

Among the *pirzade* only one married woman had received her *mahr,* and that after 40 years of marriage when her husband was about to go on the Haj pilgrimage to Mecca. The women are agreed that the *mahr* is a *mazhab ki bat* — a matter of religion — rather than a *riwaj ki bat* — a matter of mere custom — but as one woman rather curtly noted,

> the *mahr* is just a custom these days — it's never given. There are two types, the type which a man can give when he wishes, and the type which he must give when his wife asks. But then, it doesn't look nice to ask. Anyway [she added wryly, as an afterthought] I wouldn't be able to live very long on the Rs. 2000/- which were settled on me 40 years ago!

Certainly, the *mahr* is a woman's right, and she should be given it if she asks — but 'a nice, polite woman would not ask', commented a woman at whose marriage some seventy years ago a *mahr* of Rs. 2500/- was stipulated. It is shameless for a woman to persist in demanding her *mahr.* Even better than not asking for it is to 'forgive' her husband: that way she will gain merit for her generosity and he will not be punished in the after-life for failing in his obligations. One woman in her twenties said:

> My two sisters had 11,000/- each and my father would have liked the same for me, but my father-in-law set the sum at 5000/- and my father, out of respect for him, accepted that. But, no — I haven't asked for it. True enough, it is not *gunnah* [sin] for a woman to ask — but she will get *sawab* [merit] in the after-life if she doesn't.

The forgiveness rarely takes place straight after the marriage: a woman is sensible to wait until her marriage is secure, for she could forgive one day and find herself divorced the next, with no right to the *mahr* any longer. Some women talked of waiting until their husband was on his deathbed, or even until he had died before absolving him of his duty. While the *mahr* should only be forgiven 'out of happiness', not compulsion, several women talked of how men discussed the matter with their wives:

> Traditionally, the *mahr* used to be given before the husband could see his wife's face, in some families. That doesn't happen now. But if a woman asks her husband to give her the *mahr,* he's quite likely to persuade her to forgive him. He'll say he'll give it to her in the after-life, and she'll get a pearl palace to live in in Heaven — or something like that.

Other women suggested that men would use the *mahr* as a bargaining point over the custody of children if there was any question of divorce — giving the wife an option of taking the *mahr* or being allowed access to her children.

But the benefits of foregoing the *mahr* do not simply accrue in Heaven: the sums involved were generally considered to be so trivial that they would be of little use, and the position of a bride in her in-law's home so potentially vulnerable that there was no point in pressing the issue:

> The *mahr* is a woman's right. Her husband should give it if she asks. But suppose he is unable to pay. Then it is wrong of a woman to persist, especially if her husband promises to pay it in the after-life. But in any case — if a woman is well-settled in her in-laws' home, what need does she have for anything? All her wants will be provided.

Or, as another woman remarked:

> I haven't asked for my *mahr* — why should I? I'm happy and well cared for. Anyway, what would be the point? It's not worth causing a lot of illfeeling over a tiny sum of money.

It is more prudent to waive the undoubted rights in the *mahr,* for punishments in the next life can then be averted, and the in-laws have no reason to make this life unpleasant.

Although she may never receive her *mahr,* a woman receives many other items from her in-laws, even before she has been married. Once the match is settled she receives presents during festivals, and just before the marriage she is sent clothing, jewellery and toiletries, which she wears on the wedding day and the day after, the day of the 'showing of the face', when her in-laws come in turn to see the new bride, and each must present her with a gift.

Thereafter, she is entitled to maintenance from her husband. Most men contract to pay their wives a special sum — the *pitari* or *kharch-i-pandan,* the 'expenses of the areca-nut box' — which is a monthly allowance (generally about Rs. 50/-) for the woman to use as she wishes. In addition to providing her with her basic subsistence needs, many families cosset and pamper the bride who marries into their household, even for many years after the marriage. She may be given clothes and jewellery, so that she can be a *zeenat,* a 'jewel' in her husband's home, a source of honour and pride to her in-laws.

Privilege and Dependency

I have suggested, then, that the work of the *pirzada* men puts them into a common class position in relation to the pilgrims who come to the shrine. In Indian terms, their position is fortunate: they are not engaged in demeaning manual work, but in respectable priestly work. That they are also able to achieve moderately comfortable life-styles — that they can afford to eat, pay for schooling and medical expenses — places them, if not amongst the extremely affluent, at least among those fortunates who have lives which are free from financial hardship.

The men's position at the shrine also places them in a common position in relation to their womenfolk. The marginality of the women at the shrine, their exclusion from the major productive resource on which they all rely, enables the men to control the incomes which they receive there.

Different men have responded to their position in different ways, from the punctilious fulfilment of obligations and loving generosity right through to plain stinginess. Several men have insisted that their sisters take their inheritance dues, though most have not. One man gives his wife too little for housekeeping and has failed to set aside money for his sons' marriages, for he is deeply involved in litigation: but he is criticized by men and women alike, and is a lone exception.

These variations do not alter the fact that the women are dependent on their menfolk. They have little room for economic independence: they generally do not receive their entitlements, whether shares in the rota system, their inheritance or their marriage settlement, and the items which they do receive — clothing, food and some durable goods — highlight their dependence on men for their slightest subsistence requirement. In any case, the major assets of the *pirzade* are not fixed ones which could provide a stable income, but are located in the renewable human resources — the men who work in the shrine — and the continuation of their interactive skills which bring income to the shrine. Thus it is doubtful if pressing for their economic dues would be wise, for the sums of money involved are often small — and the offence caused might well be large. Economic dependence throughout their lives is a more prudent course for the *pirzada* women, and they themselves comment that their present comfort makes their inheritance rights and marriage settlement unnecessary. All their wants are provided for, and they rarely need to spend money on themselves. Nevertheless, it is still the case that all their present comfort depends on the goodwill of their menfolk.

References

1. A. Whitehead, 'Review of Jack Goody, *Production and Reproduction*', *Critique of Anthropology*, 3 (1977), pp.151-8.
2. H. Hartmann, 'Capitalism, Patriarchy, and Job Segregation by Sex', *Signs*, 1 (1976), pp.137-69. See also P.R. Sanday, 'Female Status in the Public Domain', in M.Z. Rosaldo and L. Lamphere (eds.), *Woman, Culture, and Society*, (Stanford, 1974); R. Reiter, 'Men and Women in the South of France', in R. Reiter (ed.), *Toward an Anthropology of Women*, (New York, 1975); and S. Harding, 'Women and Words in a Spanish Village', in Reiter (ed.), *ibid*.
3. M. Z. Rosaldo, 'Woman, Culture and Society: A Theoretical Overview', in Rosaldo and Lamphere (eds.), *op. cit.*, p.41.
4. E. Friedl, *Women and Men*, (New York, 1975), pp.6-7.
5. K. Young and O. Harris, 'The Subordination of Women in Cross Cultural Perspective', in Women's Publishing Collective (eds.), *Papers on Patriarchy Conference*, (Lewes, 1976). See also P. Langton and P. Halpern, 'Critique of Young and Harris Paper', in Women's Publishing Collective (eds.), *ibid*.

6. More detail on taunting in the streets is given in Chapter Six.
7. Young and Harris, *op. cit.*, p.51.
8. Langton and Halpern, *op. cit.*, p.54.
9. For general material on Sufism see R.A. Nicholson, *The Mystics of Islam*, (London, 1914); A.J. Arberry, *Sufism: An Account of The Mystics of Islam*, (London, 1950); J.S. Trimingham, *The Sufi Orders in Islam*, (London, 1971).
10. On the routinization of charisma see T. Parsons, *The Structure of Social Action*, 2nd. ed. (New York, 1968), pp.662-5. For material on Sufism in India, see W.D. Begg, *The Big Five of India in Sufism*, (Ajmer, 1972); W.D. Begg, *The Holy Biography of Hazrat Khwaja Muinuddin Chishti of Ajmer*, (Ajmer, 1960); K.A. Nizami, *The Life and Times of Shaikh Farid-ud-din Ganj-i-shakar*, (Delhi, 1955); K.A. Nizami, *Some Aspects of Religion and Politics in India during the Thirteenth Century*, 2nd. ed. (Delhi, 1974); M. Mujeeb, *The Indian Muslims*, (London, 1967). More detail on Hazrat Nizamuddin is in K.A. Nizami, 'Early Indo-Muslim Mystics and their Attitude Towards the State', *Islamic Culture*, XXII (1948), pp. 387-98 and XXIV (1950), pp.60-71; R.N. Das, 'Shaikh Nizam-ud-din Auliya', *Islamic Culture*, 48 (1974), pp.93-104; Z. Hasan, *A Guide to Nizamu-d din*, (Memoirs of the Archaeological Survey of India, No.10), (Calcutta, 1922); A.H.A. Nadwi, *Saviours of Islamic Spirit*, (2 vols.),Lucknow, 1974), vol. II.
11. Mujeeb, *op. cit.*, p.141.
12. *Ibid.*, p.140.
13. Meer Hassan Ali, *Observations on the Mussulmauns of India*, 2 vols., (London, 1832), vol. II, pp.166-7.
14. India Office Records, Government of India (Home Department), file P/8949, Vol. II, *Report of the Delhi Town Planning Committee On The Choice of a Site For the New Imperial Capital at Delhi*, para. 9.
15. From the genealogical material which I collected, it would appear that the shrine has never completely absorbed or been able to support the *pirzada* population attached to it, and this is still true today. It is only possible to speculate about the types of work which *pirzade* did after moving away in earlier times, but now several young men have received higher education and there is a doctor, an engineer, a lawyer and a businessman among the younger generation, with several young men still at college waiting to follow in their footsteps.
16. L. von Orlich, *Travels in India, Including Sinde and the Punjab*, 2 vols., (London, 1845), Vol. II, pp.32-3.
17. Menstrual and post-partum pollutions are described in more detail in Chapter Four.
18. See for instance S. Abul A'la Maududi, *Purdah and the Status of Women in Islam*, (Lahore, 1972), p.154; K. Ahmad, *Family Life in Islam*, (Leicester, 1974), p.31.
19. A.A.A. Fyzee, *Outlines of Muhammadan Law*, 2nd. ed. (London, 1955), pp.181-5.
20. *Ibid.*, pp. 335-6. See also V.R. and L. Bevan Jones, *Woman in Islam*, (Lucknow, 1941), pp.238-44; R. Levy, *An Introduction to the Sociology of Islam*, 2 vols., (London, 1931-3), Vol. 1, pp.138-41 and

205-8; *Quran Sharif,* 4:11-12. Different schools differ in details. The teaching of the Sunni Hanafi school — which is most influential in India — is based on pre-Islamic tribal law and Quranic injunctions. The Quranic regulations gave women inheritance rights, and are considered an advance over tribal laws. The details of the division are very complicated, depending on such factors as the presence or absence of children of the deceased, or just of sons.

21. Fyzee, *op. cit.,* pp.335-6; Jones and Jones, *op. cit.,* pp.242-4; Z. Eglar, *A Punjabi Village in Pakistan,* (New York, 1960), pp.45, 186-99.
22. Ahmad, *Family Life in Islam, op. cit.,* p.31; Maududi, *op. cit.,* p.154; B.A. Lemu and F. Heeren, *Woman in Islam,* (Leicester, 1976), pp.22-3; M.M. Siddiqi, *Women in Islam,* (Lahore, 1952), p.56.
23. Fyzee, *op. cit.,* 110-22; Siddiqi, *op. cit.,* pp.53-6; Levy, *op. cit.,* Vol. I, pp.137-8 and 161-3; Jones and Jones, *op. cit.,* pp.130-42 and 234.
24. *Quran Sharif,* 4:4.
25. Jones and Jones, *op. cit.,* pp.138-9; Fyzee, *op. cit.,* pp.335-6; Indian Council for Social Science Research, *Status of Women in India,* (New Delhi, 1975), p.15.

Cooking at home

3. Hearth and Home

For the *pirzada* women, the shrine is distant and alien. Even though they depend on it financially as much as their menfolk, they are excluded from economic as well as religious roles there, an exclusion which is perhaps most dramatically underlined by the prohibition on their entry into the tomb chambers of either Hazrat Nizamuddin or Amir Khusro. The shrine is the world of men — and the women have only limited access to it.

The village — and the homes in it — are, by contrast, the preserves of the women. It is here that men are interlopers and intruders. Home is not a place for a man to linger: it is the realm of the woman. Here is a world where women too may have their rotas for dividing up the domestic chores. They have their own spheres of expertise, just as the men do, and the women's ignorance about how the shrine is organized is balanced by the men's ignorance about sewing or about marriage ceremonies.

Geographically and socially there might appear to be a duality in Hazrat Nizamuddin, a duality consonant with Islamic ideas about the separation of the sexes. There is the shrine, the world of the men, and the home, the world of the women; the public and the private worlds; the sphere of production and the sphere of consumption; the competitive men's world, and the protected world of the women; the infrastructure of the economy and the super-structure of family and kinship. Taking the situation at face value, the duality appears striking. But is it the whole story? Just how profound is the gulf between the two realms?

Considerable impetus to my own thinking on this topic has come from recent critiques of the sociology of the family and from analyses of house-work under advanced capitalism.[1] Obviously, the debate on the role of the housewife in the capitalist mode of production contains elements which cannot simply be transplanted to the context of the *pirzada* women living in Hazrat Nizamuddin, for the debate is largely concerned with the benefits which capitalists reap from the housework performed by the wives of their workers. Part of the debate also considers the contradictions which some women experience between their roles of housewife and of worker. House-work under capitalism is seen as labour performed by women in isolation, which is considered an important element in their consciousness of their position. It is eased to some degree by the availability of convenience foods and labour-saving devices. And, finally, housewives under capitalism typically produce goods for use in their homes rather than for exchange in the market.

Clearly, the *pirzada* men are not employed by capitalists any more than their womenfolk are: indeed, they are not directly in anyone's employ, and so any economic benefits which might be derived from the housework which the women perform can only be rather tenuously traced out. Also, as will be seen, the households of the *pirzade* are of such a size that the women rarely have to work in isolation (though women of individual households work separately from one another), and thus there may be some effect on their consciousness, as well as a division of labour and even specialization of tasks which is rare for the typical housewife under advanced capitalism. On the other hand, housework is not alleviated by labour-saving equipment and goods to the same extent as under advanced capitalism: the *pirzada* women do not have to weave, but they do have to sew the clothes and bedding which their families need; they do not have to husk the rice or mill the wheat, but they do have to cook everything freshly each day; and the most available labour-saving devices in India are other people. Finally, the *pirzada* women do on occasion provide goods which are directly important for the work of the men in the shrine.

However, while the situations of the *pirzada* women and the housewife under advanced capitalism are not directly comparable, the literature about the latter is illuminating for an analysis of the position of the *pirzada* women. This literature levels several important criticisms at the ways in which women's housework and the family have commonly been perceived by social scientists, and analogous objections can be made to typical perceptions of *purdah*, whether those of Muslim apologists, their protagonists, or the relatively detached ethnographer. One crucial criticism is of the great divide these writers see between the worlds of the men and the women, the worlds of work and the home (a divide which is also reflected in writing about the seclusion of women). The literature about housework insists that the links between these apparently 'separate' worlds must be traced out. While there are important differences of opinion within the debate about housework under capitalism, there is agreement on several areas of common ground, and the barest bones of this debate can give direction to thinking about the work of the *pirzada* women.[2]

Much like the non-employed housewife under advanced capitalism, the *pirzada* women in *purdah* are economically dependent and yet at the same time perform vital tasks for which they are unpaid. Women living in *purdah* often appear in the literature as non-working parasites living off the labours of their menfolk, as creatures whose concern is the building of a stable home life for their children, as the *locus* of family honour, all of which is reflected in their good behaviour and fine clothes and jewellery. They depend on men for their basic subsistence needs, while the men rely on the proper conduct of their women for *their* good standing in the world outside the home.

This view is not so much wrong as incomplete, just as an analogous view of the housewife under advanced capitalism omits several important points.

Maybe such a view would be accurate for the secluded women of the extremely wealthy, whose housework consists of managing the servants' activities and whose days are spent in self-beautification and languid leisure. But among the *pirzade* the leisured wife is a creature not found in everyday reality, except maybe for the newest bride or for the elderly woman who has a bevy of daughters and daughters-in-law under her command. Most of the *pirzada* women spend their days from before dawn until well into the evening doing housework in their own homes. Their work is unpaid — just as the housewife's under advanced capitalism is unpaid — but it is work nonetheless. This is one point on which commentators on housework under capitalism are in agreement.

The exponents of housework under capitalism agree on another important point. Contrary to many perspectives, they argue that women are not simply insulated from the outside world in units which are concerned with consumption rather than production. They point to the dangers of being led astray by the invisibility of women in the outside world and the apparent separation between the world of men and the world of women. The physical absence of women in the shrine, for instance, should not be taken as an indication that women are irrelevant there, that they have no role or importance there. Analyses which concentrate on either the world of men or of women are equally partial: what is important is to uncover the connections between the two worlds, to try to locate the ways in which the apparent separation between them may conceal important features of the division of labour between the sexes.[3] The debate about housework under capitalism raises similar points: despite appearances, women are not marginal to the modern capitalist economy and the crucial economic links between the household and the outside world are not limited to the incomes which the men bring home. Women's work is indispensable, though the physical and social separation between home and 'work' masks important connections.

If the position of women is perceived as limited to consumption and the socialization of children, the home and the family might be thought of solely as part of the superstructure. But to leave the matter there would be to underplay or even ignore women's vital economic roles: the family must be seen as both superstructure *and* infrastructure, in the specific sense that women contribute to the reproduction of the labour force. On the one hand, there is the day-to-day servicing of the present labour force, ensuring by feeding, clothing and replenishing their spirits that the workers are able to perform a good day's work. On the other hand, women are also vital in bearing the children who will take up positions in later years, as workers outside the home and women who will step into their mothers' shoes. The work of women is therefore crucial in the production of new labour power.

The preceding chapter has indicated the economic dependence of the *pirzada* women and the very real power which the men as a whole have over the women. By concentrating here on the work which the women perform, the question of dependency can be turned on its head; clearly the *pirzada* men themselves rely on the women.

Housework

From early childhood, small girls help with the housework, maybe sweeping the floors or cleaning the rice or lentils before they are cooked. The tasks associated with servicing the members of the household are no prerogative of married women — as childbearing is — but are performed by all females in the household.

Pirzada women have fewer domestic gadgets and convenience foods than are commonly taken for granted in industrialized nations to ease household work. Food is rarely available in packets or tins, and refrigerators are very expensive. All vegetables and meat have to be bought daily, and spices and herbs have to be specially prepared for each dish. Wheat flour can be stored at home, but the *chappatti* (unleavened wheat bread) have to be made freshly each day. Items such as lentils, rice and sugar are sold loose and before even beginning to cook with them a thorough search has to be made for the tiny pebbles and bits of mud which are inevitably mixed up with the grains. Ready-made clothes are rare and even bedding has to be made at home, and all clothes have to be washed by hand. Cleaning and dusting the house in a dry dusty climate where rooms are open to the elements is an almost impossible and never-ending job. The languid pace at which much of the work continues, spreading the tasks over long hours, punctuating them with rests and chats, is probably also a reflection of the lack of alternative possibilities for passing the time. Nevertheless, household chores are of necessity time-consuming in the Indian context.

The position of the *pirzada* women nevertheless compares favourably with that of most women in India, and the older women are grateful for the improvements which they have experienced. In 1975 all but one of the *pirzada* households had cold running water and a supply of electricity for lighting and fans. One woman, married some thirty-five years ago, said:

> When I was married, my husband's sisters were already married and I had to care for him and also his two younger brothers. In those days we had no electricity — we used to light the house with paraffin lamps. I didn't even have a sewing-machine when we married — my parents couldn't afford to give one in my dowry — so I had to do all the sewing for the family by hand. I would get up at dawn, and first pray and read the *Quran Sharif* before making any breakfast. After my children were born I spent half an hour early in the morning massaging the baby — my husband always said that I should put the children first, then make sure that his brothers had their food exactly on time, before even bothering about him, or myself. And if guests came to the shrine, I used to cook completely separate special dishes for them too.

Her younger sister was married a few years later and commented:

> My life was terrible when the children were small. In those days we had no electricity — so we had no electric fans. That made things very difficult. In

the hottest weather, I used to sit up the entire night, fanning the small children by hand, so that they would be able to get some sleep.

Another woman of about the same age as the other two said that taps had been installed in her home about thirty years ago:

Until that time, we used to have daily deliveries of water – the *bahishti* used to bring the water in their leather water sacks and they'd pour it into tanks or earthenware pots. It was very difficult keeping clothes clean and having baths.

Housework is much easier today than it was for these women in the years just after their marriages, but, even so, it is a job with long hours.

To some extent, the burden of housework is eased by the household structure. When a *pirzada* man marries, it is rare for him to move into a separate house. Generally he and his wife are allocated a separate room in the family house, and as younger sons marry in their turn, they and their wives and their children continue to be part of the same household. In India, people commonly say 'we are one *chula* [hearth] ' to indicate that several married couples and their children, generally one particular aged couple with their married sons, live in the same house and cook and eat jointly. Some *pirzada* households do not have this kind of structure mainly because married sons generally move to separate quarters once their parents die, often before their own sons are old enough to be married. But the extended household is the common form of household structure among the *pirzade*.

According to the 1971 Census, the average household size in the part of the village where the *pirzade* are concentrated was just over four persons.[4] This merely reflects the fact that many non-*pirzade* in the village are recent migrants who are unlikely to be living with brothers or fathers and who have often not even brought their wives to live with them. Among the *pirzade,* households are generally much larger than the average: the two smallest households consist of a childless widower (who lives in a cell in the shrine) and a widow with two unmarried sons (her own and her husband's siblings went to Pakistan in 1947). Even including these two, the average size is just over ten persons, with one household consisting of over twenty persons, and around three-quarters clustering between eight and sixteen.

Thus, it is rare for a *pirzada* woman to be the only domestically competent female in the household. Daughters soon learn to be useful around the home. Brides often move directly into an extended household and are surrounded by a mother-in-law, the wives of their husband's older brothers, and his sisters who are not yet married. Moreover, since many of the women marry within the village, they may still be able to call on the help of their mothers and sisters even after their marriage. Women are generally able to share tasks among themselves, and it is uncommon for one woman to have sole responsibility for all the cooking, cleaning, sewing and childcare which is performed in her household. The oldest woman in the household normally takes a managerial role, deciding on menus and overseeing the cooking, checking that work on new bed quilts begins well before the cold season, calculating the clothes which have to be prepared for an imminent wedding in the family, and so on. New mothers are generally relieved of everything but caring for the needs of their babies for the first few months, and they do not have to bother themselves with preparing and serving food, or with sewing or washing clothes. The rest of the women share out the other household tasks.

In one household, for instance, three unmarried daughters share the cooking, dish washing and cleaning among themselves, leaving the two 'brides' free to look after their children. One sister spends an hour and a half each morning cooking the unleavened bread for the entire household, the second is responsible for preparing the midday meal, and the third cooks the evening meal. They have a three day rota for washing the pots and pans. Each sister looks after the clothes for an unmarried brother, checking that they are clean, ironed, mended and ready for him at the right time. In another house, two sisters alternate the housework: one day one does the cooking and other work in the kitchen, and the next she cleans the house and washes the clothes. Most of the *pirzada* women, then, can benefit from economies of scale and some division of labour in housework among the women of their household.

Some of the women are also able to benefit from the help which servants give. Often these are people who are paid little or nothing, who came to the shrine destitute — sometimes brought as children by their impoverished parents — and who rely on the *pirzade* for their keep. The *pirzada* women retain for themselves the main sewing and cooking tasks, and make the servants wash dishes and clothes, and even run errands in the *bazar* — a task which removes work from the *pirzada* men rather than the women. Large items needing washing — such as the floor coverings — can be sent to washerwomen rather than be washed at home.

Food preparation is a daily activity. In most homes, the day begins at dawn, when many of the *pirzade* make their first prayers of the day, and then cooking begins. All cooking in the village is done on paraffin stoves and the traditional hard-baked mud hearth fuelled by charcoal (or sometimes wood) which permits one pot to sit on top. Much of the preliminary preparation — the hulling or peeling of vegetables, and the pounding of herbs and spices — is done away from the heat of the stoves. The cook crouches on her haunches beside the pots, adding new ingredients, stirring each pot in turn to make sure nothing burns, periodically taking a small sip to check that the spices are in the right quantities. Only one of the houses has an oven, but it is sited on the roof of the house and only used infrequently to bake unleavened bread. Particularly in the hot weather, the task of sitting over a hot griddle cooking bread is such a chore that the women often send the dough ready for baking to an oven in the *bazar*. The only times when the *pirzada* women are not expected to do the cooking are when large numbers of people are invited, for instance to a wedding, and the cooking is contracted out to non-*pirzada* men from the *bazar*. Otherwise, the woman normally do all the cooking themselves at home.

On festive occasions, members of one household make every effort to sit down together for a special meal, but on normal days, mealtimes are unfixed and people often eat in groups of two or three when it suits them. Men and women may eat together — unlike in some areas of India where women may only eat separately and after the men have had their fill — but in practice they rarely do so. If a man chances to come home while some of the women are eating, he will probably eat along with them, though some men prefer to have their meals brought to them in their own room. Often, the men are too busy to come home, and a servant or a young boy of the family may be despatched with a meal which is eaten in the shrine. Even the women of one household do not necessarily eat together — one may be bothered with a sick child and has to wait until someone can take over from her, another may just not feel hungry — with the result that providing food for members of the household generally continues over several hours each day.

Another major portion of the women's work is sewing and mending. It is virtually impossible to buy ready-made clothes in India, and the *pirzada* women do not patronize tailors, since these would have to take their measurements. Thus, along with cooking, a girl must be taught to sew. All the households own at least one sewing machine, either treadle or hand-powered. The women sew all the clothes for themselves and the children of the house, and the simple shirt and *pajama* trousers which the men mostly wear. They do not sew the traditional coat with upright collar and 'modern' shirts and trousers. But old clothes must be mended, and when beyond repair, the cloth may be rescued and used to make clothes for the children. Dirty clothes must be washed by hand, and most are washed at home by the *pirzada* women themselves rather than being sent out to a washerwoman. And the men's *pajama* have to be starched, and the clothes all ironed. The women must also make all the bedding for the household, from the cotton wadded mattresses and embroidered sheets and pillow cases, to the heavy and light weight quilts which have to be emptied, cleaned and refilled every year with newly carded cotton.

In addition, before any festival, such as the Eid after Ramzan, every home sees a flurry of activity, as the women make new clothes for the family, mainly for the men and children who can go to the shrine. Several women said there is no point in sewing festive clothes for themselves since they so rarely leave their homes. Further, if there is a wedding approaching among their near kin, the women must busy themselves with preparing new clothes. The bride, with her sisters and mother, must prepare clothes which are to go into her dowry, which comprises several suits with embroidery around the cuffs and neck, handkerchiefs, and *duppatte* with lace borders delicately stitched on to them. Similarly, the women in the household where the bride will be received are also busy, preparing the suits — maybe 11, maybe 15, or even 21 or 25 — which will be sent to her before the wedding, including the suits which the bride wears on the day of the wedding and the day after for the 'showing of the face'. Some of the work may be sent out to the *bazar* if a very intricate design is required, but hand embroidered suits prepared at home are felt to be a sign of greater love for the bride. The sisters and mothers of the bride and groom must also have new suits for the wedding day. Often the sisters prepare identical suits, generally made of some gaily-coloured satin, with dresses embroidered at the neck and cuffs and *ghyrara* (long, very wide trousers) embroidered from the level of the knee down to the ground.

Then, day by day, the homes have to be kept clean: the courtyard has to be washed and swept, the cotton floor coverings must be swept and periodically sent out for cleaning. Further, since *purdah* makes it difficult to accommodate workmen, a lot of whitewashing of the walls is done by the women: the weeks before the month of Moharram are generally busy with this work and also the thorough cleaning out and sorting of the cupboards and metal trunks in which clothes and other items are stored. Apart from major structural repairs, and electrical work which is done by some of the *pirzada* men themselves, the women do all the cleaning and maintenance work around the home. The only exception to this is the cleaning of latrines. When I first arrived, the houses all had the traditional style of latrine from which the night soil had to be removed each day by non-*pirzada* sweeper women who also cleaned the open drains along the alleys of the village. In the course of the year 'flush' toilets were installed because of a government order: these toilets had no cisterns but were connected to underground drains, and after this most of the new latrines were washed by the *pirzada* women themselves.

The regular daily round of cooking, cleaning and sewing is punctuated by seasonal demands for warmer bedding and clothes and the preparations for weddings and other celebrations. Throughout the year, the women spend most of their waking lives ensuring that the household keeps functioning and that their families are properly fed and clad. Their work enables the men to concentrate on their work in the shrine, in the sure knowledge that their meals will be ready when they are hungry or that a clean white shirt and starched *pajama* can be produced for them at a moment's notice. Accordingly the normal work of the women in their homes does have an impact on the work of the men at the shrine.

In other work which the women do, the connection between the shrine and the home is even more obvious. There are several types of task performed by the women which directly enhance the status of their own menfolk, and which thereby raises the prestige and income of the men in the shrine.

Maybe half a dozen times in the year, people who are 'guests' at the shrine come from a distance to perform their pilgrimage. They may require to be housed and fed, and it is often the women who take the brunt of the re-organization which this may entail. Some of the *pirzade* have managed to erect special buildings in which their 'guests' may stay. Many households, though, have to try to accommodate their 'guests' at the same time as keeping their womenfolk invisible to them. The arrival of 'guests' may be foreshadowed by the shifting of furniture, the setting aside of a special room and the erection of drapes and screens so that the male 'guests' may come and go without being able to see the women of the house. In some extreme cases, all kitchen utensils and stoves are removed to a new site for the duration of the visit. Even if 'guests' do not have to be housed, the women are generally expected to prepare special delicacies for them to eat.

When there are festivals, the women generally also cook special food for the family at home, and many people commemorate the deaths of close relatives by preparing a *halva* or some other sweet dish over which prayers are said. In addition, the women may be expected to prepare food which is taken to the shrine to mark particular events. On the 18th of every month special prayers are said in the name of Hazrat Nizamuddin, who died on that date, and each month some of the women are expected to prepare some *halva* which is blessed and then distributed to the pilgrims. Failing that, they certainly have to prepare some *halva* for the death anniversaries of Hazrat Nizamuddin and Amir Khusro. Something should also be sent to the shrine to mark the death anniversaries of the founders of the *pirzada* Families.

During the month of Moharram, the women also have to prepare several batches of sweetmeats: on the fourth is the death anniversary of Hazrat Nizamuddin's own *pir*, and the women prepare a dish of sweetened rice and lentils; on the tenth and some other days, sweets must be prepared to mark the martyrdom of Husain (the Prophet's grandson) and his party. The month of Moharram is very important to the *pirzade*, since the whole month is set aside for mourning. Among other preparations, some of the women decorate the *taziya* – replicas of the tombs of Husain and others who died at Karbela – which are paraded round the village several times on the night of 9-10 Moharram, before being buried at the specially prepared ground two miles away. But several women felt that the restrictions which surround the preparation of *taziya* – such as setting aside a special room from which children are excluded to prevent polluting the *taziya* – were such that it was better not to prepare one at all.

Other tasks which some of the women occasionally perform include the sewing of new velvet drapes and canopies for the tomb chambers of Hazrat Nizamuddin and Amir Khusro, the material for which is provided by a 'guest' at the shrine. There are many variations among the households in what work of this sort the women actually do: some families regularly prepare sweets on the 18th of every month, while others do not but their womenfolk are involved in sewing the canopies for the tomb chambers.

What all these tasks have in common, though, is that the women work at home to prepare items which are used by the men to draw and retain the devotions of pilgrims to the shrine. It is the women who cook the *halva*, but the men who receive the religious merit of distributing blessed food to pilgrims at the shrine. The women spend hours preparing the *taziya* for a procession in which only the few women who have permission from their husbands or fathers can participate. When the death anniversaries are held, the women may make the drapes or sweetmeats, but the men control the extra income which the crowds bring to the shrine. And, just as menstruating women may not enter the shrine, so too are they reminded of their polluting capacities through the prohibition on their doing any work which bears directly on the men's work in the shrine, apart from preparing food for the men's 'guests'.

In some respects, this work of the *pirzada* women more closely approaches the vicarious achievements of the wives of businessmen and academics described by Papanek as 'dual person careers' than the Pakistani women living in *purdah* with whom she contrasts them.[5] Clearly, the *pirzada* women are performing work which furthers the work of the men: the daily feeding and clothing of the men enables them to concentrate on their work, while the special preparations for festivals and the hospitality which is extended to 'guests' more strikingly point to the connections between the two worlds of the women and of the shrine. Since the women — like the men — depend ultimately on the income which comes to the shrine, any work which they do that can enhance the prestige of their menfolk in the shrine can be expected to bring them some rewards at home, in much the same way as the business executive's wife in the West hopes that preparing tasty meals for her husband's boss will further his promotion prospects.

However, mild talk of 'vicarious achievement' evades important questions. It is insufficient just to say that a woman benefits from her husband's career and that her own inputs on behalf of his career in turn feed back to her advantage. The question of control presents a different picture. Certainly the *pirzada* men and women work for themselves and for one another, but the situation is not one of mutual interdependence, for the relationships between the men and women are asymmetrical. Through the women's work at home, the men are able to work in the shrine and the women are helping the men as well as themselves. But the women do not control the income to which their work contributes, for the men are the final arbiters of how the income at the shrine is allocated. Men and women alike work, but they are not rewarded with equal power over the income which arises from their work. This is not 'vicarious achievement' on the part of the women, but appropriation of the women-created surplus by the men, and so it is inappropriate to talk simply of mutual dependence and balanced reciprocities.

Replenishing the Labour Force

Housework represents the day-to-day contribution of the women to the reproduction of the labour force, but women's work also has a longer time-scale, that of the biological replenishment of the labour force. The question of control also arises in this context, in relation to women's sexuality, reproductive powers and the children which they bear, and this makes necessary a consideration of the matrimonial policies of the *pirzade,* and of the women's tasks of childbearing, as well as socializing the children who are born.

Sexuality and Marriage
In no human society is biological reproduction considered simply a natural process: everywhere there are rules about heterosexual coupling and about

which women may or may not bear children. Among the *pirzade* it is expected that every female will, in her turn, bear children, but childbearing is the prerogative of married women only, and the children which women bear should only be the children of their husbands. Several features of *purdah* and the way in which marriages are arranged among the *pirzade* are consistent with these expectations.

Before and after marriage, the social separation of males and females reduces the possibilities of liaisons between a woman and anyone but the man who becomes her husband. Several of the *pirzada* women also pointed to ways in which their knowledge of sex was suppressed before their marriage. The upbringing of girls (more than that of boys) is entrusted to the older women of the household, and it is largely up to them to ensure that the girls in their charge remain chaste and ignorant, in other words marriageable. Women still in their twenties tell of the *purdah* which young unmarried girls used to keep even from older *women* who might visit their mothers. As one woman put it:

> If anyone came to chat to my mother, we would all be sent out of the room immediately. I've no idea what they talked about — but I'm quite sure that I might have had more clue of what marriage would mean if I'd been allowed to stay! When I was married at sixteen, I just thought marriage was about getting some pretty new clothes, and when my mother told me simply to do what my husband told me, I didn't have any notion of what she meant. It was rather a shock, I can tell you. The whole thing is such a *sharm ki bat* [matter of shame] and my ignorance has quite spoilt my marriage. I didn't even know that I was pregnant until my mother told me — and then I was too ashamed to tell my husband!

Such innocence was compounded by the lack of formal schooling and sex education from that source, as well as the impropriety of letting young girls attend functions at which they might eavesdrop on the conversations of married women. Weddings, in particular, were not considered suitable occasions for young girls, for they provide many opportunities for rather bawdy and suggestive talk, packed with innuendoes with which the minds of the unmarried should not be poisoned. Married couples have separate rooms — where possible — and when a child is due to be born, other children in the house are kept at a distance. Sex is a matter which is not discussed openly: children traditionally used to be kept in innocent ignorance until the time of their own marriage.

In some respects, things are changing on this front. Couples still sleep separately, and it is still rare for an unmarried girl to attend a wedding, though she probably will if the marriage involves a close relative, such as a sibling. Sex education at school now forms part of the 8th class curriculum (that is for 13-14 year olds), but not all the *pirzada* girls stay at school that long. Some girls commented that their parents and most of the *pirzade* of that generation considered it most improper for sex education to be taught in school: if dealt with at all, it should be talked about at home. Perhaps the

greatest impetus to opening up this subject came through the India-wide
family planning campaign which began in earnest in April 1976, for it made
family planning in the village a daily topic of conversation with me, and often
the children of the family would listen and even participate. The woman
quoted above commented on this one day, while her 12 year old daughter was
present:

> You can see how things have changed. Many of the women of the village
> had never seen me before I was married. At least my younger sisters have
> not been treated that way. I'm glad things are changing. I have no
> intention of banishing her [indicating her daughter] when women come.
> That sort of thing holds girls back, it makes them stupid. She will pick up
> a lot of things I never knew as a child just by listening when people come
> to the house.

Even if girls no longer come to their marriages as ignorant as their mothers
and older sisters, their training throughout their childhood continues to
emphasize the importance of modest behaviour, of sitting decently and
covering their bodies properly, of learning to be dextrous with their *duppatta*
to keep silence at the right time, and to address their elders in a respectful
fashion.

By the time a girl reaches puberty, her parents' thoughts become concentrated on her marriage. Among the *pirzade,* as throughout much of India,
marriage entails the transfer of control over a girl's sexuality and reproductive
powers between two men, from her father (or guardian) to her husband.[6] In
practice, though, even the groom may have only a marginal role in the arrangement of his marriage, because *purdah* generally means that a boy may meet
only those females who are forbidden him in marriage. A man may not marry
a sister, a step-sister, a descendant or a sibling's descendant, or his mother
or grandmother or their siblings, or any woman who has been suckled by the
same woman as himself. After his marriage, he is also prevented from marrying
his wife's sister while his wife is alive, and his wife's mother. First cousins, then
are the closest relatives who can marry. Among the *pirzade,* there are no
current cases of marriage between the children of two brothers (who might
live in the same household), though the genealogical material which I collected
did contain some examples of this type of marriage. Other types of cousin
can be married — and sometimes are — and they are likely to be living in the
only homes to which young men have access, apart from their own.

Thus, the range of knowledge which young men may acquire about
eligible brides for themselves is very circumscribed. Even economic independence can rarely provide a young man with independent knowledge of
suitable marriage partners. Women, in particular, are in possession of information without which no man in his senses is likely to try to arrange his own
marriage. Even if he did try to assert his independence on this score, though,
there are sanctions: all marriages which involve a *pirzada,* particularly a man,
must be witnessed properly, not just according to Islamic regulations, but also

according to the dictates of shrine tradition: invitations should be sent to all the *pirzada* homes, and at least one member of each Family must witness and approve the match. One woman who had married secretly found that her share from the rota system was discontinued, and if men marry without approval, their children will never receive any share from the shrine, as the marriage is considered invalid. In general, young men concur with the plans of their parents, and depend on their good judgement to provide them with suitable brides.

When a match is proposed, the members of the boy's household meet together to discuss the matter in detail, and the boy is present, and may even express his opinion. If he finds the proposal abhorrent, he may say so and his wishes will generally be accepted. If he wishes to marry some particular girl — say a cousin — he may even tell his sister, who can mention it for him to their parents, and the whole affair can be arranged as if it had all been the design of the boy's elders. While the disapproval of all his family will fall on a boy who refuses to marry at all, or who wants to marry against his parents' wishes, he *can* speak up and have some influence on his marital destiny.

Compared with his sisters, his position is enviable. Likewise, they have little option other than to marry, but they are not expected to have even an interest in or influence over their own fate. Their part in the affair which seals their destiny for life is expected to be passive. When I impertinently asked a young woman about her engagement which had recently taken place, she replied:'The engagement may be *pukka* (firm), but I don't know. I haven't been told, and I haven't asked.' (She immediately changed the subject.)

For a girl to speak up or mention any preferences, even to appear interested is considered shameless: 'My marriage is not my worry. It's my parents' business. It's not my place to ask what is going on.'

Some said that it is shameless for a girl to refuse a match which her parents consider suitable, for it implies a lack of faith in their judgement, as well as an unbecoming obstinacy in not allowing her parents to perform their duty. One woman with three married daughters commented: 'Thanks to God, no daughter of mine has ever been shameless enough to refuse to marry as we have directed.'

Others said that such determination on the part of parents is less common than it once was — they talked of boys and girls alike being given no warning of their marriage, let alone being consulted — but now, if the girl has a rooted objection to a match, she may be helped to escape it through intervention on her behalf by an older sister. But if she can provide no *good* reason for rejecting a match, she will probably have to go through with it:

Our aunt was very keen for her son to marry our second sister, who was about two years younger than him. He had known us all since childhood, of course, and he was absolutely adamant that he wanted to marry our oldest sister, who is in fact about six months his senior. It is quite unusual for the boy to be younger, but he was insistent — and the difference in age is not too much. But our sister wasn't very happy. It wasn't that she could say anything wrong about him, but her heart wasn't in it. But how could she refuse? Our parents have fed her all these years — and they have all the rest of us to marry off as well. But it's all worked out quite well. He is good to her and she has grown to love him since their marriage.

Another unmarried girl told me how at 16 she had managed to persuade her family not to arrange a match which they all considered eminently suitable for her:

In all ways it did look a good match, but I heard that he smokes. The smoke always gives me a headache — so I told my parents that I couldn't face a life like that. They were disappointed, I know, because it's so hard to get girls well-married these days. But I shall have to marry sometime — that's without a doubt — not that I really want to. But my mother always asks me what I think will happen to me after she and my father are dead. Am I really so silly as to think that my brothers will want to look after me when their own families are growing up? Parents give their children life and that makes them think that they have the right to determine how much education they have and who they marry. I expect what will happen is that an offer will come which all the family likes and they'll all put pressure on me to accept it.

If the parties to a marriage are themselves so marginal to the decisions which surround it, who, then, takes the major part? Can it be said of the *pirzada* women that they are 'so many uterine pawns in a male system', as has been said of women in pre-revolutionary China?[7] In some respects this is a good, though oversimplified, approximation to the situation in Hazrat Nizamuddin. In theory, it is true, a man gives away his daughter to another man's son, or he makes moves to find a wife for his son. Indeed, settling one's children in marriage is an important duty: people gossip if a man fails to ensure that his children are properly established in life and, if a child remains unmarried, people will assume that the offers from a boy's family have been turned down, or that no offers have been received for the hand of the girl. People will chatter. They will speculate. What is wrong with the child? Maybe there is a question of a limp, a quick temper, a surly manner or a squint. Whatever the trouble, the child's guardian will be assumed to have been less than assiduous in finding a suitable match.

In several current marriages among the *pirzade,* the male head of household has clearly played a dominant role in organizing the marriages of his children. Sometimes the men build up lasting relationships with the men who visit the shrine, often with *pirzade* from other shrines. Maybe one of these contacts has a son who would make a good husband for a girl from Hazrat Nizamuddin or maybe he can suggest suitable brides to be brought in from outside the village. If a man decides to arrange the marriages of his children like this, there is little that his womenfolk can do: it is no more than his right.

One of the prominent *pirzada* men has arranged five of the marriages of his seven married children in this fashion. His second son was married to a bride from another shrine, and some years later, after the women of the two families had become friendly, the bride's younger sister was married to his fifth son. Similarly, his elder daughter was married to a *pirzada* from yet another shrine, and that man's sister was later married to the fourth son. His younger daughter was married into a family of *pirzade* in Calcutta. His other two married sons have been wedded to first cousins. His wife is happy with the brides who have come from outside, but she regrets having had to send both daughters far away in marriage. In fact, offers of marriage came from inside the village for both of them, but their father did not wish their marriages to take place in Hazrat Nizamuddin. His wishes won the day.

But even the guardian cannot have a completely free hand. He will have to make concessions to others, for any marriage which he arranges must meet the criteria of the rest of the *pirzade*. On the whole, this is a small concession, if any concession at all, since common sets of priorities are held amongst the *pirzade* when searching out suitable matches.

What is more interesting here though, is the role which women generally play in the arrangement of marriages, for men are often in practice rather marginal to the arrangement of the marriages of members of their own households. I have already indicated that the bride herself has little to say or do about her own wedding, but once she is married she is launched, like the rest of the married women, into a role which permits her the freedom to dabble in match-making on behalf of others. A woman may not control her own marital destiny, but she often influences the fate of others. Aside from their central role in making preparations once a wedding has been agreed, the *pirzada* women have often been co-opted into arranging the marriages of other women. While it is the men who have to give the final sanction to any proposed match, the women can play a vital role because of the access which they can obtain to women living in *purdah* in other households.

The parents of a girl cannot draw attention to her existence, or make suggestions about suitable matches for her. They simply have to wait until offers come for her, offers which the family gathered together discusses and accepts or rejects. But even before an offer is sent, indeed even after it has been accepted, both sides continue to search out information about the other party.

The *pirzada* men and women alike were adamant that marriages among themselves were straightforward. With some exaggeration, they sometimes talked of arranging a marriage — from the sending of the offer to the wedding day — in less than a month inside the village. But it takes several months, maybe even a couple of years, over matches with outsiders. Inside the village, the parties are well-known: the men work together in the shrine, and the women have reliable information about the atmosphere in the homes of other *pirzade*. In many cases, the idea for the match comes originally from the boy's mother, who arranges for the family to discuss sending the offer, and the men will generally bow to the superior knowledge which the women have about other women in the village. They can rest assured that the women would not suggest a match which would bring an ill-natured bride into the home, for the women in particular have to live with the bride. The women have considerable influence over marriages inside the village; but they also have considerable interests in choosing well.

For numerous reasons, though, not all marriages can be restricted to the village, and the arrangement of marriages with outsiders is considered a much more risky and difficult enterprise. Most marriages outside the village concern outsiders from Old Delhi, some four miles away, and the *pirzada* women generally play important parts in the discussions and investigations that precede the marriage.

Because of *purdah,* women who have married out of the village, or brides who have come in from outside, often know more about the existence of potential brides or the character of potential mothers-in-law than men can. Often matches may be discussed at their instigation, and they may act as *bij-wali* − women-in-the-middle or go-betweens − who can recommend families in Delhi who could provide suitable brides and grooms for the unmarried *pirzade.* They can assess with some certainty if a match might suit. This has obvious advantages over outsiders who can always be expected to indulge in deceits, big or little, about their Family, about the job which the boy does, or the skills and beauty of the girl. Outsiders can also be expected to puff themselves up and put themselves across in the most attractive light. A *bij-wali* who is not well-known to the *pirzade* cannot herself necessarily be trusted: for might she not be in league with the other party and be prepared to tell all sorts of outrageous lies which would remain hidden until the marriage had been performed? But the daughter who has been married to a man in Delhi, the beloved sister whose opinion is respected, the son's wife who always talks good sense, these are the women who can safely be used to advocate, or advise against, a match.

Every effort is made to gauge the suitability of the match. Many months may be spent checking the details of the different types of information to which the men and women have access. A boy's sisters may drop in unexpectedly to see how the girl spends her time: is she busy with housework, and is her home kept clean, or is she simply lazing around? Is she even at home? Can she embroider prettily and are her efforts at cooking edible? Similarly, the girl's sisters may want to know what the potential mother-in-law is like. Does she run an efficient and tidy home, how does she speak to her daughters-in-law? Do the brides there look happy or downtrodden? For that will be a good guide to their sister's fate if she is married there. In brief, whether they are giving away a girl or acquiring a bride, they want to ensure that the atmosphere of the bride's home and her father-in-law's home match as well as possible. There is no wish for a daughter to be unhappy in her marriage, nor for the new bride to be a misfit, for the bride is the person expected to make all the adjustments in her habits.

Other matters are also considered important − perhaps more important by the *pirzade* − especially the Family of the other party. By preference, they marry other Syed people, and checking out family trees is a task at which the *pirzada* men are adept. Through their links with men who come to the shrine, they can find out more about the Family of the other party and their reputation. Men are also in a better position than the women to check the veracity of the other party's claims about the work which their menfolk perform, and they — better than the women — may be able to investigate a potential groom's character.

One elderly man, for instance, told me in front of his Delhi son-in-law how months had been spent checking out his Family and ascertaining his character, even though the old man's cousin had known the family well for 15 years. During all this time — as is common — the bride's parents had had nothing directly to do with the negotiations, and the groom had never met his potential father-in-law, in order to avoid embarrassment if the match never materialized. Finally, when the bride's people had nearly decided that the match should proceed, they set a test of the boy's character. The old man presented himself at the dispensary where the boy worked, wearing ordinary, rather grubby clothes, and played the role of a country bumpkin with the poor fellow, checking and rechecking the details of the prescription, the dose, how often it should be taken and so forth. That the young man never once raised his voice was deemed sufficient proof that there need be no fears for the happiness of the girl.

Such examples of care are not uncommon. Daughters are not callously palmed off on first-comers. Several young women could tell me about a dozen or so offers for them which had been mulled over and investigated — and in the end rejected. It may have been a question of a lie about the boy's Family, or about the job he did. It might have concerned the greedy demands of the boy's relatives for items to be put into the girl's dowry. There might have been an unwillingness to marry a girl to a widower with small children. If there is some reason why a match is less than satisfactory, a girl's parents will turn down an offer, and will even break off an engagement if new information comes to light.

Further, girls are rarely used in the political games of their fathers: except that the children of rivals will not be married, the wider political connotation of marriage as alliance is rare among the *pirzade*. From the women's point of view, the system of arranged marriage of the *pirzade* compares favourably with other systems common in northern India.[8] Marriages within the village certainly make the wrench less for some brides, and most marriages outside the village are with people in Delhi who have been thoroughly checked out or long known to the *pirzade*. The married women play a vital role in softening the effects of the lack of control each bride has over her own marital destiny.

While girls are not often political pawns, and the married *pirzada* women play an important role in arranging marriages of their juniors, a woman — once married — has little choice about remaining in that state. In Islamic law, marriage is a civil contract which may be ended in divorce, though divorce is considered abhorrent and there are several obstacles which prevent it. The shame which faces the divorced person is often considered a major disincentive to divorce, and, in addition, the person initiating divorce generally has to forfeit the marriage settlement. Further, if a man repudiates his wife, that is, gives her *talaq,* there is a cooling-off period — the *iddat* — during which he can revoke the divorce.[9]

In theory, both men and women may initiate divorce proceedings, though divorce is in practice easier for the husband to obtain. A woman cannot divorce without her husband's consent, unless she resorts to legal proceedings in which she must specify her grounds for seeking the divorce. Given that many Muslim women live in *purdah* and have no access to private funds, the right to judicial interference is probably rather irrelevant for most Muslim women in India. Two young *pirzada* women told me that an unhappy marriage just has to be silently tolerated, for their parents have to worry about the marriages of their younger daughters, without the shameful burden of a daughter who has ended her marriage.

A husband can more easily divorce his wife. He does not need judicial interference, nor is he required to give any grounds for divorcing his wife; he can repudiate her — and revoke the repudiation during the cooling-off period too — without needing her consent. The husband's power of repudiation, in a context in which the wife cannot guarantee that her parents will willingly take her back, undoubtedly affects the behaviour of Muslim wives. Just as a *pirzada* girl — like most other Muslim girls in India — cannot determine whom she will marry, so she can have little control over whether she remains married. If she is unhappy, she may have to tolerate her marriage, while she cannot prevent her husband from divorcing her if he so wishes. The threat of divorce and the stigma which it entails (more than the reality of it) are important elements in the marital destinies of the *pirzada* women, and it represents yet another way in which individual *pirzada* women lack control over the disposal of their own sexuality.

Childbearing and Childrearing

While the status and character of a new bride are ascertained before the marriage, the test of her fecundity has to wait until afterwards. It is in this facet of married life that there is a very real sense in which women are in a 'male system' in which their uterine capacities are of vital importance. It is assumed that marriage brings children — that is not a matter for discussion — and the arrival of a new bride is a time of joy for her in-laws, as she brings with her the promise of offspring. As might have been predicted, the *pirzada* women's reproductive capacities are of the utmost importance.

Several factors determine the date of a marriage, for some dates and days are considered inauspicious and others are inconvenient for the men at the shrine. But amongst these there is another critical point: that the bride should not be menstruating on her wedding day, for then the marriage could not be consummated immediately. Rarely is the date of marriage finalized more than a couple of weeks beforehand, and this, along with the bride's lack of access to contraception (or even lack of contraceptive knowledge), means that she will probably be pregnant soon. Indeed, there must be few brides who would wish it otherwise, for they are likely to feel a failure if the signs of first pregnancy appear tardy. The absence of children in a marriage is assumed to be the 'fault' of the woman, and, perhaps above all else, the new bride must co-operate in demonstrating quickly that she is not *banjh* or barren, thereby proving to her in-laws that their choice was well made. Although none of the *pirzada* women I met is barren, they said that such a woman would be pitied — if not worse — for failing in this her essential task. She would be considered a bad omen, and would probably be excluded from some marriage ceremonies in much the same way as a widow is.

Both sets of parents are concerned about the fecundity of the bride, but in different ways. Her own parents are happy at the prospect of grandchildren. But they also hope that the birth of children to their daughter will help her to settle in well with her in-laws, and will help to ward off criticisms and humiliations which might be devised if she failed to bear children soon. For the groom's parents the arrival of children has a rather different meaning, for the affection in which his children are held is overlaid by one important element, patrilineal descent.

The *pirzade* themselves say that *'khandan bap se chalta hai'*, meaning that a person's 'Family flows from the father' — that a child takes the position of the father, not the mother. While a girl receives her 'blood' and Family membership from her father, his line stops dead with her. A daughter is merely a guest, someone whose dowry and proper marriage are constant worries to her parents during her childhood. Sons alone provide the hope that a line is not doomed to extinction. But the fulfilment of that hope is, in turn, dependent on the fecundity of the sons' wives.

This is not at all to suggest that daughters are unloved. Indeed many fathers as well as mothers have affectionate relationships with their daughters, whose marriages are as much a time of sadness and disturbance to them as they are to the brides. Yet, even though the sons and daughters of *pirzada* men may have the same affection from their parents and the same personal shares in the shrine, the structural meaning of being a daughter rather than a son is quite different. Thus a man hopes to benefit from the reproductive capacities of another man's daughter: women become the producers of private heirs for men, but there are two types of product, sons and daughters. The woman who bears only girls is structurally equivalent to the barren wife, for her husband's line will stop. Muslims do not adopt children, nor do they provide themselves with heirs through the system of the 'in-marrying son-in-law' — the *ghar jamai* — who marries a daughter of the house and whose male children can continue the line. Without sons, a line becomes extinct — as happened to one of the original four *pirzada* Families during the last century. A man can only hope to rectify the situation through taking another wife,[10] although none of the present *pirzada* women is in fact in a polygamous marriage.

The genealogical material which I collected during my fieldwork underlines all these points. Although the *pirzada* women are clearly crucial in the provision of heirs, they are not reckoned in genealogies. Denich, writing about a similar situation in the Balkans, comments that women 'leave no enduring marks of their own existence in terms of the formal structure'; the male groups so formed effectively deny the role which women play in their perpetuation.[11] Among the *pirzade,* women are genealogically irrelevant. My efforts to disentangle the patterning of their marriages proved a perilous enterprise, for knowledge about women was extremely circumscribed. One man who seriously offered to decipher his pedigree right back to Adam — I compromised with the Prophet Muhammad — could only produce details of women alive during his own lifetime. Another written document, purporting to contain a complete record of one *pirzada* Family since the time of Hazrat Nizamuddin, was clearly incomplete: the 120 men were matched by a mere 60 women.

Material which I collected orally was also dominated by males. Informants were often extremely vague about how many sisters their grandparents might have had, where they were married and so forth. Often chance comments of elderly men brought to light women who had married outside the village and were completely lost to the memories of the younger people. Outside brides would often simply be dismissed as 'from Delhi somewhere'. Few people could tell me about previous connections among brides from Delhi or between women from Hazrat Nizamuddin and the in-marrying women, but some recent examples suggest that such links were more common than the *pirzade* care to recollect. For them the system is bounded by the walls of their village. Links are traced between men and men, not women and women. Lists of a man's children tend to be given with the sons in order of birth first and then the daughters as an afterthought, a son of ten coming before a daughter of thirty. In a few generations, only the names of the sons will remain, indeed only those who have sons themselves will escape the oblivion which is guaranteed to their sisters. One man with twelve live children was completely bemused when I asked him to give me the birth orders of his children irrespective of sex: he could only think of them as two separate sets, and had to be gently corrected by a daughter who knew she was younger not older than a particular brother. If a man marries several times, either polygamously or because he is widowed, this too will tend to be forgotten, unless it is very recent: children are recorded as the children of specific fathers, not of specific mothers. Only an age gap between siblings which is too wide to be encompassed by one mother can indicate multiple marriages which have been erased from memory.

Men and women alike were incapable of comprehending my interest in collecting the names and marriages of the *pirzada* women as well as of the men, and what was particularly marked was that the genealogical knowledge of the women was, if anything, even narrower than that of the men, with respect to women as much as to men. The main point, though, is that genealogies are used to substantiate the claims of the *pirzade* to Syed status, and in that respect women are superfluous. It is in this sense that women are genealogically irrelevant: from the point of view of the Family, it does not much matter if women die, are barren, or have only daughters. And even having sons does not guarantee a woman immortality. Women are marginalized and forgotten. Their crucial physiological and socializing tasks are conveniently ignored at the level of genealogy. Among the *pirzade,* there are only two crucial nodes in their genealogies where women have any importance to them: firstly Faṭima, the mother of Hasan and Husain from whom they are descended in the male line, and who connects them directly to the Prophet Muhammad; and, secondly, the sister of Hazrat Nizamuddin, Bibi Zainab, for the Saint himself never married and the *pirzada* Families claim various, and disputed, connections to him through his sister. I hardly need to labour the interests which the *pirzade* have in remembering these two select women in their genealogies.

Briefly, then, the new bride has left her parents' house where she can have no role in perpetuating her father's line, and has moved into the home where she will spend her adult life, a home where she is expected to bear the sons which her husband requires to ensure his line's continuity. Women bear children not for their own line, but for the lines of other people. In the terminology of O'Laughlin, the *pirzada* women are alienated from their own reproduction.[12]

Moreover, the *pirzada* women claim that they had no knowledge of contraceptive and abortion techniques until recently, and that children used simply to be seen as gifts which Allah had willed on them. It is impossible to assess how typical the *pirzada* women were in this, or the extent to which *purdah* — or the *pirzada* men — might have deprived them of access to 'folk' techniques of family limitation. One point of importance, though, is that the Muslim wife is expected to receive all the sexual advances of her husband, and menstruation is the only reason which she can validly give for refusing him. Just as she has no choice over the basic disposal of her sexuality, even within marriage she has little right to control her husband's access to her. Not surprisingly, the married *pirzada* women have generally been prolific and they have had as little control over the number of children which they bear as over the choice of husband for whom they bear them. At a time when effective means of family limitation were not readily available, the cause of this could not be said to be solely the *pirzada* men. Now that contraceptive devices are more widely available, though, it appears that men and women are not always in agreement over the number of children which a woman should have, for men often seem to want more children than their wives. This is a question to which I shall return later.

There remains one final area of the reproduction of the labour force to be discussed: the socialization of the children, in which the women play a major part, particularly with girls, but also with boys for the first few years. While women may be genealogically irrelevant, this does not imply that the social status of wives is unimportant. Indeed their status is extremely significant, since women are entrusted with so much of the work of rearing children. For the *pirzade*, the most preferred bride is one who is 'noble from both directions', in other words one whose parents are both Syed. Inside the village, among the *pirzade* themselves, that can be guaranteed, but outside the village investigations have to be made not just into a girl's father's genealogy, but also into her mother's.

It is not that the bride will pass her good 'blood' to her children. Rather, pure Syed status is taken as an indication of 'breeding' in a broad sense, and the Syed girl who appears to be of good character will indeed have good qualities. Not all Syed people are virtuous, but equally the lack of breeding among non-Syed people will tell in the end, even if the girl appears good-natured. Since the mother gives the children *mysaj* or character, and *akhlaq* or morality, her breeding is crucially important. The genealogical role of women is irrelevant, but their educative roles are not: women create *insan* — human beings — by domesticating children, by the way they organize the home and through the atmosphere they create there. Bad breeding in a wife will always show through in the children, and so the selection of brides is something which must proceed with the utmost caution. While the specific identity and genealogical location of the bride are not important, her good standing, preferably her Syed status, is vital.

For the first few months after a child is born the mother has primary responsibility. Children are mostly breast-fed for at least a year, but the tasks of toilet training, teaching children to talk and lulling children to sleep may be gradually shared out among the other women and girls of the household. Men may also take a part in fondling and feeding, in talking and playing with their own children and those of their sons or brothers, but they do not involve themselves in the work of cooking food for children or in washing clothes or toilet training. Thus until the age of five or six, children of both sexes are mainly under the eye of women.

For boys, the rule of women is rather short-lived. When they attend school, they are generally taught by men, and several of the *pirzada* boys have continued their formal education to college level. Even before a boy has begun at school, though, the men of his own family take a more active role in his upbringing. Once he is toilet trained, his father or uncles may sometimes take him to the shrine and gradually he is weaned away from the women at home. Once at school he will spend little time at home, often preferring some quiet corner in the shrine to do his homework. Further, just as the women's work of reproducing the labour force has long-term aspects, so too are the men involved in perpetually re-creating the labour force at the shrine, through the informal training and the example which they provide for their sons. Small boys may be entrusted to 'sit' in the rota, even if only for short periods when they are little, and they soon become involved in flower purchasing, or sending invitations to their fathers' 'guests'.

For girls it is rather different. Until recently few girls even attended school, and they were under the close watch of the older women of their household until they were married. Now, many of them do go to school, where they generally remain until they are at least ten, though most leave before they are sixteen. Outside school hours, and once they have left school permanently, they spend practically all their time at home. Women therefore have much more control over the socialization of girls than the men do, or than the women do over the boys. The responsibility for ensuring that a girl is properly brought up, that she will not be a liability on the marriage market, that her deportment is demure and her manner becoming, and her domestic skills sufficient to qualify her as a suitable bride — all this rests primarily with the women. In other words, women play a vital role in the perpetuation of the system of sexual apartheid.

Although the question of guardianship of children only arises under some circumstances, as when one parent dies or the parents are divorced, a brief comment on Islamic law on this issue can point up the preceding discussion of childbearing and childrearing. Under Islamic law there are two types of guardianship, *hidanat* and *wilayat*.[13]

Hidanat is normally vested in women and is concerned with the rearing and training of a child. Under the Hanafi School, it lasts until a boy is seven years old, and until a girl reaches puberty, when she is likely to be married. Normally the child's mother has the right of *hidanat*, but in her absence her mother, or mother-in-law, or her own daughters or sisters have the right until the period of *hidanat* lapses. Male relatives may take over if there are no suitable women. The mother's right to guardianship is not absolute, though. She will forfeit it if she commits adultery, if she marries a man whom the child could marry, or if she fails to care properly for her child.

Wilayat is generally the prerogative of the child's father, and the mother only has this right if there are no male relatives to take the father's place. By contrast to the mother's right to *hidanat*, the father's right to *wilayat* is not conditional. Moreover, the possibility that a man will fail to maintain his children adequately is not envisaged in the *Quran Sharif*, while a mother's possible failings are.[14] The father is responsible for the guardianship of the child's property, for its education and marriage. Technically, under the Hanafi School, the guardian can only impose marriage on a child — boy or girl — until puberty, but, because of *purdah*, the guardian generally continues to exert an influence after the child has attained maturity.

Thus, in law, Muslim women have an important role in rearing their children, but they are bearing and rearing them for their husbands. A woman's rights over her children — especially her sons — are more restricted, both in scope and duration, than the rights of her husband.

Work and Control

In this chapter and the preceding one, I have been concentrating on the tasks of the *pirzada* men in the shrine and the work of the women in their homes. The jobs the women do are time-consuming and important. So, too, is the work of the men. But the interdependence between the sexes is asymmetrical, for the control which the men have over the organization of the shrine gives them the upper hand over the women. Few *pirzada* women have received the economic dues to which Islam entitles them, they have little effective economic power, and they do not even retain control over the products of much of their labour in the home. Important tasks can be delegated to the women because the men's economic power enables the *pirzada* men to retain the final say. The threat of intervention by the men, the threat of divorce or the removal of access to children, even the threat of withdrawing maintenance, *could* all be effective because of the utter dependence of the *pirzada* women.

They *can* be controlled, their position *can* be perpetuated, because of the economic power of the men.[15]

References

1. D.L. Barker and S. Allen, 'Introduction: The Interdependence of Work and Marriage', in D.L. Barker and S. Allen (eds.), *Dependence and Exploitation in Work and Marriage*, (London, 1976); M. Benston, 'The Political Economy of Women's Liberation', *Monthly Review*, 21 (1969) pp.13-27; Conference of Socialist Economists, *On the Political Economy of Women*, (London, n.d.); M. Coulson *et. al.*, 'The Housewife and Her Labour Under Capitalism — A Critique', *New Left Review*, 89 (1975), pp.59-71; J. Gardiner, 'Women's Domestic Labour', *New Left Review*, 89 (1975), pp.47-58; J. Gardiner, 'Political Economy of Domestic Labour in Capitalist Society', in Barker and Allen (eds.), *op. cit.*, pp.109-20; N. Glazer-Malbin, 'Housework', *Signs*, 1 (1976), pp.905-22; J. Harrison, 'The Political Economy of Housework', *Bulletin of the Conference of Socialist Economists*, (1973), pp.35-52; C. Middleton, 'Sexual Inequality and Stratification Theory', in F. Parkin (ed.), *The Social Analysis of Class Structure*, (London, 1974), pp.179-203; W. Seccombe, 'The Housewife and her Labour Under Capitalism', *New Left Review*, 83 (1974), pp.3-24.
2. There are differences, for example, on whether housework is productive or not, and on whether housework is a distinct mode of production or a co-opted mode.
3. F. Edholm *et al.*, 'Conceptualising Women', *Critique of Anthropology*, 3 (1977), pp.125-6.
4. India, Census Commissioner, *Delhi District Handbook Part X*, (Delhi, 1973), p.204.
5. H. Papanek, 'Men, Women and Work: Reflections on a Two-Person Career', *American Journal of Sociology*, 78 (1973), pp.852-72.
6. J. Mitchell, *Psychoanalysis and Feminism*, (Harmondsworth, 1975), pp.370-6; G. Rubin, 'The Traffic in Women: Notes on the 'Political Economy' of Sex', in R.R. Reiter (ed.), *Toward an Anthropology of Women*, (New York, 1975) pp.157-210; and B. O'Laughlin, 'Mediation of Contradiction: Why Mbum Women Do Not Eat Chicken', in M.Z. Rosaldo and L. Lamphere (eds.), *Woman, Culture, and Society*, (Stanford, 1974), pp.301-18.
7. M. Wolf, 'Chinese Women: Old Skills in a New Context', in *ibid.*, p.159.
8. For material on arranged marriages and distance, see H.A. Gould, 'The Micro-Demography of Marriages in a North Indian Area', *South Western Journal of Anthropology*, 16 (1960), pp.476-91, and 'A Further Note on Village Exogamy in North India', *South Western Journal of Anthropology*, 17 (1961), pp.297-300; A.C. Mayer, *Caste and Kinship in Central India*, (London, 1960), pp.202-13; W.L. Rowe, 'The Marriage

Network and Structural Change in a North Indian Community', *South Western Journal of Anthropology*, 16 (1960), pp.299-311.

9. A.A.A. Fyzee, *Outlines of Muhammadan Law,* 2nd. edn. (London, 1955), pp.89-91 and 123-62; K. Ahmad, *Family Life in Islam,* (Leicester, 1974), pp.26-7; V.R. and L. Bevan Jones, *Woman in Islam,* (Lucknow, 1941), pp.143-76; B.A. Lemu and F. Heeren, *Woman in Islam,* (Leicester, 1976), pp.21-2; R. Levy, *An Introduction to the Sociology of Islam,* 2 vols., (London, 1931-2), Vol.1, pp.172-6. The *Dissolution of Muslim Marriages Act 1939,* which is still in force, specifies grounds on which a woman can justify in court her prosecution of divorce proceedings, but this does not limit the husband's right to repudiate his wife. See Indian Council for Social Science Research, *Status of Women in India,* (New Delhi, 1975), pp.46-7.

10. Indian Muslims may have up to four wives if one or more of them is barren or ill, and polygamy is generally permissible after wars, but many commentators regard these as *limited* permission rather than encouragement, and the requirement that all wives be treated equally is widely considered an effective prohibition except in extraordinary circumstances. Polygamy is rare in India, restricted by the cost as well as by the fear of the tensions generated between co-wives. See *Quran Sharif,* 4:3; Jones and Jones, *op. cit.,* pp.177-93; K. Ahmad, *op. cit.,* pp.21-2; Lemu and Heeren, *op. cit.,* pp.27-9; M.M. Siddiqi, *Women in Islam,* (Lahore, 1952), pp.133-41; Levy, *op. cit.,* Vol. 1, pp.144-6.

11. B.S. Denich, 'Sex and Power in the Balkans', in Rosaldo and Lamphere (eds.), *op. cit.,* p.246.

12. O'Laughlin, in *ibid.,* p.312.

13. Fyzee, *op. cit.,* pp.171-80; Jones and Jones, *op. cit.,* pp.236-8; A.A. Thanwi, *Bahishti Zewar,* 2nd. ed. (revised and enlarged) (Delhi, 1975), pp.408-12.

14. Levy, *op. cit.,* vol. 1, p.198.

15. This view contrasts with that which considers that control over the means of reproduction is more important than control over the means of production in subsistence economies. See C. Meillassoux, 'From Reproduction to Production', *Economy and Society,* 1 (1972), pp.93-105; and O'Laughlin, *op. cit.,* p.317.

The bride

90

Legitimacy and Concord

The two preceding chapters have concentrated on the economic asymmetry between *pirzada* men and women, but this cannot be a complete explanation for the perpetuation of *purdah* in Hazrat Nizamuddin. The men's economic power is not displayed daily, and they rarely intervene in the women's work. Their ability to control the *pirzada* women is rarely openly used, let alone abused — though the threat of their intervention remains. How is it, then, that the men can entrust important tasks — without interference — to the *pirzada* women? Here the question of internalization has to be considered, for the *pirzada* women are not merely the purveyors of cultural knowledge to the children in their charge. They are themselves the recipients of a cultural tradition, and there is considerable evidence that they largely accept the propriety of the *status quo*. To the extent that they have internalized notions about the proper behaviour of women and the proper relationship between the sexes, important tasks — perhaps especially the socialization of girls — can be delegated to the *pirzada* women.

This chapter is concerned with elements of the 'taken-for-granted' world of the *pirzade,* elements which are unquestioned, those 'of course' statements which brook no questions. They are part of the natural order for the *pirzade;* they are things which have been like that 'since the beginning'.

Matters which are unproblematic to the *pirzade,* though, can be very problematic for anyone wishing to record them. Just what can be regarded as evidence of internalization, as testimony to the commitment of the *pirzada* women to the *status quo?* Merely asking the *pirzade* about the norms which guide their behaviour is insufficient. Their taken-for-granted world is something which permeates their everyday discourse on numerous topics — and something whose very diffuseness sometimes makes for elusiveness. A statement about the taken-for-granted world may be superfluous to the *pirzade,* a mere statement of the obvious. A better indication are the reactions of the *pirzade* to breaches of norms, their verbal comments and their reactions of disquiet or horror when rules are broken. Thus, the taken-for-granted world of the *pirzade* gradually emerges through hearing them discipline their children, or through their strident outrage at the 'shameless' misdemeanours of other people. But this world is also reflected in the behaviour of the *pirzade:* evidence of internalization can come from watching customary interaction and modes of behaviour which are second nature to them. Mere statements of norms can only hint at internalization, while the women's commitment to the *status quo* is more forcefully suggested in their unquestioning adherence to those norms in their behaviour. Two elements, then, seem important in assessing internalization: the behaviour of the *pirzada* women themselves, and their heated reactions to people who behave differently.

Syed Wives, Dependent Mothers

Among the elements of the *pirzada* women's taken-for-granted world are several — their Syed pedigree, their menfolk's occupation at the shrine, their ability to avoid working outside their homes, and the valued role of motherhood — all of which give rise to a positive self-image for the *pirzada* women. These elements represent ways in which they can set themselves apart from other (non-*pirzada*) people, and assert not just their separation but their superiority.

Pedigree and Breeding

Hierarchy is pervasive in India, and a major idiom in which ranking is articulated is caste, through which individuals are differentiated on the basis of the birth. The existence of 'caste' among Muslims is a matter of some dispute.[1] There are those who argue that Islam is an egalitarian religion in which there is no place for caste. Others suggest that the essence of caste is ranking based on concepts of purity and pollution which are specific to Hindus. And yet others point to the existence of groupings which have characteristics in common with Hindu castes — say, the preference for marriage within a group whose membership is defined by birth — which are to be found in Muslim populations in India and beyond, suggesting that such phenomena among Indian Muslims are not merely reflections of habits acquired in Hindu India. There is certainly evidence from the early days of Islam that pedigree was often extremely important, the egalitarian ethos of Islam notwithstanding.

The *pirzade* are imbued with notions of inferiority and superiority of breeding, and they claim for themselves an ancestry which places them at the top of the Muslim hierarchy.

Claims to high status involve tracing genealogical links through the male line to people closely associated with the Prophet Muhammad.[2] Descendants of his companions, and members of his clan — particularly of Hazrat Ali, the Prophet's father's brother's son — are granted a high position among Muslims. Pre-eminent, though, are the Syed. The Prophet had no sons who lived to adulthood, but his daughter Fatima — who was one of Hazrat Ali's wives — had two sons, Hasan and Husain. The descendants of these two are considered to have the closest connection to the Prophet himself — despite the connection through a woman which must perforce be acknowledged. The words which the *pirzade* used in this context — *qoum, nasab, nasl* and especially *khandan* — can be translated by English equivalents such as race, dynasty, breed, pedigree or family.[3] The highest level to which the *pirzade* apply these terms is the whole of the Syed, but they also apply them to the separate branches of Syed which have arisen over the centuries. The word *khandan* (which I have translated as Family), for instance, is applied to the *pirzade* as a whole as well as to the separate branches among them. Like all high status Muslims in India, the *pirzade* claim immigrant origins: many Muslims fled from Central Asia and eastern Persia in the time of Genghiz Khan, and the names of two of the four original *pirzada* Families refer to their foreign origin, the Syed Bokhari Nizami (from Bokhara) and the Syed Kashani Nizami (from Khorassan). In this way, the *pirzade* set themselves apart from low status indigenous converts to Islam: only real original Muslims can trace their connections right back to the Prophet of Islam.

It is within this context of superiority of breeding that much of the discourse of the *pirzade* takes place. They are, without question, the best sort of people. No one can compare with a Syed in purity of blood, in good breeding, even in holiness. People from low backgrounds fight and squabble, but the pure Syed is ideally noble and mild-tempered. A Syed has special excellences with which no other can compete. One woman explained to me:

> When God was making the Prophet Muhammad, he mixed together earth and water as usual, but to them he added a sweet perfume. Everywhere our Prophet went a beautiful scent surrounded him. This was passed in turn to Fatima, and her sons Hasan and Husain received the scent too. All Syed had this special fragrance. But then, after the martyrdom of Husain and his party at Karbela, it became dangerous for the Syed to be conspicuous, so the women prayed to God to take the scent away from them. This he did, to protect them from their enemies. Now the special qualities of a Syed are hidden – but they are there still.

The question of ancestry is extremely important to the *pirzade* in a number of contexts. Even some of the disputes among the *pirzada* men at the shrine – the insinuations about another's pedigree, the slurs on the veracity of a rival's claims – operate within the taken-for-granted idiom which assumes that Syed are superior.[4] One important area – and one in which the *pirzada* women are directly involved – concerns the arrangement of marriages.

No matter how suitable a match might be in terms of the relative ages, education or wealth of the potential parties, a marriage should not take place unless the *khandan,* the Family, is suitable too. A Syed should marry another Syed, if at all possible. As a last resort, Sheikh – especially Sheikh Siddiq – are considered acceptable. For the *pirzade,* no match can proceed if the other party is from a 'low' Family. Whether finding a daughter-in-law or giving away a daughter, the status of the other Family is vital. A daughter-in-law will bring up the children who will continue one's line – so she must herself be 'noble' or *sharif.* And no parents want their daughter to be married into a 'low' Family, for fear that she would be unhappy: would they not be likely to maltreat her, would she not find their uncouth behaviour unbearable?

Among themselves, the *pirzade* said, the matter is quite simple, for they all know about their ancestry. Marriage inside the village is the safest way of settling one's children properly. The question of ancestry was one reason which the *pirzade* commonly stated for preferring to arrange marriages among themselves, and the *pirzada* women continually returned to this issue when discussing how they arrange marriages.

First the Family of the other party must be ascertained, and only then can other factors, such as education or the atmosphere of the other home, be considered. As one young woman explained:

> The character of the boy or girl may *seem* fine, but that is not all that is important. If a bride from a low Family comes into the village, it always shows through in her children that her ancestry is inferior. The children will be ill-behaved or get themselves into some trouble if their mother's blood is not good. It is not that a woman passes her blood to her children — but if her own blood is not good, how can she possibly create a proper home for her children?

Thus marriages outside the village are complicated to arrange, and may take months to confirm, while the men check out the Family tree of the other party. Outside marriages are risky — for people may fraudulently claim to be Syed. One woman scornfully commented:

> Sometimes we have come across people who claim to be Syed. But they are not, they are lying. *That* shows up when we ask them to show us their Family tree. Do you know, many people don't have Family trees, so how can they be Syed? Some people don't even know what *khandan* means!

Outsiders might always be imposters: one woman even talked of 'Dalda Syed', people who pretend to be Syed just like the vegetable cooking oil marketed under the name 'Dalda' masquerades as real clarified butter or *ghee*. Inside the village they do not have to bother checking one another's Family tree, but the dangers of being deceived by liars outside mean that lengthy checks have to be made on the trustworthiness of the claims. Everyone these days, said the *pirzade*, would like to be a Syed — that is the most respectable type of Muslim to be — so they take care over the way they arrange their marriages, for their lines could otherwise be spoilt. A government suggestion that communal problems between Hindus and Muslims could be solved through marriages between the two religious groups was received with derision. One woman in her thirties was contemptuous about the proposal:

> I suppose that they might be right in saying that Hindus and Muslims fight because there are no connections between the two sides. Maybe there should be marriages — but that would have to be for other Muslims, for whom it does not matter who they marry. We Syed could not possibly do such a thing as marry other Muslims, let alone Hindus. We can only ever marry

other Syed.

Syed people have good blood, they have good breeding, and they can be expected to behave decently and honourably. By contrast, non-Syed — such as some of the people who come to the shrine — are likely to disgrace themselves by their behaviour. Sometimes people go into ecstatic trances during singing sessions at the shrine and I discussed one such occasion with several *pirzada* women. A woman pilgrim had begun to sway and moan, her movements became wilder and wilder. She raised herself to her knees, her plait became loose and her hair whipped round her head at such speed that people nearby — including myself — had to retreat to safety. After about ten minutes, she collapsed semi-conscious. The *pirzada* women were derisive. One commented later:

> We think that sort of behaviour disgraceful. We would not do anything like that. Only ignorant women who don't know any better go into ecstasy. I'm sure a lot of women are not really in a trance at all — they only do it to draw attention to themselves.

Similar attitudes were revealed during an all night session of preparations for a wedding in the village, when women gathered to put henna on their hands. While the henna was drying, they were entertained by *risque* games and singing. During the singing, one of the *pirzada* women went into ecstasy — but it was several minutes before I realized that her ecstasy was mock, and the other women in the room were stifling their laughter at her excellent mimicry of the 'ignorant women' who come to the shrine. I was later told that this was a set piece which she always performs at weddings in the village.

Disdain for the behaviour of women who come to the shrine was also shown when I attended a festival with some young *pirzada* women. My attention was continually distracted from the activities of the men by the giggles and comments of my companions about the non-*pirzada* women watching with us. One of them pointed to a woman in a cerise *burqa:*

> Isn't that just shameless. What a colour to use for making a *burqa*, and just look at all that white lace around the cape. What an exhibition! But that's a new fashion in Delhi these days. *We* don't wear a *burqa* like that. You have seen how we do it — we only wear dark colours. The whole point is to hide a woman. To wear such a bright colour is a completely *oolti* [upside down] thing to do.

Women of good breeding would not behave in that sort of fashion. Syed status provides a prima facie case for good deportment and the *pirzada* women have no inclination to mix with — and least of all to marry — people who are unlikely to know how to behave. The *pirzada* women are Syed in their own right and that places them in a position of pre-eminence among Muslims, and enables them to set themselves apart from the uncouth.

Respectability and Dependence

There is another dimension to this, for the question of occupation is very closely tied in with that of ancestry. People of high Family, such as Syed, noble and honourable people, have to think not just about their ancestry but also about their reputation in the world. Some jobs are so degrading and demeaning that Syed people should avoid them at all costs, while others are respectable and acceptable ways of earning a livelihood. This is reflected in the approach to the education of *pirzada* boys. If they show academic aptitude, they are encouraged to continue their formal education through school and college, in order to acquire some qualification for entry into a respected field, such as medicine — either Western or traditional Muslim — or the law. In these ambitions, the image of the job as well as the income which it can command are important. It is not just that the job itself entails no undignified work, but also that a man in such a job can expect a life style which will permit a comfortable existence, relatively free from financial worries. The boy who shows no academic aptitude will be expected to find work in the shrine. Rather than be unemployed, rather than establish some 'secular' trading, the young *pirzada* man should remain at the shrine, doing the honourable duties of his ancestors through the centuries. Cherishing the tomb of the Saint, caring for the needs of pilgrims, helping to cure ailments or to put the faithful on to the Way to Allah — all these are tasks which the *pirzada* men and women consider respectable, and they are tasks which are widely held in esteem in India.

Attitudes to occupations also show up in the way in which the *pirzade* arrange marriages with outsiders. After the Family has been ascertained, the next important point to establish is that the potential groom is in a respectable job, or that the potential bride's father is doing decent work. Petty tradesmen are considered unsuitable, with the exception of workers such as goldsmiths, whose craft is an honourable — and well-paying — one. Outsiders who might be linked to the *pirzada* through marriage should themselves either be *pirzade,* or in some decent occupation. Several of the young women could tell me of offers of marriage which had been rejected when the occupation of the boy had been discovered. There were the people who claimed that their son was in some lucrative business — but it transpired that he ran a wayside stall. And there was the young man who sold make-up for a living — a job which the *pirzada* woman could not accept as worthy.

An important element in the attitudes of the *pirzade* towards the jobs which men do is that the income should be sufficient to support not just the man, but his wife and children too. A *pirzada* woman feels herself entitled to be maintained, and it is a matter of great shame if such a woman has to perform work which brings money into the home. In one case, a young woman — the widow of her cousin who had lived in Pakistan — returned to her father's home and made a small contribution to his finances through doing embroidery and sewing. Similarly, a young woman married in Delhi, made some money by sewing clothes for women who lived nearby. Her mother commented:

It is a matter of great shame to us that our daughter has to work. We regret arranging her marriage in Delhi. The trouble is that it is very expensive to find somewhere to live — and her husband does not own a house. A husband should be able to support his wife, but without her efforts they would find it very difficult. I hope we shall not have to marry our other daughters in Delhi, but so few good offers come these days.

These two women were compelled to perform work in their own homes to contribute to the household income, but generally, the proud objections of the *pirzada* women to working have not been compromised. Only one young woman briefly worked before her marriage, teaching in a small school for little girls within the village. There she taught reading and writing, as well as sewing. She told me about her parents' response:

They did not want me to take the job. But I persuaded them. I think that it is important that all the girls should be able to read — and many of the children from non-*pirzada* families would never go to school at all if it were not for this school so close. My father fortunately considers that education is important, so he has given me permission — but he is still not happy and is very ashamed that I am accepting any money for the work. I get Rs. 80/- per month. But please do not tell anyone here that I am paid for the work — that would bring great shame on my parents. You see, in the old days, children used to be sent to other *pirzada* homes to be taught to read by *pirzada* women: they would teach them Urdu and how to read the *Quran Sharif*, but they were not paid for this work. It was a work of love, and when a child had completed a reading of the *Quran Sharif*, its parents would send the teacher material for a suit and matching *duppatta*. That was considered honourable work for a *pirzada* woman to do — but she should never receive any money for it. That is the trouble with my work.

But all these women are exceptions. Apart from them, none of the *pirzada* women has any independent source of income — and even these three considered that their earnings were a matter of some shame. An honourable woman does not need to work for money: her menfolk will support her and provide for all her needs.

The *pirzada* women, then, consider that they are entitled to be maintained by the men, and the older women play an important role in ensuring that the young girls in their charge are directed to a destiny of dependent domesticity. It is they who train the girls, and it is they who said a girl should know everything about how to run a home. It is the older women who insisted that the girls learn domestic tasks from early childhood, so that they will be competent by the time their marriage is arranged. The following comment — from a woman with daughters aged 10 and 12, when I offered to clear up after lunch — is typical:

No, please don't do anything. I myself will do nothing today. When the girls are at school, I do most of the housework, but on their days off they help. I think it is very important that they should learn how to do things now — otherwise they will end up being good only for the *qurban* [ritual sacrifice].

Marriage and motherhood will be the destiny of all the young women, and it is important that their childhood training equips them for their marriages — and that their husband's income is such that they are not distracted from their domestic duties by work outside the home. Motherhood itself is an important and full-time job. Women create human beings, and men play very little part in this creative work. Well-behaved children are women's products, for women give children their character and teach them how to behave. Women have an important power of moulding the children in their charge, and this — for the *pirzada* women — is the primary and inescapable responsibility of women. The job is an honoured one, but it is such a time-consuming one (if it is done properly) that a woman's attention should not be diverted on to matters beyond the confines of her home. One elderly woman put it this way:

It is not that girls cannot learn to do other jobs, but I think it is a waste of money to keep a girl at school and college. Once she is married she will have the responsibility for her home and children — and a job outside the home would mean that she could not do it properly. No husband will help her out, and servants cheat so much that it is no benefit to the family if a woman takes a job. It is better that she stay at home and do her work herself.

Thus it is, then, that the *pirzada* women who bring up the children born to them provide a training for the girls which helps to perpetuate the *status quo*. Not just through their comments but also through the socialization which they provide for the *pirzada* girls, the older women forcefully indicate the degree to which they accept that girls should become dependent mothers.

The seclusion of women is one part of stratified social systems, such as are found in Eurasia, and it is particularly characteristic of the most privileged people at the upper end of the hierarchy. Several elements of the taken-for-granted world of the *pirzade* in Hazrat Nizamuddin provide the *pirzada* women with positive evaluations of themselves and their menfolk. Their ancestry is incomparable, and, while they are not the richest people in India, their livelihood from honourable priestly work is sufficient for the women to be maintained in respectable economic dependency throughout their lives, in such a way that they can concentrate on their vital task of bearing and rearing children. These elements, in building up the self-respect of the *pirzada* women, indicate the internalization by them of evaluations which — if only at some levels — are apparently in their interests. There are, however, other elements of the *pirzada* women's taken-for-granted world which represent the internalization of matters which seem prima facie to be against their interests.

In particular, I want to concentrate here on the ways in which women behave, especially when they are in the presence of men, and on the beliefs in the 'dirtiness' of women when they are menstruating or after childbirth. The forms of deference which the women employ in relation to men suggest the devaluation of women in comparison with men, and hint at their inferiority and lack of power. Further, the belief in the pollutions which women – but not men – suffer and the shame which attaches to them are important ways in which the *pirzada* women are persuaded of their own inferiority.

The whole process of internalization thus becomes extremely problematic. If people internalize ideas and modes of behaviour which appear to coincide with their interests, socialization may be blandly represented as 'the development in individuals of the commitments and capacities which are essential prerequisites of their future role-performance',[5] through the training and example which their elders present. But if people imbibe values which seem contrary to their interests, other questions need to be put. In particular, attention must be paid to the coercive dimension of socialization – even if that coercion is more subtle than economic power – and to the way in which power differentials can result in people being persuaded to hold views against their interests.[6] It is here that it is reasonable to talk of ideological subordination, because of the acceptance by the *pirzada* women of ideas which devalue and degrade them, of values which provide them with a negative self-image.

Modesty and Distancing

The *pirzade* consider that men and women should not mix freely, and there is general agreement among them about the complex idiom of 'body language' through which men and women separate themselves. A woman should be modest in demeanour and dress, and she should not chatter in a fashion which draws attention to herself or walk around with her eyes flitting from one object to another. There should be restraint and distancing between men and women, which is achieved through bodily concealment, avoidance of eye contact, and conversational distance, to degrees which vary according to the social and spatial context. In verbal expressions of what ought to be, and in the behaviour of the *pirzada* men and women in relation to one another, and the *pirzada* women in relation to outsiders, the parallels with the 'orthodox' Muslim position on the relationship between the sexes outlined in Chapter One are clear.

Two words keep cropping up in this connection: *izzat* – honour, dignity, reputation; and *sharm* – shame, modesty, bashfulness.[7] A woman who chatters too loudly will be criticized for being *be-sharm* or shameless; the woman who feels embarrassed when her son-in-law is visiting will say that *sharm ata hai* or 'shame comes'; a young girl who covers her head when her father enters the room will be praised for being *sharmanda* or *sharm-wali*, for being modest and 'ashamed'. Similarly the man, who is *izzat-wala* or honourable, will be respected by those around him. When a person is disgraced, when he suffers an affront to his political standing or when insulting comments are made about the modesty of his womenfolk, he is said to suffer a *be-izzat*. When the phrase *izzat lena* — to take a person's honour — is used with reference to women, it refers solely to the bodily dimension of ruining her honour by debauching her. The phrases *izzat rakhna* and *sharm rakhna* both mean to guard or preserve honour and can be used when a man accompanies his wife outside their home or when a young woman covers her head 'out of respect' for her father-in-law. These two notions of *izzat* and *sharm* are central to the perceptions of the *pirzade* about the right and proper way of conducting relationships between the sexes. *Izzat* can be best kept by distancing and by various forms of modesty behaviour — and that is just what the *pirzade* do in practice.

Bodily Concealment

A major idiom through which *izzat* is preserved and *sharm* demonstrated by the *pirzade* — and indeed throughout the Indian sub-continent — is through clothing. It is not unimportant that the Urdu word for woman — *aurat*   is derived from an Arabic root meaning 'blind' or 'concealed', from which the Arabic words for pudenda and private parts — 'those which ought to be concealed' — are also derived.[8] The *sharm-wali* woman keeps her body hidden in the presence of other people, and even in the company of other women she shows no more than her hands, feet and head.

The everyday wear of the *pirzada* women conforms to this requirement. It consists of a loose dress — the *qemiz* or *kurta* — which is worn over a baggy trouser-like garment, the *shalwar* or (by some of the older women) the *churidar pajama*, which look rather like jodhpurs. The dress is not made of flimsy or transparent material and a vest will be worn with cotton lawn to give extra concealment. Also, the dress does not fit tightly, and has sleeves at least to the elbows and the neckline close to the throat. The 'trousers' are always made from several metres of thick cotton. For all females, from the time of toilet training (before which a girl may be naked from the waist down) to old age, this is the standard style of dress. For special occasions, the women replace the *shalwar* or *churidar pajama* with the *sharara* or *ghyrara*, one a skirt-like garment, the other like very full trousers which completely hide the woman's form and trail along the floor behind her. Some young women occasionally wear a *sari*, but it is considered rather unsuitable, since the blouse generally has short sleeves, and the midriff may be exposed: not only is this rather improper for social interaction, but the concealment which a woman needs for prayer or reading the *Quran Sharif* cannot easily be achieved in a *sari*.

The dress and 'trousers' represent the basic minimum of bodily concealment which is required on all occasions. The *duppatta*, by contrast, is a garment with which the *pirzada* women constantly fidget and it is here that the more subtle nuances of body language come to the fore. The *duppatta* is a piece of chiffon material about two metres long and one metre wide, generally with some decoration sewn round the border. The concealment which it affords is considered vital by all the *pirzada* women, young and old. Without it, a woman is said to have 'naked breasts'. My own clumsy efforts to keep my *duppatta* in its proper place were met with favourable comment, and my mistakes patiently corrected because I had indicated that I wanted to 'be with us'. Any woman who does not cover herself properly with a *duppatta* can only expect to be dubbed *be-sharm* by the *pirzade.*

Even in the company of other women, the *duppatta* covers most of the top half of the body. During the preparations for the wedding referred to before, there was a game in which two old women masqueraded as a priest and his wife. The latter was actually in the business of *duppatta* theft. She stood in front of several women in turn, sang a plaintive ditty about being very poor, and then, with a darting movement, snatched off the *duppatta* before the woman could protect herself. At the end of the game each *duppatta* had to be ransomed for a trivial sum, which the women gratefully did. But in the interim, amidst all the frivolity and joking, the women deprived of their *duppatta* groped for the capes of the *burqa* which were hung around the room, so that they had something to hide their 'nakedness'.

Often, the *duppatta* has to cover the head too. It is important, for instance, when the call to prayer can be heard from a nearby mosque, or when a woman is praying or reading the *Quran Sharif.* Equally, there are certain people, particularly elders, to whom 'respect' must be shown by covering the head. One unmarried teenager told me:

We don't normally cover our heads in our mother's presence. She is close to us, and we are working with her all the time. But our grandmother says that we should cover our heads and so we do when she comes, or when other older women come to talk to our mother. It doesn't look nice then to have our heads bare.

The requirement to cover the head is more strictly observed with respect to men, particularly older kinsmen, whether father, father-in-law, husband, or husband's brother. One woman, married to her father's sister's son, told me:

When I'm working in the kitchen I always have a *duppatta* with me, even though it is a nuisance, because I can never know when my father-in-law will come in and I shall have to cover myself. It isn't just because I am a 'bride' though — my husband's sisters all cover their heads when their father comes in, out of respect for him.

Covering the head is important, for a woman's hair is one of her adornments, to which she should not draw attention through displaying it. In childhood a girl may have short hair, but once she is about ten, it is allowed to grow — never to be cut again, for it must be unbraided and used as an extra concealment for her breasts when she dies. The *pirzada* women mostly wear their hair with a central parting and a single plait. Immediately after washing it is anointed with fragrant oil which keeps every tress under control — unlike the loose and flowing locks of Western 'hippies' about which the women were so disdainful. Concealment of the hair is particularly strenuously observed when a woman prays: in preparing for prayer a woman is watchful lest any part of her plait or any curl at her temple strays from underneath her *duppatta.*

Gradually, while she is being taught to read the *Quran Sharif* and to pray, a girl learns to deal deftly with her *duppatta,* although she will only begin to wear it all the time when she approaches puberty. From early childhood she has seen the instant reactions of women, the flustered redraping of the *duppatta* when a man comes in, the brief halt in kneading the dough as a woman delicately pulls her *duppatta* over her head with her flour covered finger-tips because she has caught the strains of the call to prayer, the smoothing down over the midriff of a *duppatta* which has been pushed out of the way while a woman washes clothes. Subtly, the correct ways of dealing with the *duppatta* seep into the child — and the girl herself will be continually corrected in her behaviour, and will be told to wear her *duppatta*, sometimes even while learning the Urdu alphabet. By the time she is ten or so, wearing it will have become second nature to her.

Reserve and Diffidence

In dress, then, the *pirzada* women practise the sort of bodily concealment which is considered modest for a Muslim woman. But women may also be 'concealed' socially through their deportment, and through reserve in their relationships with men. Women — and especially young women — must be socially inconspicuous too.

Even in the company of women, the youngest and the unmarried do not take a major part in conversation, for the way to show 'respect' for older women is to avoid conversing freely with them. One young woman who accompanied me to 'see the face' of a new bride in the village was explicit about this. She stayed for only a few minutes and, as she left, whispered to me:

> You can stay if you wish to. But it wouldn't look nice for me to sit and just chat to the bride's mother-in-law and sisters-in-law, since they are so much older than I am. There used to be complete *purdah* between young girls and women from other houses — 'that's finished now, but it still isn't right for a girl of my age to sit among older women chatting freely.

On another occasion, this same woman talked about etiquette among the *pirzade:*

> If a woman comes to our house we all greet her, but conversation is left to our mother. When my older sisters were small, they used to be sent from the room — but now we remain, doing our sewing or any other work,

and we can speak a little. But it just doesn't look nice to say much — that is, unless our mother is not at home, when it would naturally look very rude if we did not entertain our guest properly.

But in mixed company, within the family, the reserve and diffidence of the young women is much more marked. With older men, her older brothers as well as her father, a young woman is even more reserved in conversation. Even a man and his wife should not behave intimately to one another in front of bystanders. The freest relationships between males and females are those between older women and their juniors, such as younger brothers, or the husband's young brothers. Such relationships are often marked by a cordiality and familiarity which would be considered shocking between a man and a younger woman. The most important exception to this general rule is the relationship between a woman and her son-in-law, which is marked by distance and restraint, or *sharm*. The young man always reminds his wife's mother of his responsibility for converting her modest and chaste daughter into a married woman. It is rare, in practice, for a man to visit his wife's parents' home, because he should protect his mother-in-law from the embarrassment of having to deal with him. One woman in her fifties told me how she always feels uneasy when her son-in-law visits her home:

You maybe think this is odd, since he is my husband's nephew and considered our house as his own until he was married to my daughter. He used to play with my sons — and of course at that time I thought nothing at all about it. But since his marriage, it is all different. It is a matter of shame that he is the husband of my daughter — and now I find it hard to do more than greet him. I'm too ashamed to sit in the same room when he comes here now.

Another woman of the same age made much the same comments about her own sons-in-law, and she went on to elaborate:

It's for that very reason that we do not like the *ghar jamai* [the son-in-law who lives in his in-laws' home], for how can the man and his mother-in-law keep proper respect for one another when they live in the same house? They'll be using the same latrine, eating meals together. We think such arrangements are disgraceful. I would never permit it. When my daughter was having trouble with her mother-in-law she begged me to let her move in with us along with her husband. But I couldn't agree to that — it would bring shame on our family.

Apart from this special case, the greatest reserve and distance is maintained by young women, since there are many *pirzada* men who are their elders: they talk in lowered tones, and, except for greetings (which the junior should initiate), only respond to conversation and instructions, quietly obey, and on no account refuse or demonstrate any disagreement. Many women only talk to men with their head somewhat bowed and their hand concealing their mouth. Another element of womanly modesty is eye *purdah* – *ankhon ka purdah* – or averting the eyes, which enables women to remain physically present while socially almost absent. Instead of leaving the room or sitting with her back to a man, a young woman can distance herself by lowering her gaze.

The maintenance of respect is not just a job for the women, though. Bodily concealment is important for men too, though there is no equivalent of the *duppatta* and the hiding of the face. The men always wear a thick cotton *pajama* and a shirt. Even in summer, they wear a vest underneath their cotton lawn shirts so that they are not improperly exposed. To show respect to the Saint and when they attend any mosque, men also cover their heads. However, a man only covers his face during his wedding, when a veil of flowers protects him from the 'evil eye', a common practice among Indian Hindus and Muslims.[9]

The boy who spends little time at home is praised for having 'learnt shame'. The home is the world of women, and not a suitable place for men and boys to dally in, beyond sleeping, washing and eating: the menfolk should show proper respect by spending little time there. Men and boys come into their own homes slowly and deliberately, with their eyes averted, so that the women have a chance to collect their wits and readjust their *duppatta*. It is also improper for a man to stare penetratingly at a woman, whether in his own household or in the street, for staring is an act of sexually charged aggression and attacks the honour of the woman who is its object. One woman, the mother of eleven grown children, praised her husband to me in these terms:

> He gives proper attention to preserving honour. He meets many women who come to the shrine. I am sure you have noticed the way he talks to you. He just glances briefly, and then looks away. That is very noble behaviour. Men should not stare at women, the way a lot of young men are doing these days. It is shameless, the way they look at women.

The New Bride
There are, then, several ways in which the *pirzada* men and women maintain both social and physical distance between the sexes. The exaggeratedly demure and passive behaviour of the new bride, her more striking concealment and silence, represents a caricature of the modesty which is appropriate for all women and girls. Nevertheless, for a few years and in a few contexts, she is permitted to indulge in decoration and display which are frowned upon in old women or unmarried girls, for the passive bride is also an ornament in the home of her husband.

Sufficient freedom of mixing to enable young men and women to make wise and personal choices about marriage partners would be abhorrent to the *pirzade*. Ideally young people cannot have the opportunity to develop attachments. Ideally – and generally in practice – the young couple, particularly the bride, take little interest in the impending marriage. Once the engagement has taken place, the girl keeps *purdah* from her future husband until the day of the wedding, even if they are closely related (for instance cousins) and she never observed *purdah* from him before.

When young people violate the norms, the shocked reactions of their elders indicate the tenacity with which they believe that young people should be uninvolved in their own marriages. Young men may visit the homes of their uncles and aunts, and two recent marriages between cousins were rumoured to have been instigated by the grooms themselves. In each case, my informants insisted that I should not name them, for such an allegation would cause great offence to the parties to the marriages. They were insistent, though, that the 'shame' of a 'love marriage' is so great that, in both cases, the boy's parents had arranged the match as if they themselves had had the initial idea; for public consumption, the ideal of the uninvolved bride and groom must be perpetuated. In similar vein was the response of one elderly woman when I told her how a young man had invited me to his own wedding: she considered him completely shameless.

Generally, though, the bride and groom behave as expected of them, and the girl's marginal role in the negotiations for her own marriage is echoed in her passive behaviour during her wedding. A few days before the wedding she is massaged by her female kin, and the groom's close female relatives come to her home the day before the wedding and ceremonially do her hair and dress her with garlands and jewellery, while she sits mute with her head bent. On the wedding day itself, she is heavily shrouded in an enormous thick *duppatta* and is guided in and out of the room, bent at the waist, by a female relative who grips her firmly across the forehead. Her consent to her marriage indicates no undue enthusiasm — a grunt or a nod suffices for the modest bride. Her husband has a brief look at her as they sit together under a large *duppatta*, but she sits with her eyes closed. She is helped to the sedan chair which carries her to her husband's home and once there, her husband lifts her out and carries her into the house. In the feeding of sweets which follows, she will be so shy that her hand needs to be guided to her husband's mouth while, in contrast, he lacks no confidence. For the first few days she hardly talks, and one of her female relatives accompanies her to her husband's home to see to all her needs. The day after the wedding, she is a passive object of display and admiration while her husband's relatives come to 'see her face': she sits in the centre of the room, shoulders bent and heavily veiled and silent. Her expressionless face, with her eyes closed and lips shut is briefly exposed to each visitor who comes.

Her demeanour on this first day after her marriage sets the tone for several days — or even weeks — to come. She continues to sit quietly, with her head bent, and although she gradually relaxes with her mother-in-law and her husband's sisters and younger brothers, it may be many months before she shows her face to her father-in-law or her husband's older brothers. One elderly woman told me she had not shown her face to her husband's father until her first child was born, a year after her marriage, and even then she still had to keep her head covered in his presence. Another woman of the same age — whose father-in-law was already dead at the time of her marriage — asked if I had not been surprised to see how silent an Indian bride has to be. But, she went on, things have changed quite a lot since the time of her marriage and today's bride will remain silent for only a few days — much to her disapproval:

> I kept my face hidden even from my husband for a month or so after we were married. I was so ashamed. But there's been such an increase in *be-sharmi* [shamelessness] in the last few years. Why, the brides of today can keep quiet for even as little as two weeks, only with difficulty.

A young woman who married into the village about ten years ago explained that much depends on who the bride is:

> I kept my face hidden from my husband's father for two years. Then he said that was enough, and so I just have to cover my head when he comes in. But the next bride who came into the house after me is a cousin of her husband, and so she only had to cover her face for three or four days at most. But she still covers her head when our father-in-law comes, of course.

The silence of the new bride is also part of being an object of display. Unmarried girls still rarely attend functions even when they take place in their own homes. They wear simple clothes and are rarely allowed to put on make-up. To be otherwise is 'shameless': an unmarried girl should not be publicly paraded or admired. For the new bride, all is different. She sits quietly, doing no housework, at least for some weeks, and is the centre of attention. She is permitted — even encouraged — to spend time over dressing and putting on make-up. Among her wedding gifts will probably be a vanity case fully stocked with items with which to beautify herself. Even when there is no festival, her mother-in-law will probably want to pamper her by having henna put on her hands and feet regularly. One young woman, for instance, explained why her oldest brother's wife could not play her role in 'dressing the bride' at the time of the next brother's wedding:

> You see, our oldest sister-in-law was still a bride herself; she had only been married for a month, so she could not do anything around the house, or do the jobs which she would now do in weddings when our other brothers are married. All she had to do was sit still and wear pretty clothes. It looks good for a bride to be dressed well: she'll wear satin clothes, generally of bright colours. Often they're things which have come in her dowry or in the gifts which her in-laws give at the time of the wedding. My mother is so happy to have two brides in the house that she tries to persuade them to put henna on their hands and feet all the time, to show her happiness.

Even after her children are born, the bride is expected to bring honour to her in-laws by still wearing her finery. Women from other households will be able to admire her – and confirm that her in-laws have made a wise choice. But gradually, as her children grow up, she will become less showy in her dress. She will wear less bright colours, she will wear cotton in preference to satin when she attends weddings, she will cease to wear make-up. One woman, for instance, refused to wear the orange *duppatta* which her sister had bought: 'I couldn't wear such a bright colour. What would people say? It doesn't suit for a grandmother to dress like that'.

Several women felt that they should dress more simply once their own daughters have reached puberty. By the time a woman has daughters-in-law living in her home, and especially when she has been widowed, her dress will be very simple and underplay her sexuality. One woman in her early thirties pointed out how she feels she should dress more simply (because she has a teenage daughter) while other people consider that she is still young enough to be dressing like a 'bride':

Now that my daughter is big [has reached puberty] it looks very bad for me to wear shiny materials. My husband would still like me to, but I don't feel comfortable. People criticize me if I don't wear make-up when I go to weddings. They ask me if I am so old! There isn't any definite feeling that a woman should wear different clothes when she has a daughter-in-law, but a lot of women do, if they haven't already changed. We sometimes call an old woman who wears make-up a *heejra* [eunuch, generally transvestite] because it doesn't look nice.

One thing which will never change, though, is the bride's deportment towards her father-in-law and the older brothers of her husband. For the first few months or weeks, they may never see her face, but even after that period has passed,she will continue to cover her head when they are present, and she will always behave with the utmost 'respect' towards them – never initiating conversation and always lowering her head and gaze. She will never behave freely in front of her husband's older male kin, even if they had been related to her before her marriage. With her husband, too, she should always behave respectfully. He is her *miyan* and *khawynd* (master and lord). She will never call him by name, even when he is absent: she will refer to him as 'they' (*vo*) or, once children have been born, as 'so-and-so's father'. If she wants him to do something for her, she can never call out to him, she has to send some-one to fetch him. And when she talks to him, she will address him as *ap* (you, respectful) while he responds with *tum* (you, familiar).

Dealing with Unrelated Men

Just as the new bride's behaviour accentuates the requirements of womanly modesty, so too are the restraint, diffidence and bodily modesty which a woman shows before unrelated men heightened. Often the whole issue is evaded, for the *pirzada* women are rarely put into situations where they must deal with men who are not relatives. A woman mostly remains in her home: modesty and respect cannot be maintained if she goes out often. While permission may be given for women to make occasional trips to buy cloth at a *bazar* or to visit relatives in Delhi, this is infrequent, certainly no more than once a week, and generally less often than that. Some women — mainly elderly ones — leave the village no more than a couple of times in the year, and they rarely even visit the homes of other *pirzade* in the village.

Until about 1947, the *pirzada* women were rarely confronted with outside men. Shopkeepers in the *bazar* beyond the village stopped strange men from entering. If, perchance, a stranger found his way inside the village and knocked on a door, the women said that they would not even have answered him through the door, let alone opened it or let him inside. Even today, some women still do this, but they generally have someone else at home who answers for them. Young servant girls may be expected to find out a man's business on behalf of their mistresses. In other homes unmarried daughters may deal with callers. One such girl commented to me:

> My sister is very old-fashioned. Her husband tells her to answer the door, in case there is some important business — but she often takes so much time taking courage that people usually go away before she says anything. Our mother is like that too — she cannot bring herself to go to the door if anyone comes. So she sends me or my sisters to ask what the business is. But she does not let us show our faces.

Even malaria inspectors — checking that houses do not contain stagnant water which could be mosquito breeding grounds — are not necessarily allowed access. One elderly woman was scornful about government policy on this:

> They used to be considerate to us, and take into account that we *pirzade* women live in *purdah*. For several years they used to send quite young boys to each house to spray with DDT. That was good for us. But last year, they sent an adult man — and of course we couldn't let him come in as none of our men were at home. That is very cruel of the government. Do they want us all to catch malaria?

Only under exceptional circumstances do unrelated men enter the homes of the *pirzade*, and their arrival always puts the household into disarray. Workmen may have to come to make structural repairs or install 'flush' toilets, or there may be male 'guests' who need to be housed. Screens and curtains are erected, the women are banished to a room or to the roof and may be trapped there if the 'guests' or workmen hang around; and when the 'guests' are out, the women listen for the sound of approaching steps or the slight clearing of the throat which means that the men are returning and that they must hurriedly fasten doors and retreat into their restricted privacy. After some months, even I had begun to accept this behaviour. Once a workman delivered sand and the women fled inside and barred the door, leaving me stranded in full view. Another time some 'guests' walked in with little warning and the woman I was talking to burrowed under a blanket and left me exposed, and confused about my own feelings of embarrassment. But such intrusions into the normally private domain of the women are rare — simple repairs may be done by household members, and the *pirzada* men conduct most of their business outside their homes.

Sometimes, however, the women leave their homes. Then they are expected to be even more demure than at home, and also more concealed. There are differences of opinion about the necessity of the *burqa,* rather than an all-engulfing shawl, but there is agreement that a woman should not draw attention to herself when she is outside her home. She should not behave in an eye-catching fashion, and — if she is not wearing a *burqa* — she should at least keep her head bent, her eyes averted and be properly 'ashamed'.
Even those who question the necessity of the *burqa,* say that when a woman wears one she should only choose dull colours, and she should keep the veils over her face, rather than tossed back over her head. All the *pirzada* women over the age of twenty-five — and many of the younger women too — wear the *burqa,* and for them, the concealment has to be total. One woman of about thirty told me:

> When we go out in a *burqa,* we always wear it with both veils down. But even that is not really enough. My aunt, for instance, always takes a quick peep out of her door before she leaves the house, and if there is any man in sight, she does not come out until he has passed. And my mother is very friendly with her cousin's wife, but she only visits them after dark as they live near the *bazar* and she would not like anyone to see her features. For myself, I also feel shame when I go out: if there is a man walking in the street, then I get very embarrassed.

The *pirzada* women — young and old — condemned the immodesty of the Western hippies whom they had seen around the streets of Delhi. The following are comments from two young women, one still in her teens and the other in her twenties:

> I'm disgusted at the way some of these foreign women dress. They are so shameless. They walk around with their heads uncovered, and with long hair flying loose. And they wear dresses with such low necklines. And the cloth they choose is so thin that you can see everything through it. I really don't know why they bother to wear clothes!

> I saw one woman recently who was wearing a skirt which only went half-way down her shins, and it was badly faded. And she was wearing cheap sandals. But by the look of her face, she seemed a person who could have afforded to dress decently. What I particularly dislike are women who wear patched trousers. Trousers show up the body too much. But the patches look dreadful. It makes them look just like a *faqir ki goodri* [patched cloak which mendicants wear] and that looks very bad for a

woman to dress that way, if she can afford to dress properly.

Local women are also criticized sometimes: the girl who wears a tight blouse without a *duppatta,* or the young woman with her gauzy *sari* perched provocatively on her hips is censured for being *be-sharm.*

In sum, then, the behaviour of the *pirzada* women — and their reactions to the 'shamelessness' of other people — indicate how they have internalized notions of modesty and the importance of maintaining distance and separation between the sexes. The women unquestioningly accept that they should not talk loudly or draw attention to themselves by dressing gaudily or scantily. Men and women should not mix freely. The modest woman rarely leaves her home. And in mixed company within the home, women should be reserved and signal in numerous ways their respect, especially for older men. In their behaviour, the *pirzada* women continually draw attention to their submissiveness.

Polluting Women

The biological differences between men and women are also considered important by the *pirzade* and particular stress is laid on the pollutions which women suffer during menstruation and after childbirth.

Few of the Muslim writers who discuss the position of women in Islam give more than passing mention to the question of menstrual and post-partum pollutions. Khurshid Ahmad does not even mention them at all, and Maududi only briefly comments that menstruating women may not pray and suggests that this is one reason why women should not pray in public in a mosque, since their periodic absences would draw attention to their condition. Nevertheless, Islamic doctrine is clear that there are several bodily functions — including urination, defaecation and sexual intercourse — which are considered to pollute men and women alike.[10]

Pollutions may be minor or serious. Minor pollutions (such as caused by urination) can be removed by the ritual ablution or *wuzu,* but major pollution (such as caused by sexual intercourse) can only be removed by complete bathing or the *ghusl.* These purifications are the same for men and women and people may not pray, go to a mosque or read or touch the *Quran Sharif* until the pollution is removed. The pollutions of menstruation and childbirth are considered major, and a woman remains impure until she has performed the full cleansing bath.

There are complex definitions of menstruation or *haiz* and puerperal discharge or *nifas,* which delimit the time when a woman is 'polluted' rather than just 'bleeding'. For instance, the maximum time for *nifas* is 40 days, though it may be much less, and any bleeding after 40 days is not considered to be polluting.[11] Until a woman has cleansed herself by bathing, there are several restrictions on her activities, and failure to obey such injunctions is believed to result in various ailments or other punishments.

Among the *pirzade,* a woman's normal household duties are all permissible to her during her periods of pollution — she cooks, sews and cleans as usual, there are normally no restrictions on her movements within her home, and she does not eat separately from the rest of the family.[12] Some women, however, talked of sleeping separately from their husbands so that they could easily get up in the middle of the night to wash. For the duration of her pollution, however, she may not have sexual intercourse: this can only be resumed after her cleansing bath.

Most of the restrictions on a woman's activities relate directly to matters of *ibadat* or worship, to matters of religion — *mazhab ki bat* — rather than matters of custom — *riwaj ki bat.* Thus a woman, when she is polluted, may attend a wedding but she may not participate in those parts of it when passages are recited from the *Quran Sharif.* Likewise, she does not enter a mosque or shrine. She does not read or touch the *Quran Sharif,* and to protect the holy book from pollution of this and other sorts, most families wrap their copy in a cloth which is only removed by a person who has performed ablutions. Pious Muslims say that they like to make a complete reading of the *Quran Sharif* during the month of Ramzan, but many of the *pirzada* women find that they are unable to do so because of their polluted state. At most, a menstruating woman may help children to read the *Quran Sharif,* provided that she herself does not recite whole verses. She may not touch any coin, dish or amulet which has a Quranic verse on it, unless — like the *Quran Sharif* itself — it is covered.

Dutiful Muslims fast during the month of Ramzan, each day from just before dawn until sunset. If a polluted woman chooses not to eat or drink, her fast cannot be counted. Fasts which she misses during Ramzan should be made up later. The *pirzada* women said that Thursday and Friday are considered good days for doing this, and they gradually catch up their lost fasts after the end of Ramzan. A polluted woman may not pray either, but she may continue to set aside the prayer times for pious rather than worldly activities, by performing minor ablutions and just quietly reciting the name of Allah.

There are other restrictions which the *pirzada* women also observe. Through their connection with the shrine they are sometimes required to make sweetmeats which are blessed and distributed. A menstruating woman cannot, however, prepare sweetmeats for such purposes, and, as several of the *pirzada* women pointed out, a woman who is not living in a large household is often put in a difficult position. She may have to call on a relative to do the work for her: the absence of a contribution from her household would be a matter of shame, since attention would necessarily be drawn to her condition. One woman said that she has always been punctilious when she or her daughters are preparing sweets for the shrine, for on one occasion she cooked sweetmeats while she was menstruating and they caught fire as she was stirring them. No other woman admitted to having taken the risk. Polluted women may not consume any sweetmeats which have been prepared for a festival or, say, for the fulfilment of a vow. The only exception of which the women told me is when readings are made from books which tell of events during the Prophet Muhammad's life: menstruating women may attend and consume the sweets, but they do not take part in the reading itself.

Women may not take any part in sewing new drapes for the tombs of Hazrat Nizamuddin and Amir Khusro when they are polluted. They may not touch any of the items to be used, or enter the room where the preparations are being made. There are also restrictions during the month of Moharram. Menstruating women cannot perform the optional fast during the first ten days of the month, nor may they participate in the domestic and other rituals when sweets and drink are blessed. Most particularly, they may have no contact with the *taziya* − the replicas of the tombs of the martyrs − which some households prepare. They are not involved in any of the preparations, and they cannot enter the room which has been set aside for the *taziya*. The *pirzada* women recounted several cases which − to them − provided incontrovertible evidence for the dangers of disobeying the injunctions laid down for them. For instance, just as a barren woman might conceive after touching a *taziya* during Moharram, so − I was told − did a polluted woman, who accidentally touched a *taziya,* continue to menstruate for several extra days until she had made a special prayer and an offering of sweets.

Menstruation is a matter of embarrassment to the *pirzada* women. Partly, it is a question of cleanliness and the problems of disposal of the soiled pads made from scraps of cloth left from their sewing. These are considered so polluting that the *pirzada* women cannot clean them themselves. That is a task for the sweeper women, who take them away, and remove the pollution of the *pirzada* women for them. But the sheer inconvenience of menstruation is far outweighed by the notions of 'shame' which surround it. There are no puberty ceremonies for girls and nothing is done to draw attention to a girl's first menstruation. In private, her mother may say that the girl has become *bari* or big, or that she 'has begun to bathe', but no further note is taken of the change in the girl's condition.

Until she reaches the menopause, there will be periodic recurrences of her polluted condition. When she menstruates, she will describe herself as *gandi* or dirty, as *na-pak* or impure. Other women in the household will know of her condition, for it may affect the work which she can do around the house, and once she is married her husband will have to be informed − but menstruation is not something to be broadcast, and the *pirzada* women do their utmost to conceal their condition. Several women said that they perform a semblance of a fast during Ramzan − even knowing that they would have to catch up after the end of the month − rather than let their condition become public knowledge. It is all such a matter of embarrassment. Rather than fail to send out shares of sweetmeats, a woman should ask a sister to make some for her − otherwise the entire *pirzada* population would understand her condition. I was even told of the tradition from the early days of Islam when the Prophet Muhammad chided his daughter Fatima for being late in saying her prayers. She was menstruating, but too ashamed to admit it, and when the Prophet guessed her reason he instructed her always to apply henna to her hands and eet as a sign to him, so that he would never again confront her with her shame. The *pirzada* women do not put henna on for this reason, but they are just as ashamed as Fatima was, and just as prepared to hide their condition from others, whenever they can.

Pregnancy and lactation are not polluting conditions. After childbirth, though, a woman is polluted for up to 40 days – a condition which cannot be concealed. A woman who has just borne a child is subject to all the restrictions which apply to a menstruating woman, but, in addition, she does not wear any new clothes or leave the confines of the house where she has given birth until the pollution is over. This seclusion is called the *chilla,* a word connected with the term for 40, which refers to the special purifying bath which a woman takes about 40 days after she has given birth. Only then can she resume her normal activities. Among the *pirzade,* the first thing which a woman does is go to the shrine with her baby and several family members. Sweets are blessed and divided into portions which are shared among the *pirzade* of the different Families, and the child is placed on the threshold of the Saint's tomb chamber and then taken to 'Allah's house', that is, the mosque.

Thus, menstruating women, and women who have recently given birth, are faced with several limitations on their activities and movements. The *pirzada* women believe menstruation and puerperal discharge to be extremely polluting and they consider themselves contaminated by a 'dirtiness' that can only be removed by complete bathing. None of the *pirzada* women ever questioned these restrictions on their own activities, and they believe that the woman who fails to observe the injunctions laid down for her puts her own well-being in danger.

In the anthropological literature, pollutions of this sort – particularly menstrual pollutions – are generally considered to reveal something about the relationship between the sexes in the society in question. In their survey Young and Bacdayan, for instance, argue that menstrual pollutions reflect degradation of women and their separation from men.[13] In the sample which they examined, they found that such pollutions were particularly characteristic of 'rigid' societies, societies in which there is a lack of communication between parts of the social system – in this case a cleavage between men and women – where men are dominant and have their own exclusive male activities, and where there is strong orthodox religion and authoritarian leadership.

Similarly, Mary Douglas considers pollution beliefs in general, and suggests that they may emphasize social distinctions and the obligations attached to them, as well as frightening people into conformity.[14] Menstrual pollutions may be symbolic statements, of which two types seem particularly worth bearing in mind in relation to the *pirzada* women. On the one hand, they may assert male superiority, through the association of women with dirt and impurity. Secondly, menstrual pollutions may emphasize the separateness of male and female spheres, by limiting the intrusion of women into the affairs of men.

Menstrual pollutions, then, seem to have something to do with male superiority and with the separation between the sexes. But there is, maybe, more to them than this. Research by Jean Allan takes account of some recent developments in economic and feminist anthropology.[15] She is concerned with the relationship between ideology and the means of production, rather than just the level of ideas and symbolism. Women play an important role in reproduction and maybe also in production, but in many societies women have little control over their own reproductive capacities or over production. Allan suggests that menstrual pollutions are associated with contexts where women are controlled by men despite their crucial roles, and she sees menstrual pollutions as one ideological means of coping with this. By degrading women in comparison with men, by separating them from the world of the men, their vital roles may be masked.

This perspective is useful in viewing the *pirzada* women. The preceding two chapters have looked at the women's position, at their exclusion from the shrine and their economic powerlessness, and at their crucial role in bearing and rearing children for their husbands' lines. When the *pirzada* women are 'dirty' they must not endanger the purity of holy things. Religious tasks — prayer, fasting, reading the *Quran Sharif,* entering a mosque, and performing the pilgrimage to Mecca — are forbidden them. But more poignant and more striking for the *pirzada* women is the separation of 'dirty' women from all things connected with the shrine. They may not touch the drapes for the Saints' tombs, prepare or consume sweetmeats for the shrine, go near the replica tombs during Moharram, or enter the shrine itself. Their 'pollution' would endanger the holy world of the men — and the source of their liveli-hood. Moreover, even sexual intercourse which is one of a wife's most important obligations to her husband, is prohibited while a woman is 'dirty'. Her fecundity is crucial and her biological nature essential for the perpetu-ation of her husband's line, and yet elements of it are considered 'dirty' and shameful and necessitate her separation from her husband. Degradation and separation both figure in the menstrual and post-partum pollutions of the *pirzada* women, and form an important part of their subordination.

Ideological Subordination

To a large extent, people cannot select out elements of their culture to internalize. The taken-for-granted world comes as a package, and individuals have little freedom to pick and choose, or to accept and reject. The *pirzada* women have been confronted with and have internalized elements of a culture which simultaneously devalues them and elevates them. On the one hand, in the complex forms of modesty behaviour, avoidance and diffidence (through which they display their respect for older men), and in the pollutions of menstruation and childbirth, attention is drawn to their inferiority, to their deference and lack of power, to their separation from the world of men, and to the 'dirtiness' which being female entails. On the other hand, the culture internalized has its benefits as well as its costs. The *pirzada* women are Syed in their own right, and they partake of the special qualities which their connection with the Prophet of Islam implies. And yet even these positive elements contain their own ambiguities and shadows. Adherence to pride in their Syed ancestry also involves accepting – as the *pirzada* women do – that women do not give pedigree, that men and not women give 'blood', and that lines can only be perpetuated through men. Pride of birth carries with it the acknowledgement of women's genealogical irrelevance. Moreover, belief in their own excellence of ancestry sets the *pirzade* apart from and above other people, and the self-importance of the *pirzada* women makes it improbable that they will perceive any interest in common with the mass of Indian womankind.

They are, after all, not only superior in ancestry. The *pirzada* men perform honourable work, the women can normally expect to be maintained throughout their lives, and motherhood is an honoured role in which they can find pride. It is a sign of happiness that a married woman ornaments herself with bracelets, earrings and a nose stud, for she demonstrates thereby that her husband is alive. The removal of her ornaments when she is widowed is a dramatic display of her grief at losing her role of dependent wife. Dependence on a husband is the only proper fate for a respectable woman. But the training for dependency and domesticity which girls receive narrows their options. Dependent motherhood may be an honourable destiny, but it is also the only one open to the *pirzada* girls. For a woman to work outside the home is a disgrace – but the economic powerlessness of women is the mainstay of the *purdah* system among the *pirzade.* Dependency implies seclusion, and an existence to which the *pirzada* women are *not* wholeheartedly committed, as we shall see in the chapter that follows.

References

1. On caste among Muslims see I. Ahmad (ed.), *Caste and Social Stratification Among Muslims,* (Delhi, 1973); Z. Khan, 'Caste and the Muslim Peasantry in India and Pakistan', *Man in India,* 48 (1968), pp.133-48; L. Dumont, *Homo Hierarchicus,* (London, 1972), p.98.

2. W.S. Blunt, *The Caste System of Northern India,* (Cambridge, 1931); W. Crooke (ed.), *Islam in India,* (London, 1921); M.H. Ali, *Observations on the Mussulmauns of India,* 2 vols.,(London, 1832); R. Levy, *An Introduction to the Sociology of Islam,* 2 vols., (London, 1931-3), vol. 1, chapter 1.

3. For translations of these terms, see J. Platts, *A Dictionary of Urdu, Classical Hindi and English,* (London, 1911).

4. For more information on the men's disputes, see my paper 'Creating a Scene: The Disruption of Ceremonial in a Sufi Shrine', forthcoming in I. Ahmad (ed.), *Ritual and Religion Amongst Muslims in India* (New Delhi).

5. T. Parsons, *Social Structure and Personality,* (Glencoe, 1964), p.130.

6. On ideological subordination, see S. Harding, 'Women and Words in a Spanish Village', in R.R. Reiter (ed.), *Toward an Anthropology of Women*, (New York, 1975), pp.283-308; and more generally, in P. Bourdieu and J. Passeron, *Reproduction in Education, Society and Culture*, (London, 1977).
7. Platts, *op. cit.*, pp.725 and 761.
8. *Ibid.*, p.766.
9. For other aspects of the evil eye, see below in Chapter Six.
10. K. Ahmad, *Family Life in Islam*, (Leicester, 1974); S.A.A. Maududi, *Purdah and the Status of Women in Islam*, (Lahore, 1972), p.208; *Encyclopaedia of Islam*, (new edn.), (Leiden and London, 1960- vol.1, p.1013; vol.2, pp.167 and 187; vol.4, p.1140.
11. A.A. Thanwi, *Bahishti Zewar*, 2nd. ed. (revised and enlarged) (Delhi, 1975), pp.69-80; Platts, *op. cit.*, pp.438 and 1144; V.R. and L. Bevan Jones, *Woman in Islam*, (Lucknow, 1941), p.283.
12. In many parts of India, menstruating women may not do their normal cooking.
13. F. Young and A. Bacdayan, 'Menstrual Taboos and Social Rigidity', *Ethnology*, 4 (1965), pp.225-40.
14. M. Douglas, *Implicit Meanings*, (London, 1975), especially pp.61-3.
15. J. Allan, *Menstrual Restrictions and Production and Reproduction*, (M.Sc. thesis, University of Edinburgh, 1977), especially pp.1-10 and 36-45.

Crocheting at home

5. Complaining and Complying: the tribulations of life at home

If the men's control over the economic resources at the shrine and the women's acceptance of the *status quo* were all that could be said about the perpetuation of *purdah* among the *pirzade,* the situation could be summarized very briefly. The seclusion of the *pirzada* women could be seen as part of a closed system, overflowing with feedback mechanisms which reinforce the present position of the women. It would merely suffice to point to the economic power of the men and the success with which the socialization process has managed to persuade the men and women alike of the justice — even the naturalness — of the social order of which they are part. The overwhelming impression would be of a stable, self-perpetuating social system with little room for change, at least from within, of a system characterized by the subordination of women and their acceptance of that subordination. It might then seem plausible to view the *pirzada* women as pawns, as pathetic victims, wafted and buffeted by pressures which they cannot withstand.

But the matter is much more complex. There are loose ends. In particular, there is the insubordination of some of the *pirzada* women, the complaints which they make about their lot, the subterfuges in which they indulge to avoid reprimands. These women are no mere pawns. Thus, to broach the question of the *burqa* with them, or just to raise the issue of arranged marriages or family planning, even trying to collect genealogies was likely to trigger off a cascade of grievances. The ideological subordination of these women appears to be far from complete.

The complaints which the *pirzada* women make are rather hard to assess. They form the substance of this and the next chapter and thus it is important to indicate something of the context in which they were generated. It is certainly relevant to remember that the *pirzada* women had some idea — like most Indians — of what to expect from, and what to assume about, a white woman. They know, for instance, that there is no *purdah* in Britain. They have occasionally seen white women in the streets of Delhi, and sometimes foreign women come to the shrine for the Sufi leader Inayat Khan — who was one of those who brought Sufism to the West — chose to be buried on the outskirts of the village of Hazrat Nizamuddin. Of course, in many respects, I hardly fitted the stereotypes which the *pirzada* women held of Western women, for I always made a point of dressing 'modestly' — even though I did not wear a *burqa* — and of covering my head with a *duppatta* when talking to men or visiting the shrine. Nevertheless, the *pirzada* women clearly presumed that I was no advocate of *purdah:* by their conspiratorial tones they seemed to assume that I would not report to the men about what they said, and — judging from my invitation to tell me about their lives and their customs — I had apparently little else to do but lend a compassionate ear.

However, the complaints made by the *pirzada* women — while made in the presumption of a sympathetic reception — were not made solely because of my presence. I did not ask for complaints about seclusion. Indeed my research was not planned to cover such matters. Rather, it was in pursuit of my original intentions that the complaints of the women kept being thrown up, and almost kept obstructing my way. Conversations which I tried to keep to certain questions — how they assessed the eligibility of a potential bride, or the details of gifts exchanged during weddings — would be diverted, and run in another direction, quite out of my control. I had no need to ask leading questions on *purdah:* the women were brimming over with their own responses to their lives in seclusion.

On many occasions I took little part in conversations, but just let the women follow a train of thought among themselves. The chuckle from a woman whose daughter has just been chided for hiding away "as if she is in her in-laws' home", a comment which precipitates a serious comparison between the calm life of the beloved daughter before marriage and the harassed existence of the bride; the three young women excitedly interrupting one another in their eagerness to recount the tiniest details of the strict seclusion which was the fate of one of their aunts when she married; the knowing looks, the assenting gestures when someone expostulates about the nuisance of having to wear a *burqa:* all this suggests that the women were giving vent to opinions which they had often expressed before. The complaints appeared to be as much a part of their taken-for-granted world as their assumption that their pedigree is superior to that of all Muslims who are not Syed, or that menstruating women are 'dirty' and can endanger themselves by careless deeds. It is not that all the women complained to the same degree or about the same features of their situation; as I shall indicate in the final chapter, the *pirzada* women are not united in their opposition to *purdah*. Older women and their juniors often — though not always — take different stances. But in their complaints to me, the *pirzada* women always ensured that their audience only included other *pirzada* women whose views matched their own.

The very spontaneity of the women's comments, the way in which their complaints were so often asides — unsolicited by me — made during conversations about apparently unrelated topics, their discussions with one another in my presence, all indicate that there is something more in the complaints than just things which they thought I might want to hear.

But if complaints now form part of the taken-for-granted world of many *pirzada* women, does this mean that they are long-standing positions about the question of *purdah,* or are they notions which have only arisen in recent years? This is very difficult to assess. For the *pirzada* women there are no historical records which could shed any light on this question. Further, there are few indications about the feelings of women living in *purdah* elsewhere and at other times. Women affected by *purdah* have been rendered as silent through the ages as they have been invisible. There is only a handful of scattered reports which can give any impression of how women in *purdah* have reacted to their secluded lives in times past, and they all concern very wealthy women, whose seclusion is in spacious quarters and whose chores are greatly relieved by servants. One early report from a British woman married to a north Indian Muslim in the second quarter of the nineteenth century is about the wealthy families of Lucknow to whom her marriage gave privileged access. Her account of the houses and servants — and her passing comment that the least costly of the women's shoes were of gold embroidery on velvet — indicates that these were among the most wealthy families of the city.[1] On the whole, her assessment is favourable. She had expected that conversation with the women would be insipid, but found that the men conveyed a great deal of information to the women and that the women were 'fond of conversation, shrewd in their remarks':

> At first I pitied the apparent monotony of their lives; but this feeling has worn away by intimacy with the people, who are thus precluded from mixing generally with the world. They are happy in their confinement . . . As the bird from the nest immured in a cage is both cheerful and contented, so are these females . . . To ladies accustomed from infancy to confinement this is by no means irksome . . . the Mussulmaun ladies, with whom I have long been intimate, appear to me always happy, contented, and satisfied with the seclusion to which they were born; they desire no other, and I have ceased to regret they cannot be made partakers of that freedom of intercourse with the world we deem so essential to our happiness, since their health suffers nothing from that confinement . . . They are educated from infancy for retirement, and they can have no wish that the custom should be changed, which keeps them apart from the society of men, who are not very nearly related to them. Female society is unlimited, and that they enjoy without restraint.[2]

She makes it clear that she was not in favour of the bride and groom being 'passive subjects to the parental arrangements', and she points to the problems that poor people have in meeting the expenses of marrying their daughters. She was surprised at the extent of the women's ignorance about the appearance of fruit and vegetables while they are growing. But she was generally pleasantly impressed with the secluded women she met.[3]

Towards the end of the nineteenth century a British woman journalist visited India determined to present an unprejudiced picture of Indian women for her newspaper. She commented: '. . . life as I saw it in the zenanas was simply rather dull, rather prosaic, with few distinctive features of romance, hardship, or heroism about it.'[4] Conversation with two young women suggested to her that the restraints of *purdah* were not resented. They told her that they considered they lost little by living in *purdah:* they kept a little distance from men willingly, they had no desire to go out in the streets, and they could enjoy family parties.[5]

Similarly, Frieda Hauswirth Das, married to an Indian and herself no apologist for *purdah,* tells of a visit to a large house in Delhi in about 1930. The women had spacious quarters, and after talking to them she could not see them as 'purdah-martyrs', for she felt they were fulfilled and contented women: 'This showed zenana and family life at its best, with all its rare but actual possibilities of wide sheltering security and loving peace, of fostering a happy serene expansion untroubled by material worries.'[6]

But, at the same time, she was an ardent critic of the way women in seclusion become preoccupied with bodily adornment, how they are encouraged in their mental stultification by men who persuade them that virtuous women do not seek knowledge, and how their position in the family into which they marry depends on their giving birth to sons and only improves significantly after the sons reach adulthood and are married.[7] But what women themselves thought of all this at the time is unclear.

Katherine Mayo, whose book *Mother India* was first published in 1927 shortly before Das', and which caused a storm of controversy over its sensational concentration on child marriage and the fate of widows, quoted opposing responses from women she met at a *'purdah* party':

> You find it difficult to like our *purdah*. But we have known nothing else. We lead a quiet, peaceful and protected life within our own homes. And, with men as they are, we should be miserable, terrified, outside.[8]

Another of the women present had been to Britain and had had a difficult time adjusting to life behind *purdah* again:

> But here — here there is nothing. I must stay within the *zenana*, keeping strict *purdah*, as becomes our rank, seeing no one but the women and my husband. We see nothing. We know nothing. We have nothing to say to each other. We quarrel. It is *dull*. But they, [nodding surreptitiously toward the oldest woman] will have it so . . . And they know how to make life horrible for us in each household, if we offer to relax an atom of the *purdah* law. [9]

Jones and Jones, writing some ten years later than Mayo, also suggest that there is a variety of responses to seclusion. Older and orthodox women are likely to oppose a relaxation of *purdah* and women living in seclusion often claim that they lose little through their restrictions, for they have the companionship of women and of male relatives: 'Seclusion has been so bred into them and woven into their habits of life that women of this type do not feel *parda* to be a hardship. They neither resent it nor see any reason to abandon it.'[10]

There are plenty of critics of the bad effects of seclusion in 'dark, damp and small houses'[11] on the physical and intellectual well-being of women, and there are many who claim that seclusion is not even required by Islam, even that it is un-Islamic in spirit. Nevertheless, Jones and Jones argue, the 'modernists' who are discarding the veil are still outnumbered by those adopting it as a sign of respectability. The poor and illiterate may be as much advocates of *purdah* as the wealthy and orthodox.[12]

It is perhaps not realistic to expect that such scattered reports would throw up a clear-cut impression of the attitudes of Indian women to *purdah*. Generally, foreign women have had access only to women of the most wealthy families, and *purdah* itself is extremely variable. Seclusion in spacious apartments with access to the open air within the compound, and in the company of others — women, relatives and servants — is one thing. But seclusion of the less affluent, struggling all the while to maintain appearances, may be quite another. It may mean real damage to a woman's health, through seclusion in high, shaded buildings giving little access to sunlight to those living on the ground floor (this is characteristic of Old Delhi). And in the absence of servants and a large company of related women, it may also be a rather lonely existence in which the restraints on movements beyond the home appear as real hardships.

The available material does not permit any firm conclusions about the antiquity or generality of the complaints which the *pirzada* women make. That complaints do not predominate in the historical accounts quoted above, or indeed in the more recent ethnographic material about India, may merely reflect the very limited access to women living in *purdah*, which has been achieved by observers, whether male or female. It could be that women have had plenty to complain about through the ages — but that their complaints have never been heard outside the walls of their homes. This would imply that women have accepted the propriety of their position only within limits, and that the maintenance of *purdah* has long depended on compelling women to act in ways which they dislike. A particular feature of such a situation may well be that the adolescent straining at the leash becomes the elderly martinet insisting that her juniors behave in ways which she herself used to detest, because she is now held responsible for their deportment. Have the complaints been there for a long while? Or are the differences among the women attributable simply to shifts of opinion which each woman makes as she moves into different positions in the household, from marriageable daughter to new bride, from young mother to elderly matron with several women under her charge? This does not seem likely to be the case.

There are good reasons to suggest that the *pirzada* women have learnt to be dissatisfied with their lot only fairly recently. Even 50 years ago, those who questioned the legitimacy of secluding women were a tiny number. For most groupings in Indian society, the seclusion of women was considered an unassailable assertion of respectability. Those families who were able to keep their women in *purdah* were widely revered by those who could not. But a great deal has changed in recent times.

Reform movements within Islam and many other social changes now mean that the seclusion of women is under attack from several directions. Its appropriateness for India today is widely — though not everywhere — subjected to reappraisal. Women from wealthy families often no longer live in seclusion. The lack of *purdah* is not any more a sure sign of poverty and unrespectability. Among wealthy 'modern' families, indeed, *purdah* is more often considered a sign of 'backwardness' than of respectability.

For centuries, the shrine at Hazrat Nizamuddin has been a pilgrimage centre for devotees — mostly Muslim — of the Saint, and the position of the shrine and village near to the city which has been India's capital for much of the time since the Saint's death suggests that historically the *pirzade* have not been isolated from currents in the outside world. For the most part, it seems likely that the *pirzade* have been exposed to many of the matters of greatest concern to Muslims but it is only in the last few years — especially since the Partition of India in 1947 — that Hazrat Nizamuddin has been more directly confronted with challenges on its doorstep. Even 25 years ago, the village was in the midst of jungle. There were no secondary schools in the vicinity, and many of the *pirzada* children never attended any school at all, but were taught to read by their elders in the village. Now, the nearby refugee colonies and the old village are provided with a secondary school, which has separate facilities for boys and girls. Moreover, all the *pirzade* have radios in their homes, and some even have television.

The *pirzada* women are not such 'frogs in a well' that they are unaware of the changes which have taken place in the world outside the village. There are now new groupings in Indian society of a size and importance much greater than, say, 50 years ago: and what is more, the new colonies just outside their village walls, and the radio, enable the *pirzada* women to compare themselves with people whose lives are very different from their own. Current affairs programmes expose the women to new ways of thinking about their own position. One radio programme in particular, called *Behnen* (Sisters), discusses issues like women's rights under the law or the benefits to maternal and child health of trying to space children. I have no evidence that the men, or older women, try to prevent the younger women from listening to such programmes and several of the women said they listen whenever they can.

The new colonies of former refugees also provide alternatives which enable the women to question their way of life. Most of the families living in the colonies are Hindu or Sikh, and not only do their womenfolk go out unveiled, but some of them are also in paid employment. The secondary school also raises questions in the minds of those *pirzada* girls who are permitted to attend. The ethos of the school — through its secular curriculum, the stress on non-domestic skills, and the women teachers who themselves do not keep *purdah* — presents a stark challenge to the Islamic values which surround the girls at home. Comparisons with other people are now possible: the *pirzada* girls have clearly exposed to them the difference between their own educational fate and those of the Hindu and Sikh girls who are their class-mates on the one hand, and their own brothers on the other.

There are enormous changes taking place outside the village, many of which provide the women with new ways of looking at their own positions. Even some of the older women indicate that they have shifted their views and they talk of wishing not to hold back their daughters and grand-daughters in the way they were themselves. It seems likely that the complaints of the women have increased in recent years, rather than remaining constant. The very considerable changes which have taken place in India make this explanation more plausible than one which suggests that the women's complaints are just newly recorded examples of old resentments about the *purdah* system which have long ago been accommodated and defused. If the complaints are responses to changes in the world outside, if they are relatively new exercises in comparing the lives of the women in *purdah* with those who are not secluded, then the *pirzada* women's complaints *may* represent quite novel and serious attacks on the legitimacy of *purdah* in Hazrat Nizamuddin.

The Ignorance of Women

The complaint with perhaps the most widely ramifying implications is that seclusion makes women *be-waquf* or ignorant. Conversations with the *pirzada* women would often be punctuated by apologies and self-denigration, with shame that they were unable to answer what they considered to be straightforward questions, that they would have to refer me to the men for reliable information. Even women, now only in their twenties, said that they had to keep *purdah* from women before their marriages and it is still considered improper for a young girl to sit listening or participating in conversations with her elders. As for women now in their fifties, they said they were kept in strict *purdah* from older men and women from the age of nine or ten, and that since that time they have rarely left their homes. How, they argued, can anyone learn anything in that way? But things are changing very rapidly. One woman of about 30, who was married at 16, commented:

> When I was married it was fine for a girl to be stupid — in fact it was almost better — because her in-laws could be sure of her innocence. But I'm not going to do that to my two daughters. If they can pick up things by sitting listening, then that's all to the good. My marriage has been spoilt by my own ignorance and embarrassment. I knew nothing about marriage, about sex, about how to talk to men. But young men now want brides who have a little bit of sense and have got some social graces. Nowadays, who wants a bride who curls up mute inside her *duppatta?* It's all a question of habit. You can see the difference between myself and my next younger sister — we were brought up at home in the same way, but since her marriage in Delhi her husband even lets her meet his colleagues. It all shows in the way she behaves when there are men around, because she has learnt now how to make conversation without being dumbfounded, like I am. No — I don't want my girls to be like myself.

This woman's mother, now in her fifties, also lamented the way she had been brought up a generation earlier:

For the first 20 years of my life I stayed within the one house. I went to a tiny school in the village run by one of the *pirzada* men and learnt Urdu, but I was taken away after three years. Then, a learned man came to teach me — in the presence of my mother — but that came to an end as soon as my breasts began to grow. After that, I was in *purdah* in my own home until my marriage. I wasn't even allowed to meet my older sister's husband or my mother's sister's husband — so is it any wonder that I couldn't cope with marriage? I didn't show my husband my face at all for well over a month after our marriage. I covered my head completely with a thick shawl and just to make sure I put on a *duppatta* underneath as well! When I peeped out to have a look at him, I was terrified — he seemed so strong and large. For the first few weeks, I used to listen for him coming — in those days people used to wear wooden clogs for going outside — and pretty soon I got used to his step, so I could easily work in the kitchen and cover myself properly before he came in. What sort of a life was that? It is much better for people to be able to travel around and learn about other places and how people live in different countries, like you're doing. People only learn by going out.

Another of her daughters, the fourth of six, had been listening to this and she later commented that these ideas of her mother's were really quite new:

The first three sisters were brought up just as strictly as our mother was. I'm sure you can see the difference between them and the rest of us. It all began to change around the time when we were arranging my brother's wedding, and we spent time meeting people in Delhi. Gradually, my mother changed her mind quite a lot. Now she thinks that it is good for young people to get some experience outside their homes. She began to meet girls of our age from families in Delhi and she was struck by how much more intelligent they seemed — they were more at ease in company and could answer questions sensibly, and since then she has been happier to let us visit people and learn the sorts of manners which people expect these days.

A further aspect of this ignorance of women concerns formal education. All the women read, but few women over thirty have ever attended school. Apart from the daughters of the Imam of the shrine's mosque (who have attended college), all those who have been to school at all have left around the beginning of puberty. For the young women this is a source of considerable complaint. One old woman, for instance, is the grandmother of several *pirzada* girls in various households in the village, and with all of them she has insisted that the girls are taken away from school as soon as they reach puberty. In deference to her views, the formal education of these girls came to an abrupt end:

Our cousin was allowed to go to school until 5th class and then she was taken away because our grandmother insisted. She was the sort of girl who was keen on her studies and would have been happy to have carried on — but all because of her grandmother, she was taken away and she even began to wear a *burqa* at ten! It often makes me sad to think of all this. I would now be in my first year of B.A. if my grandmother hadn't intervened. She used to come to our home every day at the time when my sisters and I arrived home from school, and she used to shout and harangue my mother to such an extent that my mother couldn't keep up the battle against her. So — that way our education suffered.

In yet another household, the old woman also tried to prevent girls from continuing to go to school, and won her battle again:

It's not that our father is against education for girls — indeed, he's not, and he has given me every encouragement to carry on studying at home. I'm now doing 11th class, and my brothers help me with finding the books and the syllabus and so forth. The problem for my father was that he wanted us educated but with *izzat* [honour] — in other words, preferably within the village, rather than having to go some distance, as we would have done. But on top of this, our grandmother used to come here every day and make such a fuss about us big girls going to school, and that was what decided it. It seemed the only way to keep the peace. But we all resent the way that she's interfered in our lives. After all, she's old and won't be alive much longer — but we'll have to live our lives out lacking in education, and all because of her.

These are rather extreme cases, but the overall picture is one in which the education of girls at school is not considered very important by their elders. There may be no dramatic confrontation between parents and grandparents over when to take girls away from school, but even so, girls gradually drift out of formal education when they are in their teens. Indeed, many girls have never regularly attended school before that. One problem in Hazrat Nizamuddin is that there are no secondary schools really close to the village — the nearest one, about ten minutes' walk away, is considered too far by many — and any girl who attends such a school is considered in danger of developing liaisons with boys which would damage the reputation of her family. Many parents believe that their daughters can no longer be educated with honour. They fear that permitting their daughters to continue at school will hamper their marriage chances, Not only might such a girl be presumed unlikely to make a docile and obedient daughter-in-law, but there may be a suspicion that she will be incompetent at the simplest domestic chores. Without the ability to keep house, a girl may be a liability on the marriage market — and it is the duty of parents to ensure that their daughters can be well married. Several women even said that they would accept a good offer of marriage while their daughter is still at school rather than miss a chance of settling her well — and in such a case, her schooling would be stopped there and then.

The comments of girls whose education came to an abrupt and, to their mind, premature end indicate that they had several reasons for wishing to continue longer at school. The daily escape from surveillance at home is a valued freedom, and many girls also enjoyed the new experiences and ideas which they were exposed to at school. A few had hoped to continue their studies at home, but the combination of disturbance from other people and their mothers' plans to complete their domestic education meant that their hopes have not borne fruit. Nonetheless, if there is a quiet spell, the young women enjoy reading:

> You're very lucky to be able to travel and see how people in different lands live. We can't do that — so we have to make do with things like *Shabistar* [a monthly magazine for women] which tells us about the customs of people in different places, like Morocco. That's the best way we have of making up for leaving school so young.

The interest in education is not just derived from a lively curiosity about the world. Possibly more important is that the young women considered that their elders have miscalculated the current requirements for an eligible bride. Life in India has been changing very rapidly in the last few years, they argued, and people have new ideas about the qualities which a bride needs. It is not common now for domesticity to suffice (though it is still essential), and people are looking for brides with some education who can be more on a par educationally with their sons. There is also the commonly held belief, reported in several ethnographies, that the migrations of Muslims to Pakistan after 1947 have made it more difficult for parents in India to make honourable matches for their daughters.[13] It is believed that there is a surplus of unmarried women, at least among the higher ranking Families and that the parents of boys can pick and choose the brides to bring into their homes. Several girls felt that their marriage chances had been damaged by their parents' policies. Indeed, they felt their parents had been tricked by history, for they had hoped to bring up demure daughters whose honour could be in no doubt, only to find that many people now put more store by education than in keeping girls at home after puberty. Such girls feared that it will now be hard to arrange a marriage with a man who has the education and respectable job which they desire, and they did not want to be relegated as wife to some almost illiterate petty tradesman.

What makes this whole question even more piquant to the young women are the comparisons which they can make between their own fates and those of others around them. At the school which the *pirzada* girls attended, Muslims were in the minority. While they are waiting quietly at home for suitable marriages to materialize, their Hindu and Sikh class-mates of a few years ago are busily studying for their exams and maybe going on to college. Sometimes, if *pirzada* girls are permitted to attend some function at the school, they are directly confronted with the contrast — and with the teasing of their friends about waiting uselessly for their weddings to take place. How they envy the luck of the girls still at school! Seeing girls of their own age enjoying freedoms which they are denied, and coping with the world outside the home with a confidence which puts their own efforts to shame, is certainly important in changing their attitudes to *purdah*.

But there is more to it than this. In the old days, the *pirzada* girls and boys received much the same education. As tiny children, they might even be taught side by side by one of the older men or women. Boys with aptitude would probably be taught Arabic and Islamic doctrine, and maybe Persian too, by scholars from nearby mosques. But the contrast now is often very stark: a young man completing his B.A. may have a sister who has never attended school regularly and whose formal education was ended by the time she was ten. According to the *pirzada* women, radio programmes have discussed education and the arguments for and against spending money on educating daughters as well as sons. A new type of comparison is set in motion, this time across the sex barrier, with their brothers — boys who are often more interested in football than their studies, but who are, nevertheless, backed to the hilt by their parents through their school and college careers and who are encouraged to think of training in some field which will give them access to well paid and respectable occupations. Only if a boy shows very little academic aptitude will his parents take him away from school early. Throughout my fieldwork among the *pirzade,* it was clear that they are apprehensive about the long-term prospects for the shrine, and boys with ability are encouraged to remain at school, even encouraged not to waste their time sitting in the shrine when they could be studying for their examinations. As one girl put it:

> My two oldest brothers have been a great disappointment to our father. He himself is very learned, and reads Persian and Arabic, as well as knowing a little English. His own father even wrote books in Persian. He had dearly hoped that his sons would be of the same bent. So far, only my third brother has shown any inclination to study. Our father tried to encourage the older ones, but they just weren't keen. If only he'd been prepared to make such an effort with myself and my sister — we were keen enough to study! He wouldn't have needed to push *us* and cajole *us* into going to school and college. Our brothers have had all the opportunities they could wish for — and just look how they've wasted them.

Even the boy who does take advantage of his schooling is no more of a comfort to his sisters: either way, the message is clear enough, and girls can only fulminate about their bad fortune.

Girls and women alike often comment unfavourably on their own ignorance about matters which they consider simple: the middle-aged woman laughing at herself for asking her husband if Arabia was at the end of the world; the uncertainties of a young woman about which *pirzade* belong to which Family; the confusion over the organization of the rota system in the shrine and complete ignorance of the details of festivals — all such denials of knowledge would be accompanied by comments on how much my simple questions shamed them and drew attention to their ignorance. But 'frogs in a well' can hardly be expected to know about things beyond the parapets of their homes. They have only been exposed to domestic matters, so it is little wonder that they are ignorant about practically everything else in the world.

What is particularly interesting is that the women consider that their failings are rooted in their socialization and not in biology. They are ignorant because they have not been taught to be otherwise. They have not been much exposed to new ideas. They are not used to finding their way about outside alone. They never have any practice in dealing with men outside the immediate family. They rarely go to the shrine, and cannot easily quiz the men about what happens there. Women are not faint-hearted and unable to cope outside their homes because they are biologically different from men. Their answer is quite simple: they have just not been trained to any competence except in the domestic world. The 'stupidity' of women can only be cured by allowing them more opportunities to learn: only by going out more will women become *hoshyar* (intelligent, literally fully conscious). Their upbringing has thwarted their development, they said — which implies a potentially radical critique of the traditional ideology of innate differences between the sexes. This counter-ideology has not been developed much further than this, but the women are nonetheless adamant that it is their socialization which has limited their capabilities. It is their *enforced* 'stupidity' which adversely affects their staying in their homes and their going out alike.

Life in the Home

A term which is often used by the women about seclusion is that their home becomes a prison (*qaid*) where they are confined by the walls, by the requirements of family honour, even by their own 'stupidity'. While older women say they are quite used to this, young women, especially those who have attended school, say that they find it hard to adjust to a life which is carried on so completely within such a confined space.

Staying at home, they say, makes a woman ignorant, but it does more than this. 'That way, people go mad', they often say ominously. Total seclusion may give a woman time to brood over her troubles. It makes her petty and prone to gossip. Women who live in complete seclusion become narrow-minded and empty-headed because nothing of importance fills their days. Moreover, seclusion damages a woman's physical health: when the farthest a woman normally walks is across the courtyard at her home, going out, or indeed the slightest bit of extra exertion in the home, leaves her prone with exhaustion. Sweeping the courtyard or wringing out clothes can be enough to make her want to lie down. Total seclusion breeds lassitude, both physical and mental. Such are the accusations which the *pirzada* women level at their secluded existences.

A number of conversations on this topic centred on one of the *pirzada* women married outside the village and the only one to be confronted with a more strict form of *purdah* after her marriage. She was cited by several women — her sister, her niece and others less closely connected — as the prime example of the excesses of *purdah* which are no longer evident in Hazrat Nizamuddin itself. Older women could remind their juniors of what life had been like in their youth, but there was only this one example before their eyes of full blown seclusion. This woman did not wear a *burqa* before her marriage, but if she leaves her in-laws' home, the street is cleared, screens are erected and she scuttles into the car, where she sits with her veils over her face in spite of the curtains on the car windows. She is rarely allowed out, in fact, and her home is without a courtyard. When she is ill a woman doctor may come to the house, but she has had to return to her less strict parental home on several occasions when she has needed hospital treatment. To travel to her parents' home, a whole first class compartment is reserved on the train, and, armed with supplies for the journey, she is locked in and required to travel the whole distance with the blinds drawn. Her sixteen year old niece commented sourly:

> They don't even let the sparrows' chicks catch a glimpse of her. No wonder she's ill so often. But it's better than it used to be. She once told us that her mother-in-law used to have stones put inside the sedan chair so that the men carrying her wouldn't know her correct weight! Can you think of anything more stupid than that? I suppose in comparison, our life is not too bad — at least we aren't imprisoned at home.

Even so, most of the *pirzada* women spend little time away from home: they might spend an hour in another house in the village, chatting to their mother or sisters; on less frequent occasions they might go to Delhi to shop or to visit friends or relatives, but generally they are at home. And, what is more, they find a good deal to be dissatisfied with in their lives there.

They conceded that their labours have been greatly aided by the introduction of electricity and cold water supplies. They admitted that several women in one household can arrange to share tasks and alter their rotas so that their chores can be eased and days free from housework even be arranged. Nevertheless, they did not consider that their lot is much to be envied. For one thing, their work around the home seems never-ending. There are so many flies and the climate makes for so much dust that cleaning is never finished. One woman, who had spent the morning daubing mud on to a refurbished traditional hearth, was lying down to rest and soothing one of her sick grandchildren to sleep at the same time:

> You see how our work never finishes. My grandson is not well — he's always getting fevers, and won't go to sleep unless someone is with him all the time. He's a full-time job by himself. And my own health is not good — even that little job of plastering the hearth has left me with aching arms. But my work never seems to come to an end. I always get so flustered about the dirt. There are so many flies these days — the village

used to be so clean until all these milkmen arrived with their cattle — and then there's the dust. Everything gets dirty so quickly. And soon I shall have to empty and wash the bed quilts. And I shall have to refill them, as my girls can't do it neatly. And on top of that, we've had 'guests' staying — and I simply haven't had the energy yet to clean out the room where they were sleeping.

Such comments are typical, but they are only one type of complaint. The way in which the men regard the work which the women do is also a matter for discontent. The men too rarely appreciate the women's work, they said. Women plan out their work — just like the men. They have their rotas — and yet the men think that the women just sit around lazing all day with nothing to do. As much as the shrine is the men's place of work, so too the home is the women's, and in consequence they felt entitled to some consideration from their menfolk. It is not just that they resented things like being made to stop some important work so that they could iron a shirt and *pajama* for an impatient husband or brother who gives no more than a minute's warning of his needs.

The women also felt they should be consulted about alterations in the home, and indeed they usually are. Several houses in the village were in need of repair, because of damage from heavy rains, and some reconstruction work was set in train by the government order that all homes should install a flush toilet. Generally, the women were consulted about siting and design. As one man put it, his wife is his 'home minister' and it is only right that the household organization should suit her needs. Not all the women received such consideration, however, and when they do not they are not wont to keep quiet about it. On one occasion a workman had been brought in to install some new water pipes and taps. He and a son of the household head who was overseeing him had not asked the women where they wished the taps to be placed. An unmarried daughter and a daughter-in-law of the household head were sitting behind closed doors, peeping round the door every few minutes to check what was happening. The daughter-in-law was angry because she wanted her younger brother-in-law to have the tap re-sited:

The workman has just put the tap in the easiest way for himself, with no thought for the convenience of us women who will be using it everyday. My brother-in-law treats us as if we had the intelligence of dogs — he doesn't think we're worth consulting about things like that, and if we complain about the work which has been done, he wants nothing changed. His older brother wouldn't treat us like that.

The women also objected to the way the men are apt to inject chaos into the domestic scene by giving extra tasks without warning. A 'guest' may arrive at the shrine, and, without consideration for the women at home (so the women thought), the women have to make immediate arrangements to feed and maybe even house the guests for several days. That the women might have set aside that period for some particular household task — clearing out cupboards or preparing new bedding for the winter months — is not considered, and they have to discard their plans. Beds, bedding and clothes have to be shifted around so that 'guests' can be housed without coming into contact with the women; curtains have to be erected and doors kept closed so that they will not be seen, and work which they hoped to complete will have to be set aside. On several occasions, the men also forgot to remind the women of the household to prepare sweetmeats to be blessed at the shrine, and women had to do this extra work before dawn on the day when the sweets were required by the men.

Then there is also the sewing of drapes for the tombs in the shrine, which is generally done by the women of one household. The oldest woman's husband described the work as a labour of love, but the women's feelings were rather coloured by the lack of warning which they were often given. One of the women conceded that the pilgrim who gives the money for the drapes is very generous to the poor, but he is 'not quite right in his head':

> He has plenty of money and gives a lot of it away. He regards it as more or less his right to provide money for the drapes, yet he does not tell us what he wants until a day or two before they are needed. He leaves everything so late — and he gets angry if we buy material with money given by other pilgrims. My eyes get strained if I sew by electric light, and because the drapes are for the shrine no woman who is menstruating can have anything to do with the work. That means that our work-force is bound to be cut down and whatever happens several of us will be working on the three sewing machines right through the night. By the end, we're all exhausted. If only he would give us some warning of what he will want.

Marriage

Even more than housework, marriage and motherhood were subjected to close and often critical scrutiny. Marriage is inevitable. There is no escape from it: a girl just has to wait for the decisions of her elders to take their course. For the girl awaiting the offer of marriage which will seal her fate there is a good deal to fear, and much of the conversation on the topic revolved around the problems which the unlucky bride might confront.

A girl is just a temporary resident in her parents' home, a dearly loved guest, who will inevitably be exiled into an environment which may make her unhappy. It is expected that the bride will make all the adjustments to fit in with her in-laws: she is not expected to introduce changes into their home. For example, if they prefer food with more pepper than she likes, she will learn to cook and consume according to their habits. She must accept their standards of cleanliness; she must adopt their timetable for the daily round of domestic work. Even within the *pirzada* population there are small differences and the bride marrying within the village will have to make changes in her habits —

she will have to learn to be at home among new people. But how many more are likely to be the adjustments which the bride marrying outside the village will have to make. Any young girl can expect to make changes — ranging from minor to drastic — in the way she lives once she is married. All demands must be met, for her in-laws should be respected and obeyed without question, and, once she is married, she is in their hands and her parents should not intervene on her behalf. Beforehand, she can have little idea of the changes which she will have to make and, perhaps more importantly, the degree of tolerance with which her in-laws will meet her halting efforts to adjust to their ways.

There are other fears too. Prime among these is the fear that the in-laws might be quarrelsome and given to fighting among themselves. When I commented that a young woman engaged to her cousin in the village seemed to be perfectly calm about her marriage, the retort I received from a woman in her early twenties was:

> Of course she is. Why should she be worried? She knows her in-laws already and knows what sort of people they are. She's lucky to be well settled. It's different for most of us, though, unless we are to be married inside the village. Outside people can deceive so easily that it's impossible to know what they're really like until the marriage is over. I don't much want to be married, but I suppose it will not be too bad, either inside or outside the village, provided that my in-laws treat me with love, like they would a daughter.

Women whose sisters or mothers have been unhappy in their marriages are, not surprisingly, apprehensive on their own behalf. One teenager commented bitterly:

> Many people's lives have been made miserable in India because of unhappy marriages. People here say that love marriages like you have don't work, but I'm in favour of them — surely they must be happy more often than marriages where there is no love between the husband and wife before they are married?

Her cousins, in their twenties, had the example of their sister as a caution to them. One of them said that she did not want to be married at all:

> My sister is so unhappy with her in-laws. She cooks delicacies for her husband, yet still he's strict with her and sometimes is cruel to her. And her mother-in-law criticizes everything she does. Her husband talks about leaving her — but what can she do about it?

The dowry, too, is a matter of concern for a bride: how will her in-laws respond to it? Inside the village, the *pirzade* say, they do not specify what should be included in the dowry and the bride who arrives practically empty-handed will not suffer for her parents' poverty or niggardliness. But outside, it is all different. Some people may be 'noble' and make no demands, but many families have the vulgar habit of insisting that certain items should be included. Several engagements have been broken off by the *pirzade* when they find that the groom's people appear more interested in the goods the bride will bring than they are in the bride herself. One woman told me about an offer of marriage for one of her daughters:

> They began to tell us what we should put in the dowry − a particular make of sewing machine, a scooter and the like. Apart from anything else, we have other daughters to marry and cannot afford to give so much. But it is shameless for people to ask like that. What's more, they refused to set any sum for the marriage settlement, so at that point we called the match off. We've heard since that the boy was married to another girl, but that she went back to her parents after only a few months. Thanks be to God *that* didn't happen to our daughter.

This family felt themselves fortunate that they had backed out of the engagement in time, for it is not unknown for a marriage to have taken place before the trouble starts. The bride is continually questioned about what she has brought, unflattering comparisons are made between her parents and those of other brides in the household, and whenever she returns from visits to her parents she is pestered to hand over the gifts which they expect from her family. Several women were extremely cynical about the ability of the government to succeed in abolishing dowry, arguing that people would simply make secret demands and that it would just be handed over piecemeal rather than at the time of the wedding. Nevertheless, there was unanimity among the women that dowry is a bane for women, for it is often the root of their problems with their in-laws.

Other unmarried girls were more concerned about the bother and worry − *taklif* and *parashani* − which their husbands would give them, by insisting on having sexual relations with them. A Muslim wife is obliged to have sexual relations with her husband whenever he wishes. The unmarried are now more exposed before marriage to information about sex than their elders were, and they have heard about the 'bother' which some men give their wives. Although sexual relations should not take place while the wife is menstruating, one girl, screwing her face up in disgust, told of how she had heard of men who were unable to leave their wife alone even at that time. Another told of the account she had heard of a bride who had been found unconscious after her wedding night. Such rumours provide grounds for the unmarried to worry about their fate. As one girl put it:

> It would probably be better if the boy and girl could meet before the marriage and begin to make friends with one another. They are like strangers and the bride, at least, will be embarrassed and shy on the wedding night. The groom's friends will probably have teased him so much that he'll be completely shameless, and that can't make it easier for the bride.

It is perhaps easy enough to understand at a purely intellectual level how the separation of the sexes and arranged marriages can function. From my experience in Hazrat Nizamuddin, parents take their responsibility to their children seriously. The fears voiced by unmarried girls echo many of the matters which concern their parents deeply when considering matches. Indeed, parents are prepared to call off negotiations and even break engagements if some unsavoury information materializes about the other family.

Yet understanding this has nevertheless given me little insight into what it must *feel* like to have one's marriage arranged by others. My own efforts to transport myself mentally into a system of arranged marriage, to understand what it is like to show one's face for perhaps the first time on the marriage night to a man who is both a stranger and a husband, have not been far from the thoughts and worries of the unmarried women I talked to in Hazrat Nizamuddin. For them, marriage is an unknown: how their lives will evolve depends on their in-laws and their husband. Will he be kind and considerate or will he be callous and cold? Does he insist that his wife wears a *burqa* and do his parents treat the brides in their home as prisoners? Or will she be allowed to discard the *burqa*, will she have the opportunity to come and go, to visit friends and meet her relatives? What will he think about having children? Will he approve of family planning, or will he want many children? Is he the sort of man who will make every effort to love his wife and make her happy, or is he the type who heartlessly takes another wife if his first bears only daughters, without giving a thought to the problems which step-relationships and co-wives almost inevitably entail? Or might he be the sort of man who would send an innocent wife back to her parents in disgrace? Only time will tell.

However, many of the marriages of the *pirzada* women do not appear to be the trials which they feared. Often, indeed, relationships of affection and mutual respect develop out of these apparently inauspicious beginnings – the kindly soft-spoken man who asks his wife if anything is needed from the *bazar* before he will sit down to his meal; the husband who learns that his wife cannot read the *Quran Sharif* only when she asks if she may have some of the merit from his reading, and who spends the next six months patiently reciting it with her passage by passage, until she is word perfect; the wife who always cooks special delicacies for her husband; and the woman who, worried about the way her husband damages his health by missing meals, begs me to summon him from the shrine as there are no men at home to take the message. All these are, in some measure, success stories.

In other cases, the aloofness of the men from their homes, the large areas of ignorance about one another's spheres and the deference of the wife who adjusts her behaviour to fit in with her in-laws' home, probably dull any abrasiveness which there might be between a man and his wife. A husband and wife need have very little to do with one another. A few of the younger women wished for closer relationships with their husbands and would like to have more in common with them, but only a tiny number implied that their husbands hold the threat of divorce over them, and none talked of any immediate possibility of their husbands bringing a second wife into their home. Those who did talk about divorce and polygamy were unanimously critical of the power which their husband could — in theory at least — wield over their destinies; but the threat was not an immediate one in most cases.

Indeed, the person who often presents a more direct threat — and who was the subject of many complaints — is the mother-in-law. Several women said that their troubles would be over if they could live separately from their husband's close family. One woman in her twenties told me how she and her sister had both been plagued by their mothers-in-law:

> I managed to live in my mother-in-law's house for about a year after my marriage. But she is a very difficult person, and in the end I persuaded my husband to move out with me. My sister had problems too. Her mother-in-law used to give her a lot of trouble — she's her husband's stepmother — and in the end she and her husband moved out.

Motherhood

More often, though, the married women's complaints are a veritable catalogue not of the problems of married life, but of the troubles which large numbers of children bring. There should be children in every marriage. Between two and four seems to be the favoured range, and yet many of the *pirzada* women have over eight, some as many as a dozen, living children. One woman nearing forty, with five sons and three daughters, commented: 'Is it any wonder that girls try to persuade their parents not to arrange their marriages? They know very well that all their problems will come then. A woman only has peace in her parents' home.' Another woman with eight children talked of always being 'caught' by children, first by her own and now by her grandchildren, and others said that children give 'no peace'. One woman commented:

> I used to be so plump and healthy looking, but I've got weak from worry. Mostly it's about money and the children. Two of my daughters are married, but that still means that 11 people have to be fed each day and my husband doesn't make a great deal of money. And on top of feeding and clothing them all, I have to think of the cost of schooling, and of making good marriages for them when they are older.

Repeated motherhood is also ruinous to a woman's health, they said. This woman just quoted had 11 children as well as two miscarriages, and her older sister had 16 pregnancies, from which 11 children survive. Their mother had had three miscarriages, and nine children, three of whom died. The older sister's comment when she recited her history to me was: 'Is it any wonder that my health is so bad after all that?' The younger sister felt much the same:

In those days we had no wisdom — we just had children like animals do. My adult life has been spent being a baby-making machine — I'm worn out and my health is ruined. My daughters have seen what it means to have so many children and they say they want to stop after two.

Ailments ranging from general lassitude, headaches, and bad teeth to abdominal and even rheumatic pains are all considered to be the consequence of having so many children. Dark skin, in particular, is taken as a sign of poor health, and many of the middle-aged women lamented the passing of their youthful beauty when they used to be so fair. They attributed their darkness to the weakness with which many pregnancies had left them. One woman added with force her belief that her whiteness and strength had been drained out of her by suckling her children. Constant pregnancies and lactation make for weak mothers and sickly children, the women argued.

The question of family size seems to have become an acute one only in the past 30 years or so. The genealogical material suggests that sibling groups begun about 40 years ago are generally larger than those begun around the turn of the century. Going into detail while collecting the material — asking women about their own and their mother's child-bearing histories — suggests that an important change has taken place.

It is not that the *pirzada* women are now more able to conceive than they were in the early years of this century. Nor did the middle-aged and elderly *pirzada* women claim that their large families had been 'forced' on them by the *pirzada* men, in a bid to redress the population loss which occurred when about half of the *pirzade* moved to Pakistan after India was partitioned in 1947. It does not appear that their fecundity suddenly became more highly valued at that time: indeed, according to the women themselves it was something which they regretted. The change over the last 70 years is of a different sort: pregnancy and childbirth are less risky than they used to be, childhood is more likely to be survived, and even adult life is less vulnerable than it used to be.

It is not easy to summarize rather complicated material — itself made more complex by the faulty memories of the women to whom I talked — but it seems that *pirzada* women not infrequently used to die in childbirth (and their husbands might choose not to remarry), also *pirzada* children sometimes died in infancy, and certain *pirzada* men died in their prime leaving young widows. Factors such as these reduced the average size of sibling groups in earlier years.

In the past 30 years, there has been a notable decrease in infant mortality rates in most parts of India, largely attributable to improvements in public health schemes, through immunization campaigns and improvements in sanitation, as well as more widely available hospital facilities. In Delhi are to be found the most comprehensive medical facilities anywhere in India, and the *pirzade* have not been slow to use these facilities when they or their children are ill. There is a clinic about ten minutes walk away and a doctor may be summoned from there to attend a birth. Some of the *pirzada* women have even given birth in hospital, though most of their children are born at home. Other ailments can be treated by the doctors practising locally in or near the village, who have been trained in either 'Western' medicine or in traditional Muslim medicine, and the *pirzade* use both kinds. For serious complaints they go further afield to one of the numerous hospitals. Their ability to purchase drugs and pay for other treatments puts them at an advantage over many poor people. Their children are less likely to die in infancy now, and their womenfolk are put at less risk in pregnancy and childbirth than they used to be.

Lack of access to contraceptives is a vital element here. Contrary to the suggestion which is commonly made that contraceptive and abortion techniques have traditionally been the domain of women, the histories of the *pirzada* women and their own denials of any knowledge of contraception would suggest that this has not been the case here. The life histories of the post-menopausal women indicate that there has been little time during their marital careers which has been left free from pregnancy and lactation. Leaving out two women who were widowed early in their marriages (one with two sons and the other having borne a stillborn child), the average number of children born to these women, who are still alive, is just over eight. Deaths of children in infancy would slightly inflate this figure, and several women told me about miscarriages. Generally, these women were married between the ages of 15 and 20, which would give perhaps 25 to 30 years when they could bear children. This period is generally foreshortened in practice by the feeling that sexual relations should cease once a child of the couple is married and having children. In practice sibling groups seem to span somewhere between 18 and 25 years.

Like women in many parts of Asia and Africa, the *pirzada* women have been caught in a hiatus between improvements in life expectancy and the non-availability to them of effective contraceptive techniques. One woman with nine living children can serve as an example. She was married when she was about eighteen and her first child was born about a year after her marriage. As with all her children, she breastfed her son. Unlike several of her contemporaries, who made comments like 'one child was hardly out of my stomach before the next was in', she found that lactation protected her from pregnancy, but she became pregnant again almost immediately after weaning her children. There is a gap of about two and a half years between each child and the next. Her second child died in infancy and her nine children now range from 40 to 17 years of age, the youngest being born just before her oldest daughter was married. She told me that her mother-in-law had only three children who survived to adulthood, and she was anxious that her only son's wife should bear many children. Looking back she felt that a larger gap between children would have been better, so that each child could have been taught to feed and dress before the next one arrived. She approved of the five year gap between the two children of one of her sons. Equally she felt that to have three or four children was an important insurance for old age, but that more children create too many worries.

According to the accounts of the women themselves, the only way of limiting family size which was known to them until the last ten years was reducing the frequency of sexual intercourse. This was common after grand-children have been born, but is also sometimes employed by women whose children are still unmarried. But in general, according to the older women, people in the past had 'no wisdom' and just believed in the will of God. When I asked if people had not wanted many children in those days, one woman responded:

> No. They didn't at all. It's not true to say that people in the old days wanted many children and that the fashion has changed now. No. The thing is that there was no 'family plan' available then. People thought that a person's coming and going was according to God's will and nothing could be done. But we know better now. Even though God ultimately governs everything, that does not mean in Islam that a person should abandon all care: he should take proper food and pay attention to his health, and the same applies to the number of children a woman has. I suppose there may be some other changes — that's true. The radio programme *Behnen* is always telling people to send their daughters to school and people are gradually changing their ways of thinking. And educating children is costly — and there are other things to spend money on as well these days which didn't exist before, like TV — so people are now thinking that many children make many expenses, and are thinking of family planning. But now there is the knowledge to do that — which there wasn't before.

Another woman, married about 12 years and with just two daughters, said that she was happy to have a small family, though her husband would like to have a son some day. Her mother, by contrast, regretted having so many children. The daughter reckoned up that her father had sired about 17 children, though not all of these are still alive. She said that her mother was continually lamenting the worries which her enormous brood have brought, and said she would have limited the numbers if only she had known how.

At present, the women consider that men generally want more children than their wives do and that family limitation is as much a question of gaining the husband's consent as it is of availability of contraceptive techniques. Complaints about husbands were mainly directed to this question. Several women were currently having to deal with husbands who wanted them to have more children, preferably sons. One woman, who had been advised to have a hysterectomy, said that her husband would not permit the operation:

> He wants another son. If two of our three children had been boys he would have been satisfied, but we have only one son. Many men say that it is the woman's fault if there are no sons — but it isn't. It's God's will. The trouble is, how can we tell if another child will be a boy or a girl? That's what I tell my husband when we discuss the matter. I don't want any more children — whatever else, I know that it won't be my husband who will have to look after it and do all the extra housework. What trouble does a man have

from children? He doesn't have to go through nine months of trouble, then the danger of childbirth and all the problems of bringing children up which fall on the woman.

Another woman, also with three children, is under the same pressure to have another child:

> But three have been quite enough for me and my health. If he wants more children, he'll have to take another wife — that's all. The trouble is that a boy and girl don't meet before they marry, and their parents certainly don't talk about how many children they should have. It's no wonder that husbands and wives don't agree about how many children they want.

Another woman put it even more starkly: 'Some men care more about having many children than they do about their wife's health.'

It is not just that pregnancies debilitate a woman. Large numbers of children make it impossible for her to do her work properly. Large families create more cleaning and cooking, more mending and washing than small ones. These days women can expect that most, if not all, of their children will survive until adulthood. But this was not always the case. In the days when epidemics could wipe out small children within days, there was no such security. The only hope of perpetuating a line was through a woman who bore many children: only then could a man be sure that some would survive. Children could be seen as a valuable good which women should produce in quantity. Under different circumstances, children acquire a different meaning. Improved life chances mean that more of the children born survive to create more housework for their mothers, more cares about their marriages and, nowadays, more anxiety over their education and employment. A child can be costly; many children can be worryingly so. And in any case, how can a woman give adequate attention to a large brood of children? How can she ensure that they are well mannered and that they grow up to be pious and worthy Muslims? Creating 'human beings' is no insignificant job; but men have little to do with it, and the harassed housewife cannot perform her duties properly. And who but the women have all the extra work which the children's marriages will bring? For the husband, many children mean many heirs; the women have to face all the less pleasant consequences.

There are, then, pervasive undercurrents of discontent among the *pirzada* women about matters which impinge on them daily. Young women more than old resent the 'imprisonment' of life in *purdah*. Old women rather than young complain of the trials of having many children — and pray that their daughters will not have to experience what they have. The unmarried dread their inevitable marriages and young and old, married and unmarried bemoan their ignorance. These are matters in which individual women have had little control over their own lives. Marriage is not something which they can escape. They cannot decide not to be withdrawn from school, and only recently have women been able to limit the number of children which they bear. It is their fate, their *qismat,* but it is not a destiny which they all accept without regret, or without question.

References

1. See M.H. Ali, *Observations on the Mussulmauns of India,* 2 vols., (London, 1832), vol. 1, pp.111, 113-4, and 304-35.
2. *Ibid.,* pp.313-5.
3. *Ibid.,* pp.333, 339, and 348.
4. M.F. Billington, *Woman in India,* (London, 1895), p.xvi.
5. *Ibid.,* p.63.
6. F. Hauswirth Das, *Purdah: The Status of Indian Women,* (London, 1932) p.268.
7. *Ibid.,* pp.93-112.
8. K. Mayo, *Mother India,* (London, 1930), p.111.
9. *Ibid.,* p.112.
10. V.R. and L. Bevan Jones, *Woman in Islam,* (Lucknow, 1941), p.219.
11. *Ibid.,* p.223.
12. *Ibid.,* p.229, note 2.
13. See, for instance, C. Vreede-de Stuers, *Parda,* (Assen, 1968), p.10.

Women in street wearing the burqa

6. Complaining and Complying: the trials of going out

That the women complain about their lives at home is not very surprising to the European observer. Foreigners have often been quick to remark upon the health hazards of life in seclusion, and have often been prepared to argue that seclusion should be abolished for the good of the women. The *pirzada* women themselves, as we saw in the last chapter, are by no means enamoured of their lives at home: they find plenty to complain about, and say that their ignorance can only be counteracted by going out more.

What is perhaps less anticipated is that they also perceive problems in going out, and they are prepared to complain as energetically about that as they do about arranged marriages, having many children, or being 'imprisoned' at home. The street is the world of men. In many cities in north India and Pakistan, few women are to be seen out in the streets at all. The old city of Lahore, for instance, is a striking example, but in Delhi this is only true of the oldest areas of the city especially those in the predominantly Muslim areas around the main mosque, the Jama Masjid. Shoppers and shopkeepers are nearly all men and boys, and there might be just a handful of women, most of them shadowy veiled figures darting along the narrow alley ways.

For the *pirzada* women, going out is no easy matter. Often it is a traumatic experience, so much so that many of the older women said that they rarely go out at all. Their complaints have several aspects: their ignorance about the world outside their homes, having to wear the *burqa* when outside the house, and the lack of suitable facilities. All these factors deter women from emerging from their homes.

Alien Territory

Because women are so rarely given the opportunity to go out and about by themselves, the *pirzada* women argued, they do not learn how to do so with confidence. It is not just that their feet are unused to walking far in shoes — for they spend much of their time at home barefoot and only put on loose sandals to walk across the courtyard — although that certainly adds to their discomfort outside their homes. Many of the women said that their constricted lives at home mean that their bodies are not properly exercised and they consequently find even a short outing physically very tiring.

What is more important than this, however, is that women hardly ever go out alone. Generally they are accompanied by some man or boy from their immediate families, and the result, they said, is that they are never given the chance to learn the most elementary skills. Even negotiating road traffic and crossing roads is testing to women who have never had to judge by themselves the speed of vehicles. A small boy will have more confidence than a woman, and so may be entrusted with chaperoning her. Beyond this, women never learn the right way to places: they are accompanied and directed to their destinations, and when faced with the prospect of finding their own way, they are frightened and flustered. How can they ask for directions from strangers? And, anyway, strange men are notoriously likely to misdirect and confuse them, just for a joke. If they go somewhere by bus, someone will almost certainly tell them to get off at the wrong place, or they might even be told to take the wrong bus. And because they have no practice, because they cannot recognize bus routes, they cannot easily tell when they are being fooled. If they had been properly taught in the first place, there would be no need to expose themselves to such trickery, they said.

For an adult woman, such obstacles to easy movement outside the home are daunting, often sufficiently daunting to make going out unpleasant, and far from the release which it might appear to be. Older women wistfully talked of the way in which young girls have been taught 'the courage of lions', with the result that they do not find going outside their homes a frightening experience. While the men were apt to talk of the 'weak hearts' of women, the women saw such phenomena as the inevitable consequences of their upbringing. They did not deny their faint courage — indeed, it is something about which they were very open and very ashamed. One woman in her seventies was most anxious when I was about to go home alone after a function at her house which had lasted until after midnight: was I not afraid of going by myself?

No, I suppose you're used to it. It's a much better life, that women can cope in that way by themselves. You know — I hardly ever go out now. When I was younger, it was thought improper for women to go out, and we were only able to go to the local *bazar* after dark. I don't even know the way inside our own village — and if you were to send me on some errand, I'd be terrified. From childhood, our habits have been different from yours. At home, I can be as fierce as a lion. I'm in control here, I understand how to do things. I've even killed a snake in the courtyard before now. But I'm too frightened to go to lock the outside door at night, let alone wander around the village by myself. Yes — your life is better, but we've got used to not going out much.

Another woman, in her fifties, chuckled at how, when she was first married, she used to clutch her husband's shirt sleeve when they went out, so that she would not get lost:

Do you know, I did just the same when we went to Mecca on *Haj* a few years ago. There was I — a grown woman with grown-up children — clinging to his sleeve. There was such a rush of people, and I was terrified that I would get lost. I was really impressed by some of the women I saw there — Africans, my husband told me — anyway, very tall and very dark. There they were striding along with their heads erect, looking so sure of themselves — I really felt like a little mouse in comparison. I couldn't be like that outside. Why, I don't even know the way to Bhogal market, and that's only a little distance away.

While this type of response was most common amongst the older women, several of whom have tried to ensure that their own daughters do not meet with the same fate, some young women were also brought up in very cloistered surroundings, and they also commented that they find it hard to cope with going out alone. A woman of thirty gave the following account of an experience shortly after her marriage:

Just after I was married, my husband suggested that we should go to Old Delhi together. He told me that he had a couple of errands to do before we set off and said that I should make my own way to the Village Gate, where he would meet me. I suppose it never occurred to him that someone who had been born and bred in the village would not know the way — and I was too ashamed to admit my ignorance to him! You'd hardly credit it, but in the hundred yards between here and the gate, I managed to lose myself — and I wandered around, getting more and more frantic. I was panic stricken. In the end, we managed to meet up, and I can laugh about it all now — but it was a dreadful experience.

For her younger sisters and other young women, the problems presented by going out are often of quite a different order. Many of them have attended school for a while and know their way about in the localities near the village. For them, the problem more often is how to obtain permission to go out at all. Many of the middle-aged women commented that they had no wish to hold their daughters back, and yet it is still not acceptable for an unmarried girl to be seen outside her home frequently. The fear of what people will say, the fear that people will 'take our names' was often presented to me by these women as the reason why they restrict the outings of their daughters. How much the fear of gossip is merely a way of expressing what the women themselves are reluctant to permit is hard to assess. What is clear, though, is that the older women felt that they have a duty to ensure that their daughters give outsiders no cause for damaging rumours. The woman or girl who goes out often is presumed to be neglecting her domestic duties; she is somewhat shameless, something of a gadabout. The girl who goes out a lot may be suspected of liaisons with young men, and that could affect not only her own but her younger sisters' marriage chances. People gossip if parents delay in arranging their children's marriages, but the parents of girls have to wait for good offers. Theirs is not the initiative. To have adult daughters left unmarried is a matter of shame, and people will insinuate that the girls are not sought after because there is something wrong with them. Parents have to ensure that the reputation of their family is not ruined in some unguarded moment by the shameful behaviour of their young women — and the older women, who are particularly concerned with this, tend to be circumspect in the permission which they give their daughters.

If malicious gossip can punish, so too can the 'evil eye' or *nazr*. Belief in the evil eye is widespread throughout the Muslim Middle East as well as among Hindus and Muslims in the Indian sub-continent.[1] Although there appears to be some Quranic justification for belief in the evil eye, it seems likely that it was not an Islamic introduction into India. Several writers associate such beliefs particularly with complex differentiated societies in which envy may be an important element. Certainly, a general feature of evil eye beliefs is that the glance of an envious person can bring misfortune — a child may sicken, a crop may fail, a woman may give birth to a still-born child. There are many ways of warding off attacks: amulets, jewellery, and clothes of particular colours — especially red, yellow, black and white — are among the items which are said to protect a person. The veiling of women is also attributed by some to fear of the evil eye.

The evil eye can affect men, women and children, as well as animals and crops. Some of the *pirzade* suggested that 'thin blood' and fair skin are likely to make a person particularly vulnerable, and one woman claimed that envious glances at her thick hair had caused the evil eye to strike. On the whole, though, women (and children) are believed to be more vulnerable than men. The particular facet of the evil eye which is relevant here is the belief that it can 'attach' itself to women in certain conditions if they go outside their homes often. Virgins, new brides and pregnant women — that is, a sizeable proportion of all young women — are particularly likely to be attacked. The woman who wears scent and makes herself look beautiful attracts an attack, as does the woman who goes near any uncultivated areas. One *pirzada* woman was reported to have given birth to a spastic child because she had persisted in going out while she was pregnant, another blamed her frequent headaches on the envious glances which were directed at her when she attended weddings and other functions.

These represent only certain of the beliefs relating to the evil eye, but they are important in attributing the responsibility for the attack as much to the victim as to the aggressor. Women who persist in going out have only themselves to blame if they suffer from attacks of the evil eye. Along with fear of gossip, concern about the evil eye is an important mechanism which regulates the activities of the *pirzada* women, and acts as a brake on their movements outside their homes, despite their voiced desire to go out more freely.

But the women are not all of one opinion about the extent to which it is permissible for young women to go out. Often enough, women protect one another by concealing the extent of their movements from those — older women and some men — who wish them to be more restricted. Sometimes, the efforts at concealment backfire. One Friday a middle-aged woman took her teenage daughter to Delhi to pray in the main mosque and to buy a book of tales about the Prophet Muhammad. Shortly after they left, the woman's own mother arrived and enquired of the daughters-in-law where they were. They were frightened to admit the truth and said that they were visiting in the village, but the old woman found that she had been deceived and as a result was angry at the deceit as well as at the absence of the other two even on such an apparently worthy errand. More often the concealment is from the men, whose remoteness from the home generally means that no lie actually has to pass the lips of the women.

But men may have to be involved. Several young women said that they have found it made things easier to ask permission from their father as well as their mother for any outing. Within reason, permission is generally given, and care not to betray parental trust ensures that permission will continue to be given in future. The most convenient way for young women to go out is with others their own age, or at least with other women, but if the journey is somewhat distant — say to Old Delhi — they are expected to go with a male relative.

Thus, the young women cannot easily go far from their homes whenever they wish. They generally have to do so at the convenience of some man in their household. But the men may be engrossed in urgent business at the shrine or other pressing work, and they often ask the women to wait for their errands until they need to go to Old Delhi on business for themselves. In some senses, then, the demands of *purdah* mean that the *pirzada* men are often compelled to take time over tasks which they might prefer not to do. Often enough, indeed, they are expected to run errands to the local *bazar* for the women of their household, and not just to buy the food. But if a wedding is imminent, the women have to be directly involved in the purchases — material has to be chosen for the bride's suits, household goods have to be bought, jewellery has to be ordered. Even at normal times the women are continually wanting items for their needlework. Some of the *pirzada* men clearly consider that their time is wasted as they wait for their womenfolk to select threads for embroidery or lace and tiny beads for the borders of their *dupatta*. One young man, deputed to select the velvet for new drapes at the shrine, agreed to take his wife with him; but when his mother suggested that he should also take his two teenage sisters to let them have an outing, he immediately objected, half in jest, 'Do you want to drive me mad!' His bantering was taken in lively spirit by the girls and their mother, and without much further persuasion on their part he told them to get themselves ready to come with him. His comment does, however, uncover something of the attitudes of the men, who feel themselves put upon by the need to accompany their womenfolk.

If the men protest at having to go on trivial expeditions, the women themselves are not always happy that they have to tolerate the presence of a man. They feel that their privacy is infringed, that their purchases are too closely scrutinized, and that the men are unwillingly being compelled to spend their

149

precious time on matters which hold little interest for them. One young woman pleaded with me to act as her chaperon:

> I like to go shopping about once a month, and buy a batch of threads for embroidery and new designs and so forth. But I can't bear going with my father or older brother. It's not that they don't like me to go, but I do get so tired of their questions. 'Why do I need so much green thread?' 'What's wrong with that particular shade?' . . . Or whatever it might be. You see, when I go with them, they expect me to keep my face covered and stand behind them, and *they* ask the questions, with me prompting them from behind. It's so much better to be able to put my veil back and talk properly to the stall holder.

The Burqa

Of all the aspects of *purdah,* the veiling of women when they leave their homes is the most conspicuous to the outsider, and, for the *pirzada* women, it is the *burqa* which is the focus of many complaints about the problems which they meet when they leave their homes. All the difficulties which I have just elaborated are compounded by the *burqa:* young and old are vocal in their objections to it.

The *burqa* is a garment for public places. It is the most extreme way in which women can hide themselves when confronted with strangers. In the company of other women, or close male relatives, in places where there is no danger of being seen by unrelated men, the *burqa* is unnecessary. But outside the home, all the *pirzada* women over the age of about 25 regularly wear the *burqa*, and many younger women do as well. Some girls still in their teens have persuaded their parents to allow them not to wear the *burqa,* but all of them possess a *burqa* to be worn on those rare occasions when they go to the shrine, even if they do not use one to go shopping or to visit relatives in the village.

On only one occasion did I see some of the older women — and even then not all of them — outside their homes without a *burqa.* This was during the month of Moharram when the martyrdom of Husain (the Prophet's grandson) and his party is commemorated.[2] The party was besieged, until the final massacre took place on the 10th of the month. During the first ten days, prayers are said over blessed food and drink, 'military' processions re-enact the fighting, funeral dirges are chanted by the 'tombs' which represent the graves of Husain and his closest relatives, and on the day of the 10th a funeral procession takes the 'tombs' of the martyrs for burial. A constant theme is the supplying of drink to participants — for the martyrs died thirsty — and the women's ritual which takes place on the evening of the 7th is one of many which illustrates this through the use of *sharbat,* a drink of diluted sweetened milk flavoured with rose water and pistachio nuts. Most of the *pirzada* men go to the shrine, and a police guard at the gate of the village prevents strange men from entering. Late in the evening, women from each *pirzada* household congregate on a raised platform inside the village. Each one brings a jug of *sharbat*, sweetmeats and some candles and joss sticks. The *sharbat* is pooled, and then one of the *pirzada* men comes to bless the drink and the other items. To commemorate the thirst of all the martyrs, each woman in turn drinks a glass of *sharbat*. At the end, each takes away a lighted candle, 'so that there may be light in every home during the next year'.

Some of the women present when I attended were wearing their *burqa*, but all had their veils tossed back over their heads. What was much more striking, though, was the greater number of the *pirzada* women who did not wear their *burqa* at all. Among these were not just young women, but also several elderly women who had told me that they never leave their homes without their veils over their faces – even some who said that they rarely leave their homes in daylight lest their features show. Most of the women present were dressed as they would have been at home, with their *duppatta* over their heads but with their faces completely uncovered – just as they might have been if they had been the martyrs they were commemorating. In conversation afterwards, some of the women talked of 'our one night of freedom'.

On other days, though, the alleys outside their homes are public space. All the elderly women and many of the young married women and teenagers only leave the privacy of their homes when they are completely covered, even if they are only intending to walk a dozen yards to a relative's house round the corner. The *burqa* is a relatively new garment to the *pirzade*. Until about 30 years ago women would wrap themselves closely in a shawl to move around within the village, for only *pirzade* lived there then. If they went beyond the confines, it would only be in a sedan chair which would be brought right to the gate. On the whole, there is a rather grudging admission that the *burqa* has allowed greater freedom of movement outside the village. Even so, 'who likes the *burqa* these days?' was a frequent comment from the *pirzada* women.

The *pirzada* women have several objections to the *burqa*. In Delhi, cotton clothing is sufficient during the daytime even in the winter months, and during the height of the hot season in May and June, the daytime temperatures may soar well above 100 degrees Fahrenheit. So one major complaint is that the *burqa* is uncomfortably hot. It is worn over the normal dress and *shalwar* which the women wear in their homes. Even though the *burqa* is made of lightweight material – cotton or satin, often flimsy, though never transparent – the extra layer of clothing is an unwelcome addition during more than six months of the year. One young woman commented:

From the point of view of modesty, the new style *burqa* is very bad: the clinging lines show up too much of the body's lines. From that point of view, the old style *burqa* is much better – but then in the heat it is positively dangerous. The tight skull cap means that a woman's head gets very hot and there is no chance to sweat properly. Women sometimes get giddy or faint after going out in such a *burqa* in the hot weather. A shawl

151

wrapped around the body is much safer and also more modest — but even that is unpleasant when it's warm.

Several women explicitly commented that the *burqa* is a disincentive to going out at all during the hottest months of the year. If the choice is between going out in a *burqa* and not going out at all, it can be preferable to stay at home. A young woman who wears a modern style black *burqa* said that for several months of the year she hardly ever goes out:

> It's just terrible. It would be bad enough going out in that heat without a *burqa*, with the sun beating down all day. But just imagine what it's like for us having to cope with an extra layer of clothes! I always arrive drenched to the skin with sweat. With both veils over our faces, the sweat pours down in great streams, right through our scalp, right down our necks — and it has no chance to dry out as we go along. Rather than that, I prefer the imprisonment of staying at home, even though I don't like that either.

In addition, the requirement that they go out with veils over their faces means that they can see very little — so little that several women said that there is never any pleasure in going out:

> What's the point? You have to spend so much time peering out through the veil to watch your step, that you don't have any time to look around. Why, only the other day when we were going to that wedding in Old Delhi, I tripped over some grating over a drain. With hardly any practice going out, I'm always afraid of some mishap — the whole business of going out has little attraction.

That was a woman of nearly forty, who rarely has the chance to go out, except for some special occasion. A similar comment came from a girl who wears the *burqa* only when she goes to the shrine:

> It's impossible to see where you're going. I find it very hard as I'm used to walking along without trouble. The last time I went to the shrine, I missed my footing and slipped into a drain. My feet were filthy, and I had to wash when I arrived at the shrine.

Her mother, a woman of nearly sixty, had much the same complaint. One day she was asking me to describe all the sights I had visited in India. Among them, she had seen only the Taj Mahal.

> If you can say 'saw'! When my son was being married we had to go to Gwalior for the wedding, and we broke the journey in Agra. But it was daytime, and there were hundreds of tourists, so I couldn't lift up my veils to have a look. What do you imagine I could see through two layers

of black chiffon? Absolutely useless!

Much of the women's distaste of the *burqa* takes the form of wry humour about absurd situations which can arise because of it. A young woman married inside the village came to visit her mother; she was laughing as she came in, and said that a water buffalo had nuzzled up to her in the alley outside. In a flash, her mother — a woman who is very strict about wearing the *burqa* herself and insists that her daughters do the same — retorted, 'That's hardly surprising, the way you look in that thing. She probably thought you were just another buffalo!' Another time, a goat normally tethered outside the door had gone missing, and there were no men at home to go looking for it. What should be done? Amid joking and laughter it was suggested that one of the young brides in the house should put on her *burqa* and, armed with a stick, be sent to bring the animal back. But, of course, nothing was done. A *pirzada* women must act with decorum outside and it would have been quite improper for a woman — especially one in a *burqa* — to chase a recalcitrant goat through the alleys of the village.

I was also with three sisters one time, and the youngest was protesting about how their mother likes them to wear the *burqa*. The cut had to be wide to conceal their figures — with the result that they look like 'buffaloes'. The girl put on her *burqa* to demonstrate:

I'll have to bend my knees to give you a proper impression, as she would really like us to have them nearly down to the ground. Then she likes long sleeves, so I'll have to pull mine right down and hunch my shoulders so that you can get the idea. But anyway, when we go out with Mother, she makes sure that our hands are hidden. We have to hold the two sides of the cape together at the front of our neck — but from the inside!

She snorted, as she minced round the room. Amidst all the mirth which this comic turn produced, the oldest sister solemnly announced that there are two advantages of the *burqa* that should not be forgotten. Her sister stopped in her tracks in amazement. With a twinkle in her eye, the oldest sister explained:

For one thing, the *burqa* hides what you're wearing underneath. If you have to go in a hurry, you can just change your *shalwar* and nobody will know about the dirty or torn dress which you were wearing for housework! The second benefit is that you can pass men in the street without being recognized. Sometimes I want to go to the cinema with my friend so I just tell my husband that we're going to the *bazar* (which he does not question) and off we go. Sometimes we pass him on the way back home, but he's none the wiser.

Our companions rocked with laughter.

There is, however, a more serious side to the anonymity of the *burqa*. When I was in Pakistan, I had often enough thought of acquiring a *burqa* so that I could become invisible and no longer be subjected to taunts from men in the streets. During my fieldwork in Hazrat Nizamuddin, I came to realize that this would be no solution, at least not in India. Perhaps even more than the discomfort of the heat and being unable to see the way, the taunts of strange men in the street were torments for the women.

The *pirzada* women wear dull-coloured *burqa*, with the veils down, in an effort to distract attention. But all too often they do not succeed. Shop-keepers and men walking in the street often call after them or follow them. The women believed that men in non-Muslim areas think that veiled women are easily embarrassed and are good bait for teasing, provided that they have no men with them. They think that veiled women are beautiful and they leer at them and tell them to lift their veils. Several women said that the men at Bhogal market have a special name for women who wear their *burqa* with the veil down: *band gobi* (literally 'closed cabbage'). One young woman, echoing comments made by others, told me:

> If we go there without any man, we are always troubled. Even grown men will follow us in the streets saying '*band gobi, band gobi*'. Sometimes, when it's all become unbearable, I've turned on them and told them that their wives must be *khooli gobi* [open cabbages] and that silences them. But I don't really like answering back like that — it really looks rather shameless, but it's the only way to stop their tormenting.

Many of the women are so upset that they said that there are several places where they simply never go because of the teasing from men. Even going on buses is a torture, because men think that they can stare with impunity at any woman with her face veiled.

The complaints of the *pirzada* women about the behaviour of men in the streets and *bazar* are a reflection of a common phenomenon, for what is called 'Eve-teasing' is frequent enough in Delhi. I know of no systematic study which can shed light on Eve-teasing, but I am quite sure that the *pirzada* women are mistaken to assume that only veiled women are the victims of it, even though they may be more sensitive — or may be believed to be more sensitive — to it. They saw the taunting to which they are subjected as a reflection of antagonism between Muslims and non-Muslims, but it is also, I think, a reflection of another split, that between men and women.

My impression is that young rather than old men indulge in Eve-teasing, and that students from wealthy families may tease women in the streets of New Delhi or around the universities and colleges, just as do the men in the *bazar* of Old Delhi. Their victims seem generally to be young women, particularly women who are alone: this is true for the *pirzada* women, whose gait and style of *burqa* betray their age, despite their veils.

Not all men taunt women in the street, and the *pirzada* men themselves do not behave in the ways which so distress their womenfolk, and they talk scornfully about the shameless and ill-mannered men who do. But enough men *do* 'tease' women in the streets to polarize men and women, and the *pirzada* women, at least, always think of the strange man as a threat, as the enemy, and of going out as a potential trial by fire. Newspaper reports and rumours about taxi-drivers who abduct women passengers make *pirzada* women fear that their fate could be much worse than the mere verbal assaults on their modesty which they often suffer. Even the company of other women does not necessarily prevent harassment, and going out alone beyond the confines of their village is seen as a tremendous risk. The taunting which so often greets them can only be seen as a rather crude form of social control. It is not that the *pirzada* men are themselves directly implicated in the teasing which makes the women dislike going out, but, as with the threat of the evil eye, the effect is that the *pirzada* women feel that their movements are perforce constrained. Despite all the disadvantages, the only way to prevent harassment is only to go out with a male relative.

For several reasons, then, the *pirzada* women regard the *burqa* with distaste. Nonetheless, elderly women who complain about it say that they cannot easily stop wearing it: to discard the *burqa* after wearing it for years would look shameless, and people would talk. One woman in her fifties, whose older daughters still wear the *burqa,* but whose younger ones often do not, was complaining to me one day about some cotton lawn which her husband had bought for her. 'Just typical of a man', she muttered, 'to buy such poor quality stuff. There are so many holes and faults in it that there won't be any saving in the end.' When I suggested that she could have gone herself, she said that she rarely goes out in the hot season because the *burqa* is so uncomfortable. Perhaps she should throw away her *burqa,* I proposed in jest. She laughed:

> I could hardly do that! People would think I'd become shameless overnight! My own mother would be furious. It's rather different if a girl has never worn a *burqa,* but it looks very bad if someone who's worn it for years suddenly emerges unveiled. Anyway, I suppose I've got used to it – I'd feel naked if I went out without my *burqa.*

Another woman, of about fifty, whose oldest daughter is the only one to wear the *burqa,* asserted that there is nothing in Islam which demands that women should go out of their homes wearing a *burqa.* It is quite sufficient if a woman covers her head and bosom with a thick shawl: her face does not have to be covered. Yet she herself wears a *burqa* with the veil down when she leaves her home:

> Yes, I do put down the veils when I go out. My eldest daughter and I both do, though the other girls do not. But it's all a question of habit, you know, and people would be shocked that a woman of my age had become so immodest as to show her face in public. I'd be embarrassed myself.

She has put up no opposition to her younger daughters, who only wear their *burqa* to go to the shrine. But several elderly women, themselves prepared to complain about the inconveniences of the *burqa,* insist that their daughters go out only if they are fully concealed. As one young woman put it:

> Young women are quite shameless in comparison with their elders! They
> wouldn't feel any shame about going out without a *burqa*. In fact probably
> most of the girls just becoming 'big' now will never have to wear the *burqa*.
> But don't think we wear the *burqa* because we want to — it's all so that
> we shall not offend our parents' feelings. They're a bit old-fashioned
> about things like this.

One of her cousins, also in her twenties, told me how a shopkeeper in a nearby
bazar had once asked her why she likes to wear the *burqa*: 'I told him that
I didn't like it at all, but I have to wear it because of my elders. They want me
to wear it, but I'd rather not.'

Before marriage, it all depends on the parents. If they permit their daughter
to go out without a *burqa,* it is unlikely that the girls will wear it regularly. A
few mothers commented laughingly that their daughters sometimes talk of
wearing the *burqa* so that they can be grown-up, but they do not always force
the girl to wear one. One girl in her late teens, however, lamented how she had
taken to wearing the *burqa* several years earlier so that she might become an
adult:

> Then one day, I began to go out without my *burqa,* and my mother called
> me back. She was furious! How could I dare to go out 'naked' like that!
> It was only then that I realized what a silly mistake I'd made in ever wearing
> the *burqa* at all!

Several other girls talked of the battles they had had over wearing the *burqa*
Several of them had, in the end, capitulated to their parents' insistence.

> When I was about 12, I became very tall, and my mother wouldn't let me
> go without a *burqa*. But I refused. For two years I never left our house! If
> there was a birthday party for one of our cousins, or if the others went to
> visit my sister, I had to stay at home. In the end, I thought there was no
> point in carrying on like this any more. Staying at home makes people go
> mad — so I decided to wear a *burqa* only so that I'd be allowed to go out
> at all. No, of course I don't like the *burqa* any better now, but at least I
> can go out sometimes.

Another teenage girl told me that she had stopped going to school because of
the *burqa*:

> My parents were happy for me to continue at school, but my grandmother
> was not. She insisted that I should only be allowed to go if I wore a *burqa*.
> But I felt so ridiculous — no one else wears a *burqa* to go to school and
> everyone stared at me. After a while, I just got so embarrassed that I
> stopped going to school. I couldn't stop wearing the *burqa*, so what option
> did I have?

In practice, though, the wearing of the *burqa* depends on context as well as on parental wishes. If parents do not insist that a girl begins to wear the *burqa,* she probably will only wear it when she goes to the shrine. When girls wear the *burqa* to avoid offending their parents' feelings, they are more than likely to remove it or at least toss the veils back over their heads when their parents are absent. Shopping in the nearby *bazar* is made more pleasant for the young women if they can walk around with their faces exposed: not only can they more easily talk to the shopkeepers but they suffer less taunting from strange men — and they can also cover their faces quickly if a *pirzada* comes into view.

In more distant places, where they are unlikely to meet anyone who will recognize them, they are quite willing to remove their *burqa* altogether. One girl explained that she always leaves the village by a longer route than necessary so that she can avoid passing her maternal grandmother's home: only that way can she manage to go out secretly without her *burqa,* and she knows that her mother will not report her. Other girls are expected to go out wearing the *burqa,* but they are still able to create opportunities for ridding themselves of it. A visit to a married sister in Delhi can provide the freedom to go shopping or see a film in Delhi without their *burqa* — even though they may be fully veiled during their journey to and from Hazrat Nizamuddin.

Sometimes male relatives — usually, but not always, young ones — collude in the activities of the young women, and I shall take this point up again in the final chapter. On one occasion, for instance, I accompanied several young women to a fair at the school which one of them used to attend. A short distance before the school, we scuttled down a side road, they looked around furtively, removed their *burqa* and stuffed them hurriedly into brown paper bags which their young brother carried. Older brothers also take part in this sort of subterfuge. I was told of the fun which several brothers and sisters had when their parents were away on the pilgrimage: they had even had picnics in various Delhi tourist spots, and none of the young women wore their *burqa.* As far as they knew, their parents had not learnt of their 'misdemeanours'. Older men may also suggest that young women discard their *burqa:*

> When my uncle came from Pakistan on holiday he wanted to take us on treats. Our parents gave their permission, but I'm not sure how much they learnt about what we did! One day he took us to the zoo and when we were inside the gates he told us to take our *burqa* off. He was right. What would have been the point of trying to see all the animals through our veils?

Such deceits are not universally approved, though. Several women felt that a woman should either wear the *burqa* all the time or not at all. Adjusting one's behaviour to the atmosphere of the place or in relation to the presence or absence of people who might report to elders in the village, was felt by some to be an unworthy form of double-dealing. One middle-aged *pirzada* woman put it scathingly:

I just don't know what the world is coming to. The times are bad. Do you know that the girls of today think nothing of going out shopping half-naked, with their *burqa* trailing out of their shopping-baskets?

One girl of about sixteen also censured those of her age who sometimes wear the *burqa*, and sometimes do not. She felt that it was insincere to leave parents with the impression that the *burqa* continues to be worn once the girls are out of sight. Girls should be more honest. But when I pointed out that she had never been faced with battles at home about wearing the *burqa*, and even with the choice of going out veiled or not at all, she conceded that she was fortunate and might indeed behave that way if placed in such a position:

I'm sure that my grandfather would prefer my unmarried aunt and me to wear a *burqa* when we go out. But we don't want to. I hope that I'll never have to wear a *burqa*. We go out without one, and my grandfather doesn't say anything. He realizes that the times are changing. My grandmother does not want us to be held back, so she lets us go shopping with my mother and aunts and doesn't make us wear a *burqa* either.

But what would happen when she was married? That of course is uncertain. While wearing the *burqa* depends on parental wishes before marriage, the husband's wishes dominate after marriage. If he wants his wife to wear a *burqa*, she will have to comply. Several unmarried girls said that one reason why they are anxious about their marriages is that they cannot know how strict their in-laws might be until they are married, unless their wedding takes place inside the village. But, while marriage outside is marriage into the unknown, marriage within the village almost certainly means that the bride will have to wear a *burqa*. There are only two married *pirzada* women living in the village who do not wear it, both of them born in the village. On the other hand, several brides from outside have been made to wear the *burqa* for the first time after their marriage. One man was married to his cousin from Pakistan who had never worn a *burqa* there, and at first she managed to hold out against criticism when she appeared in the village without it. But after a few months, she began to wear it, at least within the village. Brides from other places in India also commented that the *pirzade* are much more old-fashioned than people from their home towns: '*pirzada* men', they comment, 'think that it is more honourable for their wives to be properly covered'.

Outside the village there is more variation, and unmarried girls consider that brides with husbands who do not like the *burqa* are fortunate indeed. The alacrity with which several young women have discarded their *burqa* after marriage should dispel any doubts about their complaints. Such women talk happily about the 'freedom' of their in-laws in contrast to the 'strictness' of their parents. For the sake of their parents' feelings, though, several of these women wear the *burqa* when they visit the village.

I'm much more free since my marriage, but that's because I married away from my mother. I always wear my *burqa* to come back to Hazrat Nizamuddin. But when I'm with my husband, I often don't. It all depends on the place. There are some parts of Old Delhi where it really looks very bad for a woman to go out without a *burqa*. On the other hand we went to see a film in New Delhi the other day and I didn't wear a *burqa* then, of course. My mother would be horrified.

The times are certainly changing. Few of the very young girls are likely to go through battles about wearing the *burqa*. Even some of the present teenagers have escaped that. But for many, the options are currently often limited in practice, either to deception, or to waiting hopefully for marriage into a family where they are not required to wear the *burqa*. While marriage outside the village may be marriage into the unknown, for many of the young women it represents the only hope they presently have of living under a less strict regime of seclusion.

Facilities for Women Outside Their Homes

Added to the complaints about the *burqa,* the *pirzada* women also claim that the paucity of suitable facilities for secluded women outside their homes acts as yet another disincentive to their going out. Their particular complaints mainly relate to the inadequate facilities which their menfolk provide for them during festivals. It is not that they want to be in the midst of the crowd of pilgrims or that they want to show themselves off to the public, but they did feel that they were entitled to see as well as hear what is happening. Sometimes there are simply no facilities provided for women in *purdah* and so there is no question that they can go anyway, but this they resent as much as the pathetic efforts which are sometimes made. Older women in particular often lamented that they have not been able to attend some of the singing sessions during the festivals as the places where they would have to sit are too public.— often without so much as a curtain dividing off the women's area from the men's.

My own experience of sampling the facilities for women at public functions lends a good deal of support to the women's complaints. There was the *'urs* ceremony held during April, when the main court of the shrine was covered with canopies to shade the male pilgrims, while the women who wanted to keep in seclusion were relegated to one of the royal tomb enclosures where they could only peer throught the marble trellis with the sun beating down on their heads. Several of the women pilgrims had taken off their *burqa* and draped them over the enclosure so that they could create some shade, which they invited me to share. Again, during Moharram, when dirges and laments were sung in memory of Husain and his party, the women were despatched into a side-room, divided from the main hall by a solid padlocked door, and the sounds which reached them were muffled and often drowned by the conversation of the men sitting just on the other side of the door. The women often enough made comments which indicated that they felt much as I did about being excluded in this way.

A few days before one of the major *'urs*, I asked a middle-aged woman if she would be attending one of the poetry and singing programmes which are held each evening during the *'urs*. She told me that she had only been once in her life:

> It was useless to go. They had placed the women's section so much to the side out of the sight of men that we couldn't hear anything properly. The poets' voices did not carry as far as us — and there's no joy in just *hearing* the singers.

Similarly, during each *'urs*, the *pirzade* hold a special commemoration for Hazrat Ali (the husband of Fatima and father of Hasan and Husain) which only the *pirzade* and their personal 'guests' attend. A meal is served, consisting of the frugal dishes which Hazrat Nizamuddin used to eat and there is a short poetry and singing session afterwards. The programme was held in a hall adjacent to the cell belonging to one of the *pirzade*, and the women were allocated to the cell. When the daughter-in-law of the cell's owner arrived, a series of protests arose: a glass-panelled door which had previously permitted the women to see the singers had recently been blocked up and the women could now only peep through the glass panels of the remaining badly placed door. A servant boy was asked why the door had been removed and he replied that it was to make a new room.

> You see how it is. The women of the family aren't even told when this sort of thing is planned. Just look how the men don't think about the women at all. We used to have such a good view of the singers, but now we can't see them at all. All we can see are our own men. We might as well have stayed at home — there's no pleasure without seeing the singers. It would be as well to hear them on the radio!

Many of the older women said they would very much like to attend singing programmes and the like at the shrine, but even if special arrangements had been made for them to go they felt they could hardly be expected to enjoy going. The arrangements outside their homes are in the hands of the men, and the women cannot expect to alter them to their own benefit. For many, the response is simply never to attend public functions at the shrine.

In sum, then, the *pirzada* women say that they often find that going outside their homes is no great pleasure. Whether they are taunted by men or lose their way, are overcome with heat in their *burqa* or are relegated to a place where they can see or hear little of a public function, leaving their homes is often fraught with difficulties and anxieties. Staying at home is no more of an unalloyed pleasure for them. It is not just a refuge from the harsh outside world, though in part it is that. It is not just a haven which the women have no wish to abandon. Apart from the few older women for whom going out is a genuine chore, staying at home all the time, doing household chores, being married to a man who may be a stranger, and bearing children for him are things from which they wish they could escape: but the world outside the home, with all the problems it presents to the *pirzada* women, provides no real escape for them.

The complaints of the *pirzada* women about their lives at home and outside indicate that there are limits to their acceptance of their position. At the same time, there are also limits to the questions which they raise about the seclusion of women: there is much that they accept and take for granted, just as there is much that they criticize and question. If they accepted everything without demur, if their ideological subordination were total, there would seem to be little room for change from within. But, if they questioned everything, if the system were merely insecurely held together by the men's economic power and threats of naked force on the one hand, and the women's compliance in the face of this on the other, it is unlikely that such a system could possibly have survived as long as it has without major threats to its stability. The stance of the *pirzada* women, is, however, a complex mixture of deep-rooted commitment and reluctant compliance, of accepting things as they are and of undermining them through their questions and evasions.

And yet, the status of their complaints is nevertheless problematic. That their grievances are probably rather new is plausible, but that they are important and fundamental has yet to be established. Often enough there is little consistency between the behaviour of the *pirzada* women and their comments. Are their complaints, then, just empty verbalizations which have little relevance to their everyday behaviour? Are their complaints just a mode of adjusting to their situation, a form of tension management, of catharsis which removes the pressure of their discomfort? Clearly, many of their complaints seem not much more than verbal protests, since they have little possibility of attaining the changes which they seem to advocate. Often enough, indeed, the women are aware that they have little choice but to grumble behind the scenes and perform as expected while in public.

However, their little acts of cheating and deceits in other contexts indicate that their comments are not just means of releasing tension, though they may also have this effect. Where there are loopholes, where there are ways round the system, where it is possible to go out unveiled without being found out, some of the women are prepared to run risks and are prepared to break the rules which are laid down for them. Over many parts of their lives, individual women often can have little influence: their schooling, their marriage, their outings and their lives at home are all matters which are often largely organized by others. In other matters, where there are openings for circumventing the *status quo,* the women — the young ones in particular — are willing to exploit them.

But there is a more fundamental problem than this. The complaints of the women may be more than empty verbalization, but just how basic are the challenges and criticisms which they make? How profound can be their influence? Are the women who complain really threatening the stability of the entire *purdah* system in Hazrat Nizamuddin? These are questions which will be taken up in the next chapter.

References

1. This account is based on several sources: W. Crooke (ed.), *Islam in India*, (London, 1921), pp. 1-83; C. Maloney (ed.), *The Evil Eye*, (New York, 1976); G. Foster, 'The Anatomy of Envy', *Current Anthropology*, 13, (1972), pp.165-202; B. Spooner, 'The Evil Eye in the Middle East', in M. Douglas (ed.), *Witchcraft Confessions and Accusations*, (London, 1970); B.A. Donaldson, *The Wild Rue*, (London, 1938).
2. More details on the Karbela massacre and Moharram practices can be found in M.H. Ali, *Observations on the Mussulmauns of India*, (London, 1832), vol. 1, pp.29-96; W. Crooke (ed.), *Islam in India*, (London, 1921), pp.151-85; India, Census Commissioner, *Moharram in Two Cities (Lucknow and Delhi)*, (Delhi, 1966); G.E. von Grunebaum, *Muhammadan Festivals*, (New York, 1974).

Putting henna on the hands

7. The Two Faces of Purdah

The keystone to the maintenance of *purdah* among the *pirzade* in Hazrat Nizamuddin is the asymmetry between the sexes and economic powerlessness of the *pirzada* women. However, it would be wrong to suggest that this alone is an adequate assessment of the situation. There is more than forced compliance, more than the surly obedience of the women in the face of superior power. There is substantial evidence that the *pirzada* women have internalized, and come to take for granted, important elements of the *status quo*. This internalization enhances the stability of the *purdah* system, and it is possible to point to the importance of ideology as well as economic factors in its reproduction. But even this is not the whole story, for internalization co-exists with pockets of resistance, and with some awareness by the women of their subordination. They appreciate how their interests may differ from those of the men. They express discontent and resentment — and their behaviour reflects their somewhat reluctant compliance as well as their active commitment. Why, then, are the women not pitted against the men in an effort to press for a change in their position?

Interest groups articulate group conflicts, but they do not arise spontaneously and their development may be blocked or even reversed. Is it, then, that the situation of the *pirzada* women lacks the conditions under which a self-conscious organized protest might arise? Just what are the structural constraints which might hamper the unity of the *pirzada* women?

Men as an Obstacle

One possibility is that the *pirzada* men have themselves prevented the women from organizing. The interest which they have in preserving the seclusion of the *pirzada* women seems obvious enough. Aside from the benefits which accrue to them from the childbearing and domestic work of the women, there is also the importance of their position in the shrine. As several women put it, 'the men like *purdah* because of *izzat* (honour)'. In other words, the men consider that the seclusion of their women has important implications for their work in the shrine, not just limited to freeing the men for that work. Their incomes, their very livelihoods, depend on the ability of the *pirzade* to persuade

165

pilgrims to visit the shrine. Apart from the pull of the revered Saint himself — which is considerable — the *pirzade* consider that their own reputations have a bearing on the success of their projects. They are subject to consumer control and thus have a special stake in the maintenance of their public respectability. Their income is uncertain and undependable. Their claims that their holiness and outstanding qualities entitle them to work in the shrine have to carry conviction — and the proper behaviour of their womenfolk is one element in this.

But if the *pirzada* men need to keep their women in *purdah,* they are in no way jointly organized to do so. They do not lock the doors of their houses when they go out. They have not organized a rota of sentries to check on the movements of the women. In some respects, they might appear rather unformidable opponents for the women, for their ranks are in notable disarray. Their work in the shrine often sets them in competition with one another: building up faithful clientele for their practices, managing to sell enough flowers to keep a family, trying to accumulate a large number of wealthy 'guests' can all set the *pirzada* men against one another, even though they are involved in joint enterprises too.

It is impossible to assess how effectively the *pirzada* men could — in some hypothetical final resort — sink their differences. Only two examples came to my notice of the *pirzada* men taking collective action against any woman, and in both cases the unity was limited to one of the *pirzada* Families. The case of the *pirzada* woman who married secretly has already been mentioned: she was deprived of her share in the rota system. In the second case, a *pirzada* man had secretly married an outside woman who would normally have been entitled to collect his share when she was widowed, but when this happened, she too was deprived of her share. Clearly, then, the men can punish those who transgress the bounds of acceptable behaviour. The women rarely referred to sanctions which the men might employ — but it is difficult to assess how much the potential power of the men is simply part of the unstated backdrop to social life among the *pirzade*, and constitutes a reality to which the women continually orient their behaviour.

Probably more important, though, is the threat that the *pirzada* men could manifest their power over the women of their own household. The *pirzada* women are dependent, but not on the *pirzada* men as a whole. The men of their household are the ones who could withdraw the provision which they make for their female kin, and the *pirzada* women are aware of this. The woman who refuses to marry cannot expect that her brother will willingly maintain his old-maid sister. Islam no doubt gives a woman economic rights, but it would be folly for a woman to press for them. A brother can hardly be expected to help his sister out if her marriage is unhappy, and he is all the more likely to wash his hands of her if she presses for her share of the inheritance from their parents. A husband, offended by demands for the marriage settlement, could — in league with his mother — make a woman's life a misery. She could be made the drudge for her in-laws, while other brides in the household might still be given pretty clothes and jewellery. She might even be subjected to the shame of a divorce. The *pirzada* women think it better not to precipitate a confrontation. The very men on whom they depend are also the ones who can most effectively punish their misdemeanours.

It would, however, leave an entirely false impression to stop there. The *pirzada* men are not a united interest group, though they wield enormous power over the women of their own households. But that power is not always employed to obstruct change. Indeed, several of the elderly *pirzada* women are so much the agents of conservative stability that some men — old and young — take the part of the younger women against them. Perhaps the men are more aware of changes in the outside world. Perhaps — to be cynical — they are prepared to permit some freedoms to the younger women because they realize that a cloistered sister or daughter might prove to be unmarriageable. Whatever the case, several young women have their menfolk to thank for improvements in their lives. A pair of brothers, for instance, were too young to influence the educational fate of their older sister, but when they were in their twenties they were able to persuade their mother to permit their teenage sisters to remain longer at school. There is also a man of 65 who protects his daughter's daughter from the wrath of her paternal grandmother, by occasionally letting her go on outings with his daughters and then taking her home himself to explain that it was he who gave permission. And several women have been able to withstand pressure from other women (say, to take their daughters away from school) by explaining — quite disingenuously — that they have to obey their husband. The greater power of the men can sometimes be manipulated in favour of the younger women.

The Women Divided

In any case, there is no powerful force of women ranged against the men, so is it the case that there is no pressure from the women themselves to form an interest group? Possibly there are structural constraints which limit the ability of the women to communicate with one another and develop joint consciousness of their common position.

One factor which might be of some importance is the isolation of women living in different households. Young and Harris suggest that this may be important in reducing the women's perception of their common interests. They argue that when the household is emphasized as a unit of consumption and production, co-operative links between women are likely to be minimized — especially where resources are limited either naturally or through surplus appropriation — because women depend on the men of their own household. The household, they suggest, 'is a key ideological construct used to divide women, to help mask their common interest'.[1]

Among the *pirzade,* while individual women are generally not isolated from one another, women in different households are. The income which the men bring from the shrine is fragmented and distributed at the level of the household. The basic unit of both production and consumption is the

household — and the men of different households are set in competition with
one another in their work. In extreme cases, the conflicts between men in the
shrine result in the women of their households breaking off links with one
another: invitations to weddings, shares of sacrificed animals, or sweetmeats
which are prepared during festivals may pointedly not be sent to the household of a serious rival. Usually the competition is muted, but the general
point remains: women in different households are indirectly in competition
with one another over the scarce resources which the shrine affords. Their
subsistence interests are oriented around the success of the particular men on
whom they depend.

In their own housework, the women are also separated from those in
different households. There is no joint work above the level of the household,
apart from those exceptional circumstances where a woman may help out
when a close relative is ill or menstruating. Women work mostly in the homes
where they are resident. Housework is expected to be time consuming and the
pirzada women spend most of their time at home doing the duties which are
expected of them. When the *pirzada* women are brought together in larger
gatherings — during weddings or when they perform readings from books about
the Prophet Muhammad — the preparations for entertaining large numbers of
guests are not done by the women jointly, but by male cooks from the *bazar*
who are paid for their services.

Even within the household, women may be divided. Closely related women
are almost expected to fight with one another, for their interests are perceived
as divergent. The images of the evil woman in popular fiction and films point
to some of the lines of potential fission within the household. The mother-in-
law who maltreats her sons' wives and vies for the young men's affections; the
jealousies between the wives of different brothers as they compete over the
resources which are allocated to the education or marriages of their children;
the bullying of a bride by her husband's sisters or the squabbles between
women married to one man: these are the stuff of fiction and often of real
life too.

In Hazrat Nizamuddin, the tensions are recognized, but they generally
remain beneath the surface. The fears of unmarried girls about how their in-
laws will treat them; the turning down of offers of marriage from widowers
lest a girl is charged with favouritism once her own children are born; the
woman who turned down an offer of marriage for her step-daughter from a
man known for his quick temper, commenting that 'people would say I would
never have done that to my own daughter — that I was only being step-
motherly'; the expectation that the wives of brothers will fight in due course,
for their interests are inherently divergent and only the overarching control of
the elderly mother-in-law can prevent an untimely split in the social and
spatial fabric of the household; in all this, the *pirzade* are but reflections of
much more general patterns.[2] Women are likely to quarrel, though older
pirzada women generally manage to keep their households intact with their
married sons and their wives and children living under the same roof. Once the
linking parent is dead, however, the cracks in the fabric can no longer be

concealed.

The *pirzada* women, then, are divided from one another: those in different households, even those within the same household, have interests which diverge. Women are constantly being pulled apart from one another.

On the other hand, there are grounds for suggesting that these divisions among the *pirzada* women are not insuperable barriers to the development of an interest group, and, indeed, that there are factors which might actually facilitate joint action by the *pirzada* women. Two factors seem particularly likely to countervail the divisions among them.

Firstly, the *pirzada* women are resident in a small compact village, and they are able to move around within its confines without a male chaperon. Further, the village is the preserve of the *pirzada* women for much of the time, because the men spend so much of their lives in the shrine or going elsewhere on business. On the face of it, the possibilities for the growth of corporate action by the women seem considerable — though they have not taken advantage of them.

Secondly, the pattern of marriages among the *pirzade* would seem to contribute further to erasing the divisions among the women. In northern India, a bride typically moves several miles away from her parents' home, into a home which is peopled with strangers. Her husband is unknown to her, and so too are her mother-in-law, her husband's sisters and the other 'brides' in her husband's household. The new bride — though briefly pampered — is powerless, and enters on the lowest rung in an alien environment.

While not all marriages concerning the *pirzade* take place within the village, many do. A *pirzada* bride may move yards rather than miles, and her husband's close kin may be known to her parents — if not to her — over many years. Most of the women married to *pirzada* men are simultaneously 'daughters' and 'daughters-in-law' of the village of Hazrat Nizamuddin. Moreover, several of the *pirzada* women who have been married outside have returned to Hazrat Nizamuddin, either after being widowed or having persuaded their husbands to take a house in the village. Including these women, the married *pirzada* women living in the village outnumber outside women by nearly three to one. When the unmarried 'daughters' of the village of marriageable age are taken into consideration, outside women are outnumbered by over five to one by those born in the village. All but two women from outside live in the company of several women from the village itself, and outside women do not form a separate or excluded grouping.

While a married woman is expected to involve herself most closely in the household affairs of her in-laws, her links with her mother and sisters persist, and they may live only a few yards away along an alley. Moreover, the women in her in-laws' household may be known to her: her mother-in-law might even be a beloved aunt (though generally the relationship is more distant than this), while the other women in the household may have been her playmates or cousins whom she has known since infancy. Bonds of affection link women whose interests might diverge. A formal analysis of kinship among the *pirzade* would stress pedigree and links through men, but conceal the vital ties among the women which could be the kernel of a women's organization. Despite the divisions among the women, between households as well as within them, there are important cross-cutting ties, which suggest that the *pirzada* women *could* organize jointly. Even this is not straightforward, though, for marriage within the village means that a woman's father and brothers are also nearby, and they could exercise pressures which might support or even, perhaps, contradict the powers of her in-laws over her. It is difficult to assess the structural factors which might affect the development of a women's pressure group. But in the case of Hazrat Nizamuddin some appear to limit, while others seem to facilitate, such a development.[3]

The Women's Interests

Maybe, in any case, structural factors are less important, in this case, than the effectiveness of the ideological subordination of the *pirzada* women. Perhaps they are incapable of formulating a programme for joint action. Maybe there is no ready framework within which they could justify pressing their claims. Possibly the interests of the women have yet to be fully articulated and made manifest. Maybe the *pirzada* women are a 'muted group' whose ability to formulate a coherent programme for change is obstructed by the culture in which they are embedded. Certainly, there is substantial evidence of internalization, of the terms of their discourse being set by the dominant culture.[4]

This is evident even in the complaints which they make. Their objections are not directed against their destiny as wives and mothers, but at the ways in which they are unable to perform these roles adequately. Their complaints amount to requests that their lives should be made more pleasant within the same overall framework. They do not wish to be set loose to earn their own keep, but they do want their positions as wife, mother and domestic worker to be improved. They want permission to go about outside their homes more freely, to visit their relatives, to go shopping, to see films — but not to work. To be able to go out unveiled or to have enough formal education to command a respectable husband on the marriage market, to take on the responsibilities of motherhood without being harassed by the demands of numerous children — these are the improvements which the young women, in particular, seek Their vision of how their lot can be improved is far from revolutionary. They tinker with the system, they press for small changes which would make their position more palatable to them, but which cannot be said to strike at the root of the *purdah* system.

The divisions among the *pirzada* women, their economic dependence, their need to avoid antagonizing their male protectors, and their acceptance of much of the ideological buttressing on which their seclusion rests — while important — cannot give a complete account of the *pirzada* women's position. The women themselves take an additional dimension into account, which would suggest that they would be mistaken to demand profound changes. This is not at all to negate the foregoing picture, but to round it out. If *purdah* has its dark side, it also has its light one. *Purdah* is both abhorrent and attractive, both deprivation and privilege. The *pirzada* women are pulled in contradictory directions, and the interest which they have in maintaining — rather than undermining — the *status quo* has to be assessed too.

Purdah: A Negotiated Privilege

The imbalances between the *pirzada* men and women have perhaps been too starkly drawn in the preceding chapters. The *pirzada* women may be economically powerless, but they are not completely reduced to the status of pawns. Several writers suggest that women can be actors and strategists even when they are restricted to the domestic sphere. When major decisions are made outside the home, they work at a disadvantage with respect to men, but they can nonetheless exercise some influence over their own lives and those of other people.[5]

For the *pirzada* women this influence is largely restricted to the women's sphere, in the homes in the village. It is there that the women are embedded in a domain in which they can be powerful and at ease, in contrast to their powerlessness and unease in the outside world.[6] It is there that they can organize rotas for housework and socialize the young children in their charge. Many of the ceremonies during weddings are the prerogative of the women and they may also hold their own readings from sacred books to mark festivals. The women's world is where valued relationships with other women can grow relatively undisturbed by men's intrusions.

Perhaps most important of all is the control over information on which the men rely. Through networks of friendship and gossip from which men are excluded, the women can build up banks of information about suitable marriage partners. Women can often best assess the eligibility of young women to marry grooms in the village, for they have access to the homes of other people and can view potential brides. The women depend on the goodwill of their menfolk for their maintenance, but the men too rely on the women not to sabotage the system seriously. The economic power of the men is crucial but its exercise is checked by the possibility of retaliation by the women. It is in this sense that Friedl talks of the crucial power of the apparently weaker party, and Nelson of the negotiated order, for all the power is not on one side.[7]

The *pirzada* women are not equally able to strategize and exercise influence, though. Respect for the elderly is an important idiom in Hazrat Nizamuddin and women consider themselves entitled to the respect of their juniors, whether male or female. This is another dimension on which women may be divided from one another. Seniority is largely, but not exclusively, a matter of age. A mother is senior to her daughters, an older sister to her younger sisters. Within an extended household, the seniority of brides follows the order of birth of their husbands. Women are also junior to their older brothers' wives, even if the brides are younger in age.

Seniors are entitled to a display of respect from their juniors. Amongst sisters and sisters-in-law juniors rarely cover their heads, but grandmothers or middle-aged women visiting the house can expect their juniors to honour them by keeping their heads covered. In days gone by, young girls were sent from the room and it is still considered disrespectful if a girl takes an active part in conversation with older women. Seniors are also addressed respectfully: generally, a senior calls a junior by name, but the junior reciprocates with a title. A senior can expect obedience without question and the junior who 'gives answers' is roundly criticized. Several married women avoid offending their mothers-in-law by simply never making requests which will be refused. The rule of the elderly should be a rule of love, with instructions given gently and criticisms gently voiced, and generally it is. But it is rule nevertheless, and respect for elders is one very important way in which older women can exert an influence over the lives of their juniors, even though elderly women are just as economically dependent on the men.

There are shifts in power during the life-cycle. Young women can look to the future for, and the elderly have, a considerable stake in the *status quo*. Deviance could be costly, while patience should bring its own rewards in time. By playing the game according to the rules, a woman can hope to win a position of influence, albeit only limited influence.

Promotion does not come simply with age, though. The benefits which can come to a woman are best exemplified through a consideration of marriage and motherhood. Despite the women's complaints about some aspects of these roles, a woman has to be married and become a mother if she is to taste the rewards which are available to elderly women. The aged spinster — actually unknown in Hazrat Nizamuddin — has no place, nor the barren woman nor the woman with no sons.

At the time of her marriage, the bride steps out of her position as *larki* (girl) and becomes an *aurat* (woman). No unmarried woman is regarded as a 'woman' by the *pirzade* — marriage and adulthood go together for them. During the showing of her face the day after the marriage, the bride is launched into adult obligations. Gifts presented to her are the first of a series of exchanges which the *pirzade* call *len-den* or 'taking-giving' which continue for the rest of her life. Each donor's gift is noted down and the bride should reciprocate when there is some 'happiness' — such as a birth or marriage — in the donor's house. Thus is set up a chain of giving and receiving which binds the adult women. The unmarried have no part to play in these exchanges. Through her choices about how much to give, which links to acknowledge and which to ignore, a married woman can develop her own network of allies.

The *pirzada* women consider that the best marriage for them will be inside the village. Marriages outside are risky adventures into the unknown, while there is less danger of being deceived by other *pirzade* about the character of the groom or his mother. The bride faces a break from her parents which is less stark than if she is married outside, and fewer changes of her habits will be required of her than if she is married distantly. Her kin will be at hand if she needs help and she can visit them without transport costs or needing her mother-in-law's permission for a lengthy absence. Further, the *pirzade* rather haughtily assert, demands are not made within the village about the contents of the bride's dowry and the bride who goes to her in-laws almost empty-handed will not be taunted or maltreated by them. 'We give what we can, out (happiness' was the standard formula and the dowry is not a matter of haggling or unpleasantness among the *pirzade*. Marriage makes a girl into a woman, and marriage inside the village enables a woman to retain links forged in childhood throughout her adult life.

The occasion for the greatest jollity during my fieldwork was the marriage of a pair of cousins, the children of two *pirzade* sisters married inside the village. Throughout, joking turned on the double roles which everyone could play: all the *pirzade* were simultaneously 'bride's people' and 'groom's people'. The day before the wedding, the *pirzada* men — as 'groom's people — bore gifts to the bride's home. They were given tea and soft drinks — then they became 'bride's people' and conveyed their gifts of the groom's wedding clothes to his house. On the day of the wedding itself, the groom's parents — in their roles of bride's uncle and aunt — presented him with 'greetings money'. The next day the bride's mother — in her role of groom's aunt — came to 'see the bride's face', while the assembled women jested about the bride's coyness with the 'groom's aunt'. And later that day, when the bride's siblings came to take her back to her parents' home for a few days, there was joking among her brothers, her husband's brothers and the sons of their mother's brother. The groom's oldest brother should have hosted the affair, but he arrived with the bride's brothers, asserting that he was entitled to be a guest since he was her 'cousin-brother'. He was jokingly upbraided for just wanting an excuse to eat more of the food which his parents provided. The young hosts attempted to wash the hands of their guests before sitting down for a meal — but guests and hosts insisted on changing roles half way through the job, and as a result, clothes were soaked and the courtyard flooded with puddles of soapy water. And the bride, meanwhile, with her head slightly bent and making no contribution to the bantering, was finding it difficult to conceal her own laughter. Her mother-in-law later said that weddings inside the village are so happy that the *pirzade* should ensure that marriages only take place outside when there are no possible matches among the *pirzade* themselves.

But marriage by itself will not give a woman much influence. Sons are important for men — for the continuation of their line — but they are also important for women. The mother of daughters cannot expect much power in her old age, but the mother of sons can. A home without sons will be an empty home in later years, while sons can give a woman the expectation of brides and of the expansion of the women's world in which the elderly mother of sons will be accorded respect and obedience by her daughters-in-law.

The women's world of the home, then, provides benefits to women in turn. The unmarried teenager does housework as directed and marries where she is told to. She will be expected to obey her husband and accommodate herself to the expectations of her mother-in-law. It is on the young women that the weight of male power and the influence of elderly women rest most heavily.

But as the years pass, when her children grow up and she arranges their marriages, once her mother-in-law is dead, she can come into her own. This is the only acceptable route to *some* power, to *some* influence over the lives of others which the *pirzada* women can realistically take.

The benefits of conformity become all the more clear when the perspective is broadened beyond the confines of Hazrat Nizamuddin. My own concerns in most of the preceding pages are as restricted as the 'frogs in a well', and such a narrow perspective, while important, is at best partial. The lot of the *pirzada* women is unenviable in many ways, but another dimension must be added. A study of Syed women must be sociological both from the bottom up and the top down. It is in this paradox of inequality within the family, coupled with high status in a stratified society, that the complexity of *purdah* resides. If the *pirzada* women appear to be a 'muted group' this is perhaps less a reflection of their inability to formulate their joint interests than of their awareness of their ambivalent position.

The elitism of pedigree in which the *pirzada* women participate legitimates their separation from others. They have little social contact with non-*pirzada* women living in the village, with sweeper women and domestic servants, or with the women living in the new colonies around the village. Their major contacts are with their own kin — people who by definition are their equals. They are largely cocooned in isolated self-importance.

Also, while bodily modesty and displays of deference accentuate the women's dependence on men, they can also be seen as signals of female fragility which enable the *pirzada* women to opt out of earning a livelihood. Making a bid for independence is not something to be lightly done in the Indian context, where the economic independence even of many men is not guaranteed and where few people have access to any unemployment benefits or pensions. The *pirzada* women talked of being well cared for and of not needing money. Their dependence enables them to retreat into a sheltered existence behind the *purdah*, where they can avoid having to attend to earning a livelihood.[8] They appreciate the folly of pressing for their economic dues, for they might be challenged to be really independent, and hence the caution and conservatism which moderates the women's complaints. Being 'immured in a cage' has attractions over the degradation of impoverishment and back-breaking work.[9] Seclusion also makes the *pirzada* women inaccessible to outside men by a security which poor men cannot afford to provide.[10] The *pirzada* women are constrained in their movements outside the home, each has little control over her own destiny and they are economically dependent, but that is a price worth paying, for their *purdah* does not entail poverty, inadequate diet and the inability to pay for sound housing or medical expenses.

Outside the realm of orthodox Islam, *purdah* rarely gets a sympathetic press. The mental foot-binding, the 'frogs in a well' syndrome, the submissiveness of the young bride and the inability of adult women to cope with the world outside their homes — all this has been trenchantly criticized many times over. Calls for the abolition of *purdah*, however, should not fail to relate the seclusion of *some* women to the wider system of stratification into which it is integrated. We cannot anticipate the end of *purdah* without profound changes occurring in the Indian economic structure, changes which, despite political rhetoric, would not necessarily guarantee any improvement in the lives of Indian women as a whole in relation to men. But changes of a radical nature would be changes which the *pirzada* women would not want: they are unlikely to be in the vanguard, for they are playing a game in which they reap benefits which would be lost in the wake of a peasant revolution. The signs, in any case, are not set in the direction of any such a profound upheaval — and the *pirzada* women have gradually managed to ameliorate their position, the girls can hope to become the dependent (but not necessarily secluded) wives of prosperous men. They still see themselves within the framework of a stratified system, in which women are divided from one another by their economic position.

References

1.   Women's Publishing Collective (eds.), *Papers on Patriarchy Conference,* (Lewes, 1976), p.49.
2.   This is a common theme in many ethnographies of India. See also L. Lamphere, 'Strategies, co-operation and conflict among women in domestic groups', in M.Z. Rosaldo and L. Lamphere (eds.), *Woman, Culture, and Society,* (Stanford, 1974), p.104; and M. Dobkin, 'Social Ranking in the Women's World of Purdah: A Turkish Example', *Anthropological Quarterly,* 40 (1967), pp.65-72.
3.   See also N. Leis, 'Women in Groups: Ijaw Women's Associations', in Rosaldo and Lamphere, *op. cit.,* who talks of divided loyalties in a matrilineal-patrilocal context inhibiting group development, whereas in a patrilineal-patrilocal context a women's group did appear. See also N.S.S. Tapper, *The Role of Women in Selected Pastoral Islamic Societies,* (M.Phil. thesis, University of London, 1968).
4.   S. Ardener, 'Introduction', in S. Ardener (ed.), *Perceiving Women,* (London, 1975), pp.vii-xxiii; and S. Harding, 'Women and Words in a Spanish Village', in R.R. Reiter (ed.), *Toward an Anthropology of Women,* (New York, 1975).
5.   J.F. Collier, 'Women in Politics', in Rosaldo and Lamphere, *op. cit.,* pp.89-96; L. Lamphere, 'Strategies', in *ibid.,* pp. 97-112.
6.   L. Paul, 'The Mastery of Work and the Mystery of Sex in a Guatemalan Village', in *ibid.,* pp. 281-300.
7.   E. Friedl, 'Position of Women: Appearance and Reality', *Anthropological Quarterly,* 40 (1967), pp.97-108; C. Nelson, 'Public and Private Politics: Women in the Middle Eastern World', *American Ethnologist,* 1 (1974), pp.551-63. See also C.M. Pastner, 'Accommodations to Purdah: The Female Perspective', *Journal of Marriage and the Family,* 36 (1974), pp.408-14, for a discussion of strategies the women may employ.
8.   H. Papanek, 'Purdah: Separate Worlds and Symbolic Shelter',

   Comparative Studies in Society and History, 15 (1973), pp.289-325.
9.   M.H. Ali, *Observations on the Mussulmauns of India,* 2 vols., (London, 1832), vol.1, p.313.
10.   V. Das, 'Indian Women: Work, Power and Status', in B.R. Nanda (ed.), *Indian Women from Purdah to Modernity,* (New Delhi, 1976). pp.143-4.

Statistical Appendix:
Tables

Table 1

Indian Women's Participation in the Workforce by Age: 1961 and 1971

Age Group	1961 Urban	1961 Rural	1961 Total	1971 Urban	1971 Rural	1971 Total
0-14 years	1.6%	7.6%	6.6%	0.8%	3.0%	2.6%
15-34 years	15.8	49.8	43.6	10.1	21.3	18.9
35-59 years	22.9	49.6	47.6	13.8	22.8	21.2
60 years plus	11.4	24.3	22.4	6.4	11.3	10.5
All Ages	11.1	31.4	28.0	6.6	13.1	11.8

Source: Indian Council of Social Science Research, *Status of Women in India*, (New Delhi, 1975), p.162.

Table 2

Distribution of Indian Women Workers by Industrial Sector, 1971

Industrial Sector		Rural (%)	Urban (%)	Total (%)
I	Cultivators	32.6	4.2	29.6
II	Agricultural labourers	54.4	17.5	50.4
III	Forestry, fishing, plantations etc.	2.6	2.0	2.5
IV	Mining and quarrying	0.3	1.0	0.4
Va	Household industry	3.6	10.0	4.3
Vb	Other industry	1.6	12.9	2.8
VI	Construction	0.4	2.0	0.6
VII	Trade and commerce	1.0	8.2	1.8
VIII	Transport etc.	0.1	3.2	0.5
IX	Other services	3.4	38.1	7.1
	Total workers	100.0	100.0	100.0
	(Numbers in '000s)	(27,966)	(3,332)	(31,298)

Source: D. Jain (ed.) *Indian Women*, (New Delhi, 1975), p.68.

Table 3

Distribution of the Indian Female Population by Marital Status, 1971

Age Group	Never Married	Married	Widowed	Divorced and Separated
10-14 years	88.1%	11.7%	0.1%	0.0%
15-19 years	42.9	56.3	0.3	0.4
20-24 years	9.1	89.4	0.9	0.6
25-29 years	1.9	95.6	1.9	0.6

Source: Jain (ed.), *op. cit.,* p.155.

Table 4

Average Number of Children Born Alive to Current Mothers, by Age Groups, Rural India, 1969

Age Group of Mother	Average Number of Children
15-19 years	1.3
20-24 years	2.1
25-29 years	3.5
30-34 years	4.8
35-39 years	5.8
40-44 years	6.4

Source: Jain (ed.), *op. cit.,* p.157.

Table 5

Expectation of Life for Males and Females, by Age, India, 1951-60

Age	Expectation of Life (Number of Years)	
	Males	Females
At birth	41.9	40.5
5 years	48.7	47.0
10 years	45.2	43.8
20 years	37.0	35.6
30 years	29.0	27.9
40 years	22.1	22.4
50 years	16.5	17.5
60 years	11.8	13.0

Source: Jain (ed.), *op. cit.,* p.146.

Table 6

Educational Enrolment as Percentage of Indian Population in Corresponding Age Groups, 1950-1976

Selected Years	Ages							
	5 to 8		9 to 11		12 to 14		15 to 16	
	Boys	Girls	Boys	Girls	Boys	Girls	Boys	Girls
1950-51	55%	20%	21%	5%	11%	2%	3%	1%
1955-56	60	25	26	7	15	3	5	1
1960-61	74	35	36	13	21	5	8	2
1965-66	90	48	50	21	29	9	12	2
1970-71	110	69	67	33	34	12	15	4
1975-76	110	97	82	56	41	17	17	5

Source: Indian Council of Social Science Research, *op. cit.*, pp.147-8.

Bibliography

Abu-Zahra, N.M. 'A Reply', *American Anthropologist*, 72 (1970), 1079-88.
Ahmad, A. *Islamic Modernism in India and Pakistan, 1857-1964* (London, 1967).
Ahmad, I, (ed.) *Caste and Social Stratification among the Muslims* (Delhi, 1973).
Ahmad, I. (ed.) *Family, Kinship and Marriage among Muslims in India* (Delhi, 1976).
Ahmad, I. (ed.) *Ritual and Religion among Muslims in India* (Delhi, 1978).
Ahmad, K. *Family Life in Islam* (Leicester, 1974).
Ali, M.H. *Observations on the Mussulmauns of India*, 2 vols, (London, 1832).
Ali, S.A. *The Spirit of Islam*, rev. ed. (London, 1922).
Allan, J, *Menstrual Restrictions and Production and Reproduction* (M.Litt. thesis, University of Edinburgh, 1977).
Altekar, A.S. *The Position of Women in Hindu Civilization*, 3rd ed. (Delhi, 1962).
Antoun, R.T. 'On the Modesty of Women in Arab Muslim Villages', *American Anthropologist*, 70 (1968), 671-97.
Antoun, R.T. 'Antoun's reply to Abu-Zahra', *American Anthropologist*, 72 (1970), 1088-92.
Appadorai, A. (ed.) *Status of Women in South Asia* (Bombay, 1954).
Arberry, A.J. *Sufism: An Account of the Mystics of Islam* (London, 1950).
Ardener, S. (ed.) *Perceiving Women* (London, 1975).
Baig, T.A. (ed.) *Women of India* (Delhi, 1958).
Barker, D.L. and S. Allen (eds.) *Dependence and Exploitation in Work and Marriage* (London, 1976).
Barth, F. *Political Leadership Among Swat Pathans* (London, 1965).
Begg, W.D. *The Big Five of India in Sufism* (Ajmer, 1972).
Begg, W.D. *The Holy Biography of Hazrat Khwaja Muinuddin Chishti of Ajmer* (Ajmer, 1960).
Benston, M. 'The Political Economy of Women's Liberation', *Monthly Review*, 21 (1969), 13-27.
Billington, M.F. *Woman in India* (London, 1895).
Blunt, W.S. *The Caste System of Northern India* (Cambridge, 1931).
Boserup, E. *Woman's Role in Economic Development* (London, 1970).
Bourdieu, P. and Passeron, J. *Reproduction in Education, Society and Culture*, (London, 1977).
Cohen, A. *Arab Border Villages in Israel* (Manchester, 1965).
Conference of Socialist Economists. *On the Political Economy of Women*

(London, n.d.).

Coulson, M. *et al.* 'The Housewife and her Labour under Capitalism — A Critique', *New Left Review,* 89 (1975), 59-71.

Crooke, W. (ed.) *Islam in India* (London, 1921).

Das, F. Hauswirth. *Purdah: The Status of Indian Women* (London, 1932).

Das, R.N. 'Shaikh Nizam-ud-din Auliya', *Islamic Culture,* 48 (1974), 93-104.

Das, V. 'The Structure of Marriage Preferences: An Account from Pakistani Fiction', *Man (New Series),* 8 (1973), 30-45.

Dawood, N.J. (trans.) *The Koran* (Harmondsworth, 1968).

de Souza, A. (ed.) *Women in Contemporary India* (Delhi, 1975).

Dobkin, M. 'Social Ranking in the Women's World of Purdah: A Turkish Example', *Anthropological Quarterly,* 40 (1967), 65-72.

Donaldson, B.A. *The Wild Rue* (London, 1938).

Douglas, M. *Implicit Meanings* (London, 1977).

Douglas, M. (ed.) *Witchcraft Confessions and Accusations* (London, 1970).

Dumont, L. 'Marriage in India: The Present State of the Question III: North India in Relation to South India', *Contributions to Indian Sociology,* 9 (1966), 90-114.

Dumont, L. *Homo Hierarchicus* (London, 1972).

Dutta, R. and Joshi, P.C.(eds.) *Studies in Asian Social Development No. 1.* (Bombay, 1971).

Edholm, F. *et al.* 'Conceptualising Women', *Critique of Anthropology,* 3 (1977), 101-30.

Eglar, Z. *A Punjabi Village in Pakistan* (New York, 1960).

Encyclopaedia of Islam, (London and Leiden, 1960—.

Foster, G. 'The Anatomy of Envy', *Current Anthropology,* 13 (1972), 165-202.

Friedl, E. *Vasilika: A Village in Modern Greece* (New York, 1962).

Freidl, E. 'Position of Women: Appearance and Reality', *Anthropological Quarterly,* 40 (1967), 97-108.

Freidl, E. *Women and Men* (New York, 1975).

Fyzee, A.A.A. *Outlines of Muhammadan Law,* 2nd ed. (London, 1955).

Gadgil, D.R. *Women in the Working Force in India* (Delhi, 1965).

Gardiner, J. 'Women's Domestic Labour', *New Left Review,* 89 (1975) 47-58.

Gibb, H.A.R. *Islam,* 2nd. ed. (London, 1975).

Goody, J. *Production and Reproduction* (Cambridge, 1976).

Goody, J. and Tambiah, S.J. *Bridewealth and Dowry* (Cambridge, 1973).

Gould, H.A. 'The Micro-demography of Marriages in a North Indian Area', *South Western Journal of Anthropology,* 16 (1960), 476-91.

Gould, H.A. 'A Further Note on Village Exogamy in North India', *South Western Journal of Anthropology,* 17 (1961), 297-300.

Glazer-Malbin, N. 'Housework', *Signs,* 1 (1976), 905-22.

von Grunebaum, G.E. *Muhammadan Festivals* (New York, 1964).

Harrison, J. 'The Political Economy of Housework', *Bulletin of the Conference of Socialist Economists,* (1973), 35-52.

Hartmann, H. 'Capitalism, Patriarchy, and Job Segregation by Sex', *Signs,* 1 (1976), 137-69.

Hasan, Z. *A Guide to Nizamu-d Din* (Memoirs of the Archaeological Survey of India, No. 10, Calcutta, 1922).

Husain, S.A. *Marriage Customs Among Muslims in India* (New Delhi, 1976).

India, Census Commissioner. *Religion* (Series 1 — India, Paper 2 of 1972).

(Delhi, 1972).

India, Census Commissioner. *Delhi District Handbook Part X* (Delhi, 1973).

India, Census Commissioner. *Moharram in Two Cities (Lucknow and Delhi)*, (Delhi, 1966).

India Office Records, Government of India (Home Department), file P/8949, Vol. II, *Report of the Delhi Town Planning Committee on the choice of a Site for the New Imperial Capital.*

Indian Council for Social Science Research. *Status of Women in India* (New Delhi, 1975).

Jacobson, D. *Hidden Faces: Hindu and Muslim Purdah in a Central Indian Village* (Ph.D. thesis, Columbia University, 1970).

Jain, D. (ed.) *Indian Women* (New Delhi, 1975).

Jones, V.R. and Jones, L.B. *Woman in Islam: A Manual with Special Reference to Conditions in India* (Lucknow, 1941).

Khan, Z. 'Caste and the Muslim peasantry in India and Pakistan', *Man in India*, 48 (1968), 133-48.

Laxminarayan, H. and Tyagi, S.S. 'Some Aspects of Size-distribution of Agricultural Holdings', *Economic and Political Weekly*, XI (1976), 1637-40.

Lemu, B.A. and Heeren, F. *Woman in Islam* (Leicester, 1976).

Levy, R. *An Introduction to the Sociology of Islam*, 2 vols. (London, 1931-3).

Madan, T.N. *Family and Kinship* (Bombay, 1965).

Maloney, C. (ed.) *The Evil Eye* (New York, 1976).

Matthiasson, C.J. (ed.) *Many Sisters: Women in Cross-cultural Perspective* (New York, 1974).

Maududi, S.A.A. *Purdah and the Status of Women in Islam* (Lahore, 1972).

Mayer, A.C. *Caste and Kinship in Central India* (London, 1960).

Mayo, K. *Mother India* (London, 1927).

McEachern, D. 'The Mode of Production in India', *Journal of Contemporary Asia*, 6 (1976), 444-57.

Meillassoux, C. 'From Reproduction to Production', *Economy and Society*, 1 (1972), 93-105.

Misra, R. *Women in Mughal India (1526-1748 A.D.)* (Delhi, 1967).

Misra, S.C. *Muslim Communities in Gujarat* (London, 1964).

Mitchell, J. *Psychoanalysis and Feminism* (Harmondsworth, 1975).

Mujeeb, M. *The Indian Muslims* (London, 1967).

Myrdal, G. *Asian Drama*, 3 vols. (London, 1968).

Nadwi, A.H.A. *Saviours of Islamic Spirit*, 2 vols. (Lucknow, 1974).

Nanda, B.R. (ed.) *Indian Women from Purdah to Modernity* (New Delhi, 1975).

Nelson, C. 'Public and Private Politics: Women in the Middle Eastern World', *American Ethnologist*, 1 (1974), 551-63.

Nicholson, R.A. *The Mystics of Islam* (London, 1914).

Nizami, K.A. 'Early Indo-Muslim mystics and their attitude towards the State', *Islamic Culture*, XXII (1948), 387-98, and XXIV (1950), 60-71.

Nizami, K.A. *The Life and Times of Shaikh Farid-ud-din Ganj-i-Shakar* (Delhi, 1955).

Nizami, K.A. *Some Aspects of Religion and Politics in India during the Thirteenth Century*, 2nd. ed. (Delhi, 1974).

von Orlich, L. *Travels in India, including Sinde and the Punjab*, 2 vols. (London, 1845).

Papanek, H. 'The Woman Fieldworker in a Purdah Society', *Human Organization,* 23 (1964), 160-3.

Papanek, H. 'Purdah: Separate Worlds and Symbolic Shelter', *Comparative Studies in Society and History,* 15 (1973), 283-325.

Papanek, H. 'Men, Women and Work: Reflections on a Two-person Career', *American Journal of Sociology,* 78 (1973), 852-72.

Parkin, F. (ed) *The Social Analysis of Class Structure* (London, 1974).

Parsons, T. *The Structure of Social Action,* 2nd. ed. (New York, 1968).

Parsons, T. *Social Structure and Personality* (Glencoe, 1964).

Pastner, C.M. *Sexual Dichotomisation in Society and Culture* (Ph.D. thesis, Brandeis University, 1971).

Pastner, C.M. 'Accommodations to Purdah: The Female Perspective', *Journal of Marriage and the Family,* 36 (1974), 408-14.

Pehrson, R.N. *The Social Organisation of the Marri Baluch* (New York, 1966).

Peristiany, J.G. (ed.) *Honour and Shame: the Values of Mediterranean Society* (Chicago, 1965).

Peristiany, J.G. (ed.) *Mediterranean Family Structures* (Cambridge, 1976).

Pickthall, M.M. (trans.) *The Meaning of the Glorious Koran* (New York, n.d.).

Pitt-Rivers, J. *The Fate of Shechem or the Politics of Sex* (Cambridge, 1977).

Pitt-Rivers, J. (ed.) *Mediterranean Countrymen* (The Hague, 1963).

Platts, J. *A Dictionary of Urdu, Classical Hindi and English* (London, 1911).

Pocock, D. *Kanbi and Patidar* (Oxford, 1972).

Rauf, A. *West Pakistan: Rural Education and Development* (Honolulu, 1970).

Reiter, R.R. (ed.) *Toward an Anthropology of Women* (New York, 1975).

Rodinson, M. *Mohammed* (London, 1971).

Rosaldo, M.Z. and Lamphere, L. (eds.) *Woman, Culture and Society* (Stanford, 1974).

Rowe, W.L. 'The Marriage Network and Structural Change in a North Indian Community', *South Western Journal of Anthropology,* 16 (1960), 299-311.

Schneider, J. 'Of Vigilance and Virgins', *Ethnology,* 10 (1971), 1-24.

Seccombe, W. 'The Housewife and her Labour under Capitalism', *New Left Review,* 89 (1975), 59-71.

Siddiqi, M.M. *Women in Islam* (Lahore, 1952).

Srinivas, M.N. 'The Changing Position of Indian Women', *Man (New Series),* 12 (1977), 221-38.

Tapper, N.S.S. *The Role of Women in Selected Pastoral Islamic Societies* (M.Phil. thesis, University of London, 1968).

Thanwi, A.A. *Bahishti Zewar,* 2nd. ed. (Delhi, 1975).

Thomas, P. *Indian Women Through the Ages* (London, 1964).

Trimingham, J.S. *The Sufi Orders in Islam* (London, 1971).

Vatuk, S. *Kinship and Urbanisation* (Berkeley, 1972).

Vreede-de-Stuers, C. *Parda: A Study of Muslim Women's Life in Northern India* (Assen, 1968).

Ward, B. (ed.) *Women in the New Asia* (Paris, 1963).

Whitehead, A. 'Review of Jack Goody, *Production and Reproduction',* *Critique of Anthropology,* 3 (1977), 151-8.

Wiser, W. and Wiser, C. *Behind Mud Walls 1930-1960,* rev. ed. (Berkeley, 1971).

Women's Publishing Collective (eds.) *Papers on Patriarchy Conference*

(Lewes, 1976).

Yasin, M. *A Social History of Islamic India,* 2nd. ed. (New Delhi, 1974).

Young, F. and Bacdayan, A. 'Menstrual Taboos and Social Rigidity',
    Ethnology, 4 (1965), 225-40.

Index

Zed Books Ltd

is a publisher whose international and Third World lists span:

- **Women's Studies**
- **Development**
- **Environment**
- **Current Affairs**
- **International Relations**
- **Children's Studies**
- **Labour Studies**
- **Cultural Studies**
- **Human Rights**
- **Indigenous Peoples**
- **Health**

We also specialize in Area Studies where we have extensive lists in African Studies, Asian Studies, Caribbean and Latin American Studies, Middle East Studies, and Pacific Studies.

For further information about books available from Zed Books, please write to: Catalogue Enquiries, Zed Books Ltd, 57 Caledonian Road, London N1 9BU. Our books are available from distributors in many countries (for full details, see our catalogues), including:

In the USA
Humanities Press International, Inc., 165 First Avenue, Atlantic Highlands, New Jersey 07716.
Tel: (201) 872 1441;
Fax: (201) 872 0717.

In Canada
DEC, 229 College Street, Toronto, Ontario M5T 1R4.
Tel: (416) 971 7051.

In Australia
Wild and Woolley Ltd, 16 Darghan Street, Glebe, NSW 2037.

In India
Bibliomania, C-236 Defence Colony, New Delhi 110 024.

In Southern Africa
David Philip Publisher (Pty) Ltd, PO Box 408, Claremont 7735, South Africa.